Alan Thorne

JEALOUS JUSTICE

The story of a top-ranking police officer whose career was
wrecked by jealous rivals

Alan Thorne

JEALOUS JUSTICE

The story of a top-ranking police officer whose career was
wrecked by jealous rivals

MEREO
Cirencester

Mereo Books

1A The Wool Market Dyer Street Cirencester Gloucestershire GL7 2PR
An imprint of Memoirs Publishing www.mereobooks.com

Jealous justice: 978-1-86151-839-2

First published in Great Britain in 2017
by Mereo Books, an imprint of Memoirs Publishing

The address for Memoirs Publishing Group Limited can be found at
www.memoirspublishing.com

Cover design and artwork - Ray Lipscombe

The Memoirs Publishing Group Ltd Reg. No. 7834348

The Memoirs Publishing Group supports both The Forest Stewardship Council®
(FSC®) and the PEFC® leading international forest-certification organisations. Our
books carrying both the FSC label and the PEFC® and are printed on FSC®-certified
paper. FSC® is the only forest-certification scheme supported by the leading
environmental organisations including Greenpeace. Our paper procurement policy
can be found at www.memoirspublishing.com/environment

Typeset in 12/18pt Century Schoolbook
by Wiltshire Associates Publisher Services Ltd. Printed and bound in Great Britain
by Marston Book Services Ltd, Oxfordshire

Printed on FSC approved paper

To Shel, the girl who made my life.
To Gill, the girl who kept it going.

INTRODUCTION

I have just embarked on my seventh decade. During my working life I was a serving police officer for some 27 years, rising to a relatively high rank. When I retired and found that I had time, that very expensive commodity, on my hands, I began to enjoy delving into Britain's history through the pages of well-researched and light-heartedly written books, and on the odd occasion, when a natural pause occurred, I would lift a glass of chilled chardonnay to my lips and find my mind just slowly wandering; I would look upwards, my stare fixed on something which had no relevance to the moment whatsoever and I would see images of my life's memories slowly passing before my eyes.

Now my life, I am sure, has no more significance in this universe of ours than those of millions of other folk, but my journey to date has been something of a rollercoaster ride. Sitting there in my favourite chair, a myriad of thoughts would sail past and very often I would become conscious that I had a smirk on my face, sometimes a smile – or, far too often, I would become aware of small, delicate, yet very wet tears meandering down the wrinkled folds of my cheeks.

Only weeks after my birth in 1944 it was clear to a few close members of the family into which I had been delivered that I was not going to be afforded a typical childhood with parental care and guidance. I was certainly too young to comprehend that, but I believe my mother had an inkling. I was, as it turned out, nurtured under the care of my maternal grandmother and due to her loving and competence, I like to think I developed into an acceptable member of society. In fact, she moulded me to a level which enabled me many years later to reach one of the of the highest ranks in the British police service.

In recent years, the literary world has been bombarded with autobiographies written by or on behalf of celebrities, politicians or other notable people, usually published just in time for the summer holiday period or before the Christmas stockings are hung up. There are a few where the subject is still in early middle age and these give a clear indication to the reader that there will be a 'part two' to follow. Those make me a little suspicious. Are there more interesting tales to tell, or is it more of a commercial exercise?

Forget celebrities and other notables – each of us has a story to tell which may well be far more interesting to read than fiction. My journey has been somewhat painful at times and when I first considered committing my tale to paper I had deep reservations, as following certain events, it has taken me several years to regain some form of equilibrium in my life, and I was afraid that the disturbance of old and often unpleasant memories would instigate feelings of remorse, anxiety or even depression.

I mentioned to a few close family members that I had thoughts of penning a few words. This received an enthusiastic response from my younger son, and when I discussed the subject in depth with my wife and best friend, she had no hesitation in showering me with support – what more could a man ask?

As Max Bygraves used to say, 'I'm gonna tell you a story'. It's about my life, where I came from, where I've been and what I did, with all the ups and all the downs. It will demonstrate how someone's life can be torn apart with no regard for loyalty and dedication, and how a travesty of justice can be considered fair game for the 'establishment'. Everyone sometimes stops, thinks and ponders about decisions they have made along life's journey, and I am no exception, but this task on which I am embarking gives me the opportunity to review in some depth more than 70 years of modern history in which at times, I had a prominent role. If just someone, somewhere, absorbs an ounce of enlightenment, I'll be happy.

CHAPTER 1

What's the very first thing you can remember? This is a question that's often brought up at the odd social gathering or celebrity interview. Goodness knows why because, generally speaking, no one has any great desire to know, but it does prompt conversation and occasionally, amusing answers.

It is, however, a question I can answer with some clarity. I would have been no older than 12 or 13 months and being held in the arms of my maternal great-grandmother, who was standing in the front doorway of a small terraced house in the village of Argoed, the place where I was born. Argoed is a small but spread-out community situated some five miles north of Blackwood in the Sirhowy valley, in a corner of South East Wales. There were three or four family members present, including my grandmother, Amelia, who was waving goodbye to her sister Marion. Great Aunt

Marion was a career-minded spinster, married to the nursing profession. She had been visiting, having driven her small saloon car down from Merthyr Tydfil General Hospital, where she held the esteemed post of Matron. My mother was one of three sisters and two brothers and no doubt, Aunt Marion was the influencing factor within the family that prompted my mother, Ceridwen, and her sister Joan to pursue nursing careers.

Some years before I was born, my mother had been appointed District Midwife for Argoed and the surrounding area. It was a busy role and because of her employment I was to spend most of my childhood in the care of my grandparents, living under their roof well into my teenage years. My father's name was James Thomas Thorne, but he was known all his life as Jim. He was born in Plymouth, into a working-class environment, and on leaving school with no significant educational qualifications he joined the Army as a professional soldier. My parents met just before the Second World War in Wellington, Somerset. I have never ascertained why my father had drifted north from Plymouth for what was a life-changing event for them both, but my mother had been sent to this pretty West Country town to complete her domiciliary midwifery training after undergoing residential tutorship at Crumpsall Hospital in Manchester.

I arrived into this big wide world via the small front bedroom of my gran's house in this Welsh mining village on a typical bright, breezy March day in 1944. My mother was attended by her colleague, Nurse Pritchard. They were professionally responsible for different areas of the valley but covered for each other during periods of sickness or leave.

The midwife was a well-respected pillar of the community, on a par with the local doctor, village bobby and chapel minister. I mention chapel because the vast majority of the valley population were staunch Welsh Baptists, with a smattering of Methodism. There were very few Church in Wales followers. My mother, even at the age of 97, was still receiving Christmas cards from, as she put it, some of her babies, many of whom she had delivered more than 75 years before.

The work of a district midwife in those days was not easy, with the hours long and varied. No expectant mother was admitted to hospital for the birth in the post-war period unless there was a pre-determined medical condition which could cause risk to mother or child. It was the district midwife who dealt with everything, perhaps with a little help from a close family member. Very often, hot water and other sundry items were ferried to and fro by a very excited dad who, if the truth be known, didn't really want to be there. Because of her involvement with the community, everyone got to know my mother and she them, and although I felt some pride for her on occasions, it caused me considerable consternation well into my teens when I was introduced in company as 'Alan Thorne', because the response was usually 'ah, Nurse Thorne's son'!

What's in a name, some may ask. Well, a great deal to me, because the name that was recorded on my birth certificate was to cause me annoyance, frustration and anxiety for the next 65 years. Choosing a name for one's offspring is an important pre-requisite to parenthood; it is a task which I believe should not be taken lightly and should be a joint and agreeable decision made, whenever practicable, by both parents. The surname 'Thorne' had been pre-determined by my father's ancestry and the sole name 'Alan' was amicably decided upon, or so I am reliably informed by my mother. It was to be spelt that way because that was the custom in our slice of the Welsh valleys.

After completing her training in Wellington, my mother was living at home with her parents when I was born. It was my father who registered my birth, so he must have been home at the time. I know he was present at Dunkirk and that he left Britain for the D-Day landings in June 1944, so he could well have been on leave shortly after my birth, before the big Allied push back into France.

He visited the local authority offices and registered my birth in the name of Frederick Allen Thorne. When I became old enough to discuss what to me was a serious issue, I ascertained from my gran that the name Frederick had been chosen by my father, as he explained, in memory of his brother, who had lost his life at sea in the Atlantic naval battles. The spelling of Allen seemed, he said, to be the natural way, and the only way that came to mind in the Registrar's office. As far as I am concerned, if my father had wanted to commemorate his brother by the naming of his own son, then he must have given thought to the subject; it would not have suddenly entered his mind at the time of registration. My father and I never did become natural conversationalists. In my view his actions were at best thoughtless and at worst devious.

Now let me make it quite clear: although the name Frederick gives me no joy – in fact, I just do not like it – I have no wish to cast aspersions as to its adoption anywhere or anyhow. In fact, there have been many great figures in history so named. However, it was not a good 'handle' for a child born into a deprived Welsh valley community in the post-war years. As a toddler it was bad enough, but history has dictated that I would be saddled with it throughout the enlightened fifties and swinging sixties, at an age when I had need to make my mark on the world. Whatever anyone else thought, it became my own unswerving view that my officially-declared name was a millstone around my neck, causing me untold embarrassment. In primary school there would be a hushed snigger rippling around the classroom every morning as the teacher marked the register.

I was too young at that stage to explain that I wanted to use the name Alan on a day-to-day basis and when I reached my teens and was able to converse in a matter-of-fact manner, people would reply, very often with a sly smirk, telling me that 'Allen' is a surname and as a Christian name should not be spelt that way. I have never discussed this subject in any depth with my mother, but I would have thought she would have been annoyed at the time. My gran was the one to whom I could talk and I know that she certainly was.

My parents and I were in no way close and I never could engage in any meaningful, sincere or harmonious conversation with either. Furthermore, it is sad and perhaps tragic that I was never able to have any kind of relationship with my father throughout my whole life. I am extremely grateful for the support and care he afforded me whilst I was growing up, but in any deep and lasting relationship there must be understanding and love. I lived with the result of my father's actions throughout my teens and most of my adult life and kept explaining to everyone, and I think subconsciously convincing myself that it didn't matter. However, I became very annoyed with my situation every time my name was called out in the dentist's or doctor's surgery. In our doctors, the blasted thing was piped over the tannoy. I used to imagine there were several persons lurking there who knew me and were secretly chuckling. Furthermore, in recent years, my wife and I have been accustomed to taking holiday cruises and as many will know, the moment you embark on the vessel you have selected, you no longer have the need for cash. You are duly photographed and your whole life is governed by your 'boarding pass'. This card contains brief cruise details and your name. The name is taken from the passenger's inventory which is, in turn, taken from your passport. To be brief, it lists the name imprinted on your birth certificate. The pass has to be produced to everyone and everywhere, and I soon found that I was being addressed by everybody as Fred.

I did eventually do something about it. In my 69th year I officially changed my name by Deed Poll to a simple Alan Thorne. My wife duly organised notification to all bodies and organisations that legally needed to know and at last, I no longer have any literature being posted through my front door bearing the name Frederick Allen. Had I known that the process was so easy I would have done it years ago.

As far as I can recall, I had a relatively settled and happy childhood. With my father away doing his bit for our country, my pre-school years were spent living with my mother in my grandparents' home. Because of my mother's duties I was brought up on a day-to-day basis by my grandmother, of whom, over the following 16 years, I grew extremely fond. We developed a bond, which looking back, was something really very special.

My grandfather, a relatively short man with a temper to match, was a coal miner all his working life. I must admit that in my early years I was really afraid of him. His level of tolerance was extremely low and he would shout and rant if the slightest thing displeased him. His strait-laced Victorian values were inflicted on me at every family Sunday dinner, as I clearly recall. It was always a roast and whenever possible my mother, and sometimes visiting relatives, would also be there. This was the only meal of the week when there would be a bottle of Corona pop on the table, with me having the honour of choosing the flavour from the four-bottle crate which was delivered once a month. I would be permitted one half-glass of this celebrated liquid, but my grandfather decreed that not one drop was to pass my lips until my plate has been cleared of every morsel of food. Now what was that all about?

The whole family appeared to me to hold the view that my grandparents were a happy, devoted couple and neighbours, friends and acquaintances would have assumed likewise. After all, they remained together for over 60 years and parented five children. But I grew to know differently. My grandmother not only had to endure domestic hardship through the lack of financial stability, she was subjected to marital verbal abuse, stopping just short of violence, which was perhaps accepted as the turmoil of married life in the first half of the 20th century but would certainly be condemned in our modern era. However, the words 'separation' and 'divorce' were never mentioned in pre-war society, not even quietly within families. The only advice given out then was 'you made your bed, you lie in it'.

My grandfather hailed from the heads of the valleys, an area described in graphic detail by Mr Cordell in his widely-acclaimed book *The Rape of the Fair Country*. After their marriage, they settled in the small village of Tafarnaubach, but the depression of that time forced him to seek work further afield and they moved to the house where this story began. My grandfather had secured work in Markham colliery, a little way up the valley, and I understand that within several years they were able to afford a mortgage on the property. In 1958 my grandmother was like the proverbial dog with two tails when she persuaded my grandfather to have a bathroom extension built on the rear ground floor. Before that, in my pre-school days, I can remember only too clearly my weekly scrub in the tin bath in front of the living room fire.

They occupied this house until they were both well into their nineties. What a social transformation and technological advancements they both witnessed throughout their lives. They could both clearly recall the invention of the motor car, which was initially restricted to 4mph with the attendance of a man with a red flag walking in front. Then, decades later, they both sat in their living room and watched Neil Armstrong on television as he set foot on the moon.

I visited the avenue in which I grew up a short time ago to acquaint Gill with my 'glorious past' and found that several new detached houses have been built on the nearby field where my friends and I created all kinds of games. There were rows of multi-coloured plastic rubbish bins lined up where our goal-posts used to be, but what really brought a lump to my throat was the large 'TO LET' sign which had been staked into my gran's front garden. The sign was almost as big as the patch of grass in which it stood. In the few minutes I was there, hundreds of thoughts flashed through my mind, but the one which lingered most was the fact that my gran had never been really happy living there. And that hurt.

1945 saw peace once more settling throughout our islands and family life for most folk was again becoming normal, with thousands of dads returning from Europe. Mine was amongst them, and it soon became obvious that we could not all live in the small terraced house. In addition to myself and my parents, my grandparent's youngest, Uncle Dave, was unmarried and living at home.

The election of July 1945 saw a Labour government take power, and amongst many of the nation's problems was a serious shortage of housing. This issue was partly solved in some areas by the design and manufacture of the 'prefab'. These were relatively small prefabricated houses of approximately 635 square feet when assembled. Each component was no more than seven and a half feet wide, to enable every part of the building to be transported from the factory to the site on the back of a lorry. The prefabs could be bolted together on a previously-prepared concrete base in less than a day. There were several different types manufactured from a combination of asbestos, cement, steel, wood and aluminium.

The Bedwellty Urban District Council, which was the local authority governing our area, decided to erect a small estate of these prefabs in the adjoining village of Markham and my mother, who had requested council housing and who, for the wellbeing of the community needed to remain in the area, was allocated one. I would have been four or five years of age, and I can remember seeing the lorries chugging past the end of the avenue laden with these large, strange-looking deconstructed boxes, one of which was destined to be my home for the next 16 years. These temporary houses were designed for no more than 10 years' use, but it was 21 years before they finally replaced them.

The village of Markham was only some one and a half miles up the valley. It had approximately 1000 inhabitants and had mushroomed around the deep shaft colliery owned and operated by the National Coal Board. The pit produced a very good quality steam coal and I did hear, on more than one occasion, that the quality dug from Markham was such that it was used in the engine of the royal train, but I cannot vouch for the truth of that.

Markham was situated right on the top of the mountain, approximately 500 feet above sea level, and our home was erected on a barren windswept field on the edge of the village. There were 22 dwellings on the little estate and our small family moved into number 6 David Street. You will now be aware that I am one for simple names, so it well suited me. The local councillors who had decided on the names at their planning meeting must have lacked inspiration because they named our neighbouring street 'John Street'.

I attended the local primary school from the age of five and soon accepted that this daily incarceration was going to be my fate for the foreseeable future. Like all youngsters of that age I did my best initially to disrupt this course of action, but it proved fruitless.

I progressed through to the junior school, which was really in the same building; our daily access was simply through a different gateway and the two playgrounds were divided by a high close-mesh fence. This is the time of life when most children start to gradually understand what life is all about, and I was no exception. I made friends with certain classmates and drew away from others because my senses told me to. I made firm and positive impressions on the teaching staff, and naturally, the good vibes came from the teachers who took the lessons I enjoyed; English, history and woodwork.

There was one person at this time, the PE teacher, Mr Maynard, who really was a thorn in my side. It was not because I loathed games or gymnastics, because I didn't. In fact, I was pretty average at rugby and played for the school team in latter years. However, this particular member of the teaching profession just kept picking on me. Everything I did and every answer I gave was wrong. I finally came to the conclusion after two or three terms that the reason was that our Mr Maynard, a married man, was conducting an extramarital affair with Miss Richards, the music and arts teacher. I, along with other classmates, had sussed this out, and I believe he knew that we knew. But why did he only pick on me?

My home life was still being disrupted, because with both of my parents working I was still spending most of my non-school time with my gran. Every weekend and all through the holidays I would live and sleep at my gran's house in Argoed, and when school finished on other days, I would walk, or usually run, the two miles or so to her house, taking the shortcut through fields. During term time, I would make my way back up to the prefab to sleep in order to attend school the next day. The time for my homeward bound trek was usually about half an hour after the street lamps came on, and I use the term 'back up' because the route between Argoed and Markham traversed Penylan Road, which was a hill with a one in six gradient and approximately three-quarters of a mile long. It was just perfect for free-wheeling down on our bikes, but I never looked forward to that evening climb back up after gallivanting about with my mates.

If I give the impression that my childhood was being disrupted by my parents' work, I was not bitter in any way about it. I didn't care – I enjoyed every minute with my gran.

I lived with this form of dual residency from the age of about eight through to my late teens, because by the time I gained employment at the age of 16, all the friends I had made lived in Argoed, so even through secondary school I had this semi-nomadic lifestyle. I just used the prefab as a place to rest my head and the older I got, the later in the evening I would arrive. I would have any social or family conversation with my mother as and when our paths crossed, which gave me the opportunity to ask, when the need arose, that age-old question "can I have...?" I rarely had any kind of discussion with my father and then only when my mother thought that he should intervene because of some misdemeanour on my part.

CHAPTER 2

I was an industrious young fellow, and I was able to secure gainful employment in my tender years. My first job was an evening paper round through Markham village, for which I was paid the sum of five shillings a week. I secured this prestigious position at Edward's Newsagents, one of seven shops in the village, primarily because the proprietor, Harry, ran a taxi business and had a contract with the health authority to convey my mother out on her rounds and to emergencies, as she never learned to drive. She was in a prime position to vouch for my character. Like most youngsters, I soon became fed up with the role, not because of the effort required or the miserly recompense but because the round took at least an hour to complete and that was vital time, especially during the shorter days, which I could have spent travelling down to Argoed and my friends.

There is a macabre and tragic twist to this part of my

tale. After giving my notice to Harry Edwards, he took on a young girl who was about my age, 10 or 11, the younger of two sisters who lived no more than 100 yards from us. My mother knew the family well and had in fact, delivered the youngster. She had been engaged on my paper round for no more than three weeks when one evening she was reported missing. Her body was found the following day, partially hidden in undergrowth some 600 yards from the last house to which she had to deliver. A middle-aged man, known by everyone in the village as Wally, was arrested. Wally was mentally impaired, and took on any menial task he was offered around the village to supplement his allowances. As in any close-knit community, the talk around the village for weeks revolved around that classic statement "who would have thought it?" Well, the poor girl's family was left thinking for a long time, because at his subsequent trial, Wally pleaded guilty to murder and was sentenced to life imprisonment.

My second job was in Argoed with a Mr Hyde, who operated a mobile greengrocer's van around the village. He took me on as an extra pair of hands, but he wouldn't allow me to serve anyone or have anything to do with cash transactions, which was no reflection on my character. Tudor Hyde, like his father, who had run the business before him, was just tight, the typical modern-day Scrooge. The role didn't last for more than three months and was confined to weekends because the hours were long. I would be off with him in the van mid-morning and eventually finish late evening at anything up to 10 pm after loading the goods for the following day. For this, I would receive a few apples or other fruit that was in season and maybe a bar of

Fry's Five Boys chocolate; quite popular at the time. I can really thank my gran for freeing me from this role. She could see that I was being exploited and introduced me to my third part-time employer, Bill Collier, who was a farmer and had the sole milk delivery round in the village.

Bill's farm was on the other side of the valley in an outpost called 'The Grey'. It was a three-and-a-half-mile walk, and Bill was not happy unless he began his round by 6 am. This meant an early rise for me at 5 am so that I could arrive in good time to load the van with sufficient crates of pasteurised milk and ample eggs – Bill didn't like missing a sale of eggs. It was a weekend and holiday job and it became part of my life for five and a half years, and I loved it. Bill was a man I could look up to and respect, and in turn he trusted me implicitly, giving me responsibility for all aspects of the role.

The morning ritual would unwind as I arrived between twenty to and a quarter to six, and as soon as his kitchen light flickered I would tap the window and be welcomed by Bill's wife, Irene. The Rayburn would be springing to life and I would be presented with my mug of coffee – a little milk and one sugar. Whilst waiting for Bill to appear I would gaze at the plaque hanging on the right-hand side of the chimney breast; it displayed the poem 'If' by Rudyard Kipling and within weeks I knew it off by heart. I would read it over and over in my mind, giving my voice different inflections as if I were performing in the Royal Albert Hall in the guise of Richard Burton or some other prominent actor.

Bill would suddenly draw my attention back to earth with his appearance and practise his daily ritual, which was to drink two inches of sherry from a glass containing a raw egg, before enquiring about my health. Both of them really made me feel part of their family, even though they had two sons of about my age fast asleep upstairs. Having donned his flat cap from behind the kitchen door he would shout "come on young man!" and we'd be off. It was not many mornings that I left the yard without a quiet word with Dobbin the carthorse, and then we'd start trundling down the lane towards Cwm Argoed in the old Thames van with the bottles rattling so loud that it was pointless trying to talk to each other.

I think Bill was the man who gave me my lifelong interest in the automobile, because during the round, when we came to a safe place, he would allow me to jump into the driver's seat, slip the handbrake off and roll to the next stop. It was a real dream when in 1955, he purchased a new van; a long-wheelbase Bedford CA which had sliding front doors. I really loved these times. I was as happy as the proverbial pig in the farmyard.

The weekend social life in Welsh valley villages in the mid-20th century took two forms, depending on whether your family was religious or otherwise. If otherwise, the men of the family would spend most of their time in the pubs or working men's clubs, with their womenfolk shopping for provisions and tending to their family's needs. The clubs were a widespread feature in Wales and more so in the mining valleys, because of their industrial labour force; they evolved as a direct result of the Sunday licensing laws, which applied throughout the Principality. The law prohibited the sale of intoxicating liquor on the Sabbath and to counteract this, all types of institutes and associations would register themselves with the Magistrates' Licensing Committee, which allowed the supply of intoxicating liquor to bona fide members. These two words are important because 'supply' did not, in law, amount to a 'sale' and therefore drinks could be legally consumed. It has been said many times that the law is an ass. Well, I couldn't possibly comment!

Another farcical aspect of this situation, which I soon became aware of at the commencement of my later police training, was that the Licensing Act empowered police officers to enter any licensed public house at will to prevent or detect offences, but because these 'clubs' were registered and not licensed they were deemed private premises, so in the event of any suspected offence being committed, a search warrant was necessary for the police to gain lawful entry.

Now, if a family was in any way religious, and mine was, the situation was completely different. The devout Welsh Baptist was a moral crusader who supported abstention. Regular attendance at chapel was the norm; three times each Sunday with various meetings and services during the week. My grandmother hailed from Maesteg with a very devout Baptist upbringing, and she was instrumental in fostering a similar lifestyle in her offspring. My grandfather, on the other hand, was something of an enigma. He portrayed very Victorian values, but it was a case of 'do as I say, not as I do'. He never gave me the impression of having any religious leanings. On the contrary, he must have had some thoughts on hell and damnation, as one or both of these words were included in his vocabulary each time he blew a fuse, which to me, at my young age, seemed quite often.

It therefore followed that I was encouraged to tread the 'straight and narrow', which resulted in me accompanying my gran, and my mother when available, to services at Argoed Baptist Chapel at 10 o'clock each Sunday morning and again at six in the evening. I was now eight years old. I hadn't got a clue what the services were all about, I was utterly bored, and the only thing that made the whole experience bearable was the never-ending supply of Mint Imperials produced from Gran's pocket.

As I became older and was able to step out into the wide world unaccompanied, I was encouraged to attend Sunday School at two o'clock each Sunday afternoon. Looking back, it was this that gave me the opportunity to further my horizons, allowing me to develop into adulthood.

Yes, it has probably been the same for millions of other youngsters; you suddenly find yourself in an arena where you can meet people and make some meaningful friendships. It just happened to be that particular Sunday School for me. I was not in any way religious, certainly not at that young age; I didn't develop any religious inclination and I'm certainly not religious now. What life has showered on me has made me question whether there is in fact anyone up above looking out for us at all, as will become clear.

At Sunday school I became friendly with two or three boys, but more importantly I became acquainted with a few girls, and one in particular. Her name was Eirlys Dodd. She was my age, one of two sisters and lived in the village. Her mum had sadly died a few years earlier and her dad was the headmaster of the local primary school. If we had been 10 years older and at the local dance hall in Blackwood, I could have said I'd 'pulled'. It was however, much more subtle. I was somehow attracted to her and I'm positive she felt the same. We would each suddenly become coy and shy if we became aware that the other was paying attention. What subdued my emotions at that age was the fact that at any gathering or activity our friends would laugh and joke and make fun of our apparent relationship, but there is no doubt that I was hooked.

Over the next few years our relationship grew; purely platonically, I would add. We would have both been in our 13th year before we shared our first kiss. My attendance at Sunday services continued, but I was now sitting upstairs in the gallery along with the other youngsters, where our time was spent poking fun and giggling. We even embarked on screwing up sweet wrappers and using Mrs Harris, the organist, as a target – something she didn't like one little bit. I can add here that at the age of 11, my parents enrolled me for piano lessons with Mrs Harris, which I detested. It was not the piano which I disagreed with but the fact that for two one-hour long evening lessons each week I was marooned and missing my leisure time with our 'gang'. As I grew older I would come to regret not having persevered with the piano, though if I had a pound for every time I've heard someone say the same, I'd be a very rich man.

In addition to chapel each Sunday, my friends and I, which obviously included the girls, were now attending various other religious sessions throughout the week. There was Young People's Guild on a Tuesday evening, which was really a discussion session with the aim of encouraging interaction between those who saw their futures happily embraced within the body of the church. Then there was Band of Hope on Thursday evenings, which was again designed as a session when the minister or a church elder would try to convince us of the evils associated with drink. I had no interest in any of it, and neither did Eirlys or any of our friends. If that had not been the case, we would most certainly have not been 'an item'. Our whole weekly charade was a reason for friends to get together for social intercourse and general fun whilst having the support and encouragement of our families. Although these gatherings at church were enjoyable, what we all really looked forward to were the country walks we'd embark on afterwards. We would walk for miles through the narrow lanes that criss-crossed the surrounding villages.

This period of my life seemed like Utopia and the school holidays seemed endless. When I hear the doom and gloom about global warming from what seems an over-abundance of environmentalists, I immediately think of what seemed the endless scorching summer days of my youth. I can clearly remember many occasions when the road's tarmacadam melted from the strength of the midday sun. Three or four of our gang would regularly set off armed with a small pack of sandwiches and water, or a drop of that Corona pop if we were lucky, and make our way, usually over the mountain, for miles, where we'd spend the day bird-nesting, building a camp or catching newts. We'd usually arrive home about five and find time for food before embarking on an evening's entertainment pestering the girls. Even school time didn't put too much of a damper on it for me; I was out of class and on my way down to my gran's by three-thirty each afternoon. But to be honest, I can't say I had a strong dislike for school. Apart from that PT teacher, I seemed to get on with most of the staff and although I was in no way academic, I got by. I say 'got by' because I was bitterly disappointed when the results of the 11 plus examination revealed me as a failure. My parents didn't seem to mind, or at least neither spoke to me with any seriousness about it. I was more concerned about what my gran would say, but I found I had no reason to worry there, as she understood.

My worries were dispelled somewhat when I found that most of my friends were in the same boat, so I was not the only duffer. My biggest worry was that Eirlys has passed, and although she had been attending a different junior school in Argoed, she would soon be transferring to the county grammar school in Pontllanfraith, some seven miles away. That would surely disrupt our lives and our relationship. For some months up until this time, we had been meeting up at various locations where we could steal some time on our own without interruption from friends.

Nearly all those who had been unsuccessful in this now infamous examination were destined to attend the secondary modern school, but in our county of Monmouthshire there was an established boys-only school, Pontllanfraith Technical School, known throughout the county as Pont-Tech, and like the grammar school it was in Pontllanfraith. Entrance was governed by selective examination, but I was thrilled to attain a pass, and during the summer of 1955 I made several shopping expeditions with my gran to obtain the statutory uniform. Pontllanfraith, which is really a suburb of Blackwood (though residents wouldn't agree), was about a mile and a half from the grammar school. All pupils of both schools living higher up the valley would need transport to and from school, which meant I would very often be on the same bus as Eirlys.

Pontllanfraith Technical School was the first of its kind in Wales and therefore to some extent it had the task of setting the standards for the future. There was an all-male teaching staff who wore their gowns at all times and I clearly remember that the chemistry teacher actually wore his mortar-board cap. The headmaster, Mr Glyn Price, always referred to as the Principal, was a strict disciplinarian. No misbehaviour would be tolerated in class and if any teacher had the slightest need, you would be marched to stand outside the Principal's office to await his deliberation.

I, along with two classmates, was sent on this frogmarch one afternoon for alleged misbehaviour, discovered when our technical drawing teacher suddenly returned to class, having left us to quietly get on with our work. The Principal kept us standing in trembling anticipation for about half an hour before advising us in his sharp, incisive voice that he would deal with us at assembly the following morning. A very anxious sleepless night followed. We all received six of the best, three on each palm, before the whole school. I was only 12 years old at the time, but I did not dare tell anyone, apart from claims of bravado to my mates. One thing was certain; I never did again disrupt a class for the remaining four years at that establishment.

The original school, which is still in use as a youth club, was actually a disused chapel which was only just big enough to accommodate four classrooms; the remaining school buildings were spread around the neighbourhood. It was a walk of half a mile to where the metalwork forge and woodwork benches were housed. However, apart from the brutally-inflicted corporal punishment, I enjoyed my time there. As the school's name would suggest, the theme of the education was to prepare young lads for a future within an industrial environment, and although we were taught the basic academic subjects there was no real emphasis placed on them, which suited me.

My time at this secondary school was uneventful and I fitted in as one of those 'run of the mill' pupils who made up the numbers. I do recall quite well that I was fortunate that my parents (and when I say parents I am really referring to my mother, as she was the main breadwinner) were in a position to be able to pay for me to participate in two school trips, both to Austria. The first was to a suburb of Vienna and the second was much more interesting, to a small village called Zirl in Tyrol in Austria. Both trips were part of life's learning curve; we had no educational projects to complete. It just seemed to be a great holiday for us lads and to a certain extent, for the staff as well. I suppose they did have to care for our welfare and safety, but it didn't stop us sampling the local bitter on a few occasions as far as I can recall.

One memory of school life whilst in my middle years was of the Head Boy. Like my classmates, I was somewhat wary of him. He was called Mike Dixon, quite tall, full of his own importance and liked to display it at every opportunity. I kept my distance and our paths never crossed at school, but I came face to face with him some 10 years later when I found that he was one of 80 traffic patrol car drivers under my supervision. He never recognised me from the past, but I kept a careful eye on him to ensure that he had grown out of his slight arrogance.

My social life at this time had graduated from those long walks when we'd go looking for nature's weird and wonderful, and my time was spent cycling or playing football with the occasional visit on a weekday evening to the village institute, where we spent many a happy hour consolidating our misspent youth playing snooker. On a Saturday, we would journey to Blackwood to see one of the latest releases in one of the two cinemas. Sunday was chapel and courting. Eirlys and I still saw each other, but not as often. Actually, I believe that it was about this time that my mate Glen told me she was seeing someone else who'd been spotted arriving by bus to visit her home. I shrugged it off as not important enough to bother me – or did it?

Christmas 1959 had passed and I was embarking on my final term at Pont Tech. There was provision for pupils to stay on after reaching 16 years of age to further their studies, but I definitely wanted to move on into employment. There was virtually no assistance from the school in this respect, no careers advice and no visits to or talks from potential employers. I had no discussions either with my parents. The only information one could assemble in one's mind was from discussions with mates or adverts in the papers.

As the summer months approached and the end of term loomed, I had formulated a few ideas. I had seen adverts for apprenticeships at the electricity board and openings with the BBC in Cardiff as technicians, but I was really interested in becoming a police cadet. The Monmouthshire Constabulary was one of the few forces which at that time took on youngsters aged 16 as cadets, employing them on basic office and administrative duties with the hope of moulding them into more than suitable police entrants three years later. My initial application was swiftly answered; I was told they would have no vacancies for the foreseeable future. In fairness, the force, because of the financial implications, never employed more than 10 cadets at any one time and in the absence of any concrete evidence to the contrary I will assume that was the reason for my rejection. However, several years later when I had sworn the Queen's Oath myself, and with some experience under my belt, it became clear that to secure a position as a police cadet it was a matter of who and not what you knew. Nepotism was rife. In the late 1970s, when left-wing academics started to gain significant influence on police training, the post of police cadet was abolished nationwide.

As far as my career was concerned, it was now one down, two to go. I didn't fare a lot better with the BBC. My initial letter was answered with an application form for completion together with a pile of leaflets and advertising material which would have been sufficient to paper my gran's back kitchen. My heart wasn't really in the BBC post; I suppose the sheer glamour had attracted me, so I wasn't too disappointed with their subsequent rejection. This left me with the electricity board. I thought I stood some chance here; at least most of my family were customers. After scrutinising my application form, they invited me to their divisional headquarters in St Mellons for written and practical tests. But alas, it was not to be.

Then a few weeks later, as if by magic, my Uncle Dave asked me if I would be interested in a job at the garage where he was employed. He worked at Chaston's of

Blackwood within their sales department and was well thought of by management. Chaston's was a family run business in the 1960s, headed by the founder's son, Alfred, who had built it into a renowned and respected dealership. It was affiliated with the British Motor Corporation brand together with Wolseley, Riley and Morris, which together later formed British Leyland. The added kudos was that they also sold and serviced Jaguars, Land Rovers and several other unique marques. Uncle Dave had spoken to the Service Manager, who had agreed to let me start on a month's trial with a view to a five-year apprenticeship. I nearly bit his hand off. Wow! To hell with nepotism!

The garage accountant, Mr Jones, wrote to me officially confirming that my trial would commence after the school holidays. I was in heaven for those last few weeks, or at least I would have been if it not had been for my love life. The liaison between Eirlys and me was seriously cooling from her point of view. She always had something else to do when we spoke about meeting up and the bond between us snapped clean apart the evening I actually witnessed some yobbo getting off the bus from Blackwood and entering her house, which was just yards away from the bus stop. I learned that he was a pupil at her school and was probably a nice lad, but to me he was a total undesirable. I had no further contact with her from that evening on.

CHAPTER 3

It was 7.40 am on Monday 5 September 1960. I was sixteen and a half years old and standing outside the large roller-shutter doors which gave access to the bottom workshop of Chaston's garage. The building was on the northern edge of Blackwood town in a prominent position on Pentwyn Road, to the rear of the Miners' Welfare Institute and just 100 yards down from the memorial Cenotaph. I was clutching my sandwiches, which would hopefully sustain me through my day's hard labour, and anxiously waiting to announce myself to the big new world of employment.

The service manager, Mr Colin Evans, to whom I had been told to report, arrived at 8.00 on the dot to open up. There was no way I intended to be late, so my father had dropped me off at 7.30 as he drove to his employment as a progress chaser at South Wales Switchgear, further down the valley.

As I've mentioned, Chaston's was a relatively large commercial undertaking, not only in its spread of business but the size of the premises it occupied. It had two adjoining workshops, the larger being about the size of a hockey pitch, with a separate body repair area incorporating two spray booths. The sales department building could house in excess of 30 cars where they were prepared for sale, with a first-floor office suite for administration. In addition, some 100 yards away on the A4048 main valley road was a vehicle showroom, together with fuel pumps and forecourt to serve passing traffic.

There was a workforce of around 50, with 12 time-served mechanics who each had an apprentice. This was the section of which I was to become a member. Well, not exactly, at first. In addition to the facilities I've mentioned, there was a machine shop staffed by Len Hutton. Len was a proper gent; he was in his 60s, approaching retirement and had worked as a mechanic there for 20 or so years. Len had been moved into the machine shop to lighten his workload somewhat and it was the pattern that all new starters did their initiation with Len for perhaps six months or so until a suitable vacancy arose in the workshop. In addition to assisting Len in any way he wished, the mundane side of my initial duties included making tea for the whole workforce during the official morning break and the collection and packing of dirty overalls each week so that they could be collected by the cleaning company.

The main purpose of the machine shop was to supply the mechanics with all the facilities required to undertake the more technical aspects of their role. It was equipped with all types of measuring devices (calipers, dividers and micrometers etc) and also housed a large free-standing lathe which was used quite regularly to re-bore engine cylinders, because the automobile trade was a different animal back in those days. Engines and gearboxes were routinely stripped down, cleaned and reassembled with new parts where necessary. Quite often, if a gearbox cog or shaft was not readily available from the manufacturer, Len would produce one with the array of tools in what he called his 'Aladdin's Cave'.

The other specific roles that were down to us were the making and fitting of number plates for all new vehicles and the fitment of radios when customers required them as an extra. It was only at about this time that manufacturers fitted vehicle heaters as standard equipment. My initial role in the machine shop was not filled with the glamour I had envisaged, but I did enjoy it. The drudgery of the tea making and overalls meant that I got to know every member of staff in a short period of time, and they me. The engineering aspect of the role gave me a detailed knowledge of how the internal combustion engine worked before I really began to get my hands dirty under the bonnet.

I didn't have to serve in the machine shop all that long, because about four months later Len announced his retirement, which he assured me personally had nothing to do with my arrival. The management decided to implement a cost cutting measure and Len's position was not filled. Each mechanic was to be responsible for his own machine shop activities. I had by now signed my apprenticeship papers indicating my intention of completing a five-year training programme and I was teamed up with a relatively young mechanic named Elwyn Newman. Elwyn was in his early 30s and we got on like a house on fire. Having tuned in to each other's mannerisms and idiosyncrasies, over the next few months we became a good team.

The widely-acclaimed Mini was introduced to the world in August 1959, so by the time I was Elwyn's lad they were rolling through our workshop for pre-delivery inspections at a rate of about 10 a month. The service manager had decided that Elwyn was to become the firm's 'expert' on this new revolutionary mode of transport, so it was we who were given the task of analysing any problems as they were fed to us by the stream of new owners. This procedure worked because as the number of Minis coming into the workshop increased and other mechanics had to be utilised to work on them, Elwyn was able to share his knowledge, with everyone else being able to pick his brains when necessary. This was the recognised practice in all large garage workshops; other mechanics working alongside us would have their own expertise in other makes and models.

A fact that was perhaps held back from the press and general public by the British Motor Corporation shortly after the Mini's launch was that it had a few technical design faults which became apparent to new owners well within the 12-month warranty period. The defect that cost BMC by far the most in initial warranty claims was clutch failure. This was caused by the plate becoming contaminated with oil, which leaked through a small seal fitted in the clutch housing. The seal was approximately two inches in diameter and would probably have cost, in those days, no more than 10 shillings (50p). The major problem was that to replace the seal, the clutch housing had to be removed and to remove the clutch housing, because it was a front-wheel drive vehicle, the whole power unit – engine and gear box – had to be completely removed from the vehicle. This was a major financial problem for BMC, because for the first few years of manufacture almost 50% of Minis sold developed clutch slippage in the first 12 months of use. To ease their fiscal problem, the boffins at BMC allowed their dealers and distributors throughout the country only a very restricted amount of time to carry out this work. As an example, the first few drive units that Elwyn and I removed and replaced took an average of three hours. Our firm was only allowed to claim back from the manufacturer the cost for one and a half hours – they were allowed to stipulate the time allowance under the terms and conditions of the dealership. No one needed an accountant to point out that the figures would not add up. There must have been thousands of garages around the country in a similar situation but none, including Chaston's, could afford to lose their BMC dealership. That was what was at stake if anyone had refused to undertake the work.

The service manager, after talking to Elwyn, decided to adopt a 'production line' approach, based on the principle that the more often you do a job the faster, and hopefully better, you'll do it. Elwyn and I were given almost every Mini clutch replacement that was booked through the workshop, certainly all that we could cope with, and just before I moved to another mechanic for further experience some 10 months later, we were completing the job in 50 minutes. Elwyn often joked in the years that followed that he found he could do it slightly quicker after I'd left – yes, he was joking. Wasn't he?

My introduction into the British workforce had gone

well; I was really enjoying myself. My 'on the job' training in the workshop was complemented by having to attend the local Technical College on a day release basis once a week, to undertake a City & Guilds course in mechanical engineering. It was for three years, and attendance was a condition of my legally-binding apprenticeship. The social side of working in Chaston's suited me also. There were a dozen apprentices aged between 16 and 21, a few young lads working in the body shop and a lad called Mike Davies who worked in the stores. He not only worked on the retail counter, selling to the public, but also supplied the workshop staff with our components. We all got on like the proverbial house on fire and there were always at least six of us who would get together each weekend.

Friday night would see us meet in the Tredegar Arms at the top end of the High Street, the proprietor of which was Ernie Young, who also worked as manager of our tyre department. As a group of young lads, we would never wilfully misbehave, but Ernie, knowing us all, would very often let us get away with some over-excitement, when some other landlord would have moved us on.

Saturday night would again see us all meet in the 'TA', but this was the evening when we'd soon drift up the road some 300 yards to the Miner's Institute, the type of building which could be found in almost every South Wales town. They were established with contributions from the area's mining workforce and dedicated to house their out of work pastimes and leisure. In the case of Blackwood, the ground floor provided snooker tables and upstairs there was a concert hall with a beautifully sprung floor which provided a first-class ballroom.

The Saturday night dance at Blackwood 'Stute' was renowned throughout the eastern valleys, and I mean that in the nicest possible way. It had a widespread reputation for live acts and good music and attracted members of the community, which obviously included young ladies, from far and wide. That is probably the reason why the lads from Chaston's spent their Saturday nights there.

Talking of the dance prompts me to mention that at about this time I was elected onto the firm's social committee. I really don't know why; I was probably told by Elwyn that I was their choice and I had no option. The committee met bi-monthly in an upstairs room at the 'TA', with sandwiches and one drink each provided by Ernie, who no doubt obtained reimbursement from somewhere in the organisation, as he was as tight as a duck's behind. The committee consisted of a member from each of the garage departments and we really had two roles. One was to devise and organise treasure hunts for the staff, wives, partners and friends, which we'd run three or four times a year; the course would traverse the county and we would arrange to terminate at some hostelry where we'd determine winners and present prizes culminating in a buffet. They were popular and we would often attract more than 20 cars.

Our second responsibility was to arrange the firm's annual dance each September, which was considered the local event that hundreds from far and wide wanted to attend. It was held in the 'Stute' ballroom and tickets would be on sale in the locality for about two months beforehand. As time drew nearer, tickets would become scarce and the dance was so popular that some say it was easier to get hold of a ticket for the East Terrace of Cardiff Arms Park for a

Wales v. England rugby fixture. There is no doubt that its popularity was due to the fact that some bright spark in years gone by had secured the attendance of Bob Miller and the Millermen, who proved such a success on their first visit that the welfare committee kept on booking them a year in advance.

Bob Miller and the Millermen were an instrumental band of the 1950s and early 1960s who appeared regularly on radio and television. They also toured with such names as Shirley Bassey, Cliff Richard and Bobby Darin. I met the band leader himself a few times during his visits whilst I was serving on the committee and he told me that for some reason, he always enjoyed bringing his musicians on this annual pilgrimage to our relatively quiet backwater in Wales. I think, from his point of view, it was one of those bookings where his band could just relax and enjoy themselves with nobody giving any criticism. Of course, the fee did help, which to my recollection was about £500, a great deal of money in 1960, but the price of our tickets ensured that the books balanced.

One of the really enjoyable perks we apprentices had, even from the early age of 16, was being allowed to drive all the vehicles we worked on. This was only inside the garage premises of course for those of us too young to hold a licence, but as I've pointed out, the workshop was a considerable size, so even the distance between our workbench and the lifting ramps mounted up during the working week to quite a few miles. With all the reversing and shunting that took place, we lads soon had the ability to handle most vehicles with a fair degree of expertise. It therefore followed that we only had to master the finer points of road craft before we were ready for our MOT driving tests. I passed mine in the pretty border town of Abergavenny two months to the day after my 17th birthday.

It was shortly after this time that the owner of the firm, Alfred John Chaston, generally referred to by the staff as 'AJ', sold the whole business to a larger organisation, Howell's of Cardiff, who also bought within the next few months a large firm in Newport and one in Swansea. Howell's of Cardiff was now one of the biggest BMC dealerships in the UK. We in Blackwood saw no consolidation. In fact, we saw expansion in our sales department, which was obviously reflected in greater activity in the workshop.

We soon learned that our regional organisation had secured a massive deal to supply British Road Services with new vehicles for use by their area sales representatives. This company was established in 1948, formed by the nationalisation of Britain's road haulage industry, and by the 1960s it consisted of BRS, who were transporters of all imaginable goods, BRS Parcels, later rebranded as Roadline, and Pickford's, who we all still know today. For those who have an interest in our industrial past, it may be of interest to know that in 1969, British Road Services was renamed the National Freight Corporation, which in 1982 was sold to its employees in one of the first privatisations of state-owned industry by Margaret Thatcher's government.

Well, that small slice of social history illustrates that BRS was a sizable organisation with a large number of sales representatives. Our contract with them was to supply Austin A40 Farina models, together with Austin A60s, all finished in light grey. The main aspect of this contract which excited us apprentices was that each vehicle had to be delivered to its allotted office, which were located countrywide, and it was obviously cost-effective to use low-wage apprentices to undertake this task. Most of us, by now, were fully licensed to drive, so we had a glorious few months being nominated to visit the four corners of England and Wales. The journey both ways was by car, because used vehicles were bought back in part exchange. This whole programme did cause some temporary jealousy and friction between us boys because our nomination depended on the workload of our particular mechanic or by our day release studies. Nevertheless, I was fortunate to secure several trips to some exotic places including Falmouth, Poole and Chester. Who said that work was a bind? At the age of seventeen and a half, I thought it was great.

Young lads in their late teens like to believe that they have become men, not only from a psychological point of view, but also biologically. Young ladies were always in the forefront of our minds, not only when out socially in mixed company, but when idly chatting with a cup of tea around a workshop stove. We had four large stoves in the workshops so we all did a fair bit of chatting. I had not attracted any girlfriends since leaving school, so on Friday and Saturday nights, together with one or two of my closer mates, we would endeavour, whenever possible, to inflict our presence on as many groups of young ladies as we could and attempt to sort the wheat from the chaff.

Over the next few months, several weekend dates came my way, but we were usually accompanied by one or two of my mates and their individual conquests. However, at one Saturday dance I shared some time with Hannah, a girl of my age who lived a short distance down the valley in Cwmfelinfach. I probably didn't set her world on fire, nor she mine, but we got along well enough and the relationship must have lasted all of six weeks. It was brought to an abrupt end when I bumped into a girl called Janet Morgan, again at the dance, and being unattached that particular night, I took her home. She was actually from my village, so that saved some petrol. I was able to have the use of my father's car at this time as he rarely took it out anywhere apart from the work run, due to my mother's duties, but a few of my older mates actually had vehicles of their own, which were purchased literally from scrapyards and refurbished using the works facilities.

I had been dating Janet for just a matter of weeks when we garage lads decided to arrange a night out to celebrate one of our birthdays. When I use the term 'celebrate' I don't wish to give the idea of some wild orgy, our 'celebrate' was to meet at some local public house for a laugh, a good natter and on the odd occasion, a game of cards. This night however, must have been a bit special because all the girls were invited and Janet mentioned that she was bringing a colleague from work.

Tuesday 27th March 1962 is a date that has been indelibly etched on my mind ever since. We all met up at the Church Inn, an olde-worlde building dating back to the 17th century and still in business today. It is situated in the tiny hamlet of Bedwellty, which gives its name to the surrounding parish and was the name adopted by Neil Kinnock, the local MP, when he was elevated to the House of Lords.

Our gang had occupied the small back room, which we

had more or less to ourselves, and it soon filled up as everyone started to arrive. Janet showed up fairly early with her friend, a brunette, who was about five feet four inches tall in fairly high heels. She sat with Janet and the other girls on the other side of the room, only 15 feet from me, and within minutes I was smitten. I could not take my eyes off this gorgeous young lady and desperately wanted to believe that she couldn't take hers off me. The only problem was that she had a turn in her left eye and when her head was at a certain inclination, she seemed to be looking at someone to my right. It didn't make a scrap of difference; I was convinced that I was in love. We had no conversation all evening. I was nervous and somewhat shy, but as the evening broke up I somehow managed to ask if I could take her home. She agreed without hesitation. In any event, I had convinced myself that she was leaving with me and no one else.

Bedwellty is somewhat 'out in the sticks' as they say, and although I remained a perfect gentleman, I did park up for a short while and we both took the opportunity to elicit as much information as possible about each other. I eventually dropped Shelby (I thought her name was great too) off at her home, arranging to telephone the following day. I drove the three miles home to Markham flying at 10,000 feet, totally convinced that I'd met the girl I wanted to share the rest of my life with.

For some strange reason, I never bumped into Janet Morgan again after that night, but some 10 years later I found that her brother Christopher was one of my uniformed sergeants when I was deputy commander at Ebbw Vale. Shelby never questioned me about the uceremonious manner in which I had dumped Janet on the night we met, and I never enquired about any discussion they may have had, though I know that Shelby would have dealt with it in her own inimitable way.

I have mentioned earlier that I was really enjoying my role as an apprentice. The work was interesting and I had become involved with a nice group of colleagues and was spending most of my social time with them. But now I was happier than I could ever imagine. Everyone must experience the same feeling at some point in their lives, but when it happens to you, wow, it's special.

I saw Shel, as she was always known to her family and friends, every evening and weekend for months and rang her at work from a local call box almost every lunch hour. She accompanied me on all social activities with my workmates and we both became good personal friends of my instructor mechanic, Elwyn, and his wife. My life had been lifted up a notch and everywhere I went was with a spring in my step.

Only three weeks after we met, Shel invited me to a social evening, when most of her family were getting together to say goodbye to her older brother, who was leaving for overseas duty having recently joined the RAF. My introduction to her mum and dad seemed to go fine and I'm sure that her prior description of me matched their anticipated perception. To them I was, after all, Nurse Thorne's son!

I think that at this point it's worth mentioning my short foray into the thespian world, which, with a good agent, might have propelled me into the West End and beyond! The very suave sales manager at the garage was one Raymond Davenport, who I would describe as a real gentleman. Raymond was gay, a fact which in those days would only have been acknowledged by the individual's close circle of friends. Of course, all the garage staff were aware of Ray's sexuality and fully accepted it, because he really was the nicest of guys with an endearing personality. Anyway, besides being a damn good sales manager, he was a leading light in the Blackwood Amateur Dramatic Society, which regularly put on productions at the Little Theatre in the town centre.

During the autumn of 1962, Ray was to be the producer of their next show, *The Boy Friend,* a 1950s hit musical written by Sandy Wilson. It had a relatively small cast, the nucleus consisting of a group of young boys and girls enjoying themselves on the French Riviera. Now, you don't generally find many youngsters involving themselves in amateur dramatics, so where did Ray hope to find some of the boys? Yes, you've got it. The garage apprentices. He tried to recruit several, but was only successful in securing the efforts of two, me and Jeff Lewis, who at 19 was a year older than me. God knows why we agreed. Perhaps it was the proposed cast of young girls which spurred us on, but that shouldn't have influenced me as my mind was fully occupied by Shel.

For several weeks following our initial commitment to Ray, he totally ignored all our lame excuses for pulling out, and we both found ourselves at the first evening rehearsal when we had our initial read of the script. Jeff came away that evening having been cast in the ensemble with a few other young lads and I found myself in the supporting role of Bobby Van Husen. This production, as a musical, meant that I was involved with all the others in the songs, choruses and other activities, but as this guy Bobby, I found myself having to sing a duet with Maisie, another supporting role and with only us two on stage at one point we had to dance the Charleston.

Well, both Jeff and I saw it through, culminating in four live performances before the paying public. Shel was looking forward to her visit on the last night and brought her mother along to enjoy the entertainment, which went well until we met up for the journey home. You see, I hadn't fully explained over the previous weeks that as Maisie and I concluded our duet, the script dictated that we had to slowly sink onto a chaise longue, positioned centre stage, and there, whilst the curtain slowly closed on Act Two, we should engage in a romantic kiss. It took several days for me to talk Shel round, but she eventually calmed down. The drama critic of the local paper described my performance as 'adequate'.

My relationship with Shel was, in my mind, becoming as serious as it could get; it was special. But what it did for me was to make me think about the important things in life. At 18 years of age, a young man like me in the full flow of youth thinking that the world is his oyster doesn't often contemplate the future with a serious mind and appreciate what responsibilities lie ahead, but on the odd occasion I did.

I really enjoyed my work as it was; although the money was rubbish as an apprentice it would increase slowly over time, but would it improve enough to enable me to raise a family in relative comfort? And did I want to spend 20 minutes each evening after work at the kitchen sink, trying to scrub the grease and oil from my fingers? To be honest, my heart and soul were still pushing me towards the Police Service. After several discussions with Shel I decided that it was for me, and if that was the case, then the sooner the better. The age for entrance to the Force was 19 years and that was only a few months away. So my application letter winged its way to Police HQ at Abergavenny.

The procedure at that time was to ask all applicants to visit the local Sub-Divisional Commander, so that their presence and bearing could be scrutinised during a short chat, and so it was that one evening I presented myself before Chief Inspector Edwin Williams at Blackwood Police station. C/I Williams was an ex RAF Wing Commander and had the handlebar moustache to prove it. He was a formidable sight in full uniform behind his desk to a simple valley lad who, by this time, was an expert only at draining oil from an engine sump.

He listened to my tale, to my hopes and aspirations and, more importantly to me, he listened with interest and concern (qualities which, as I came to acknowledge a few years later, are essential in a good police officer). He finalised our meeting with some straight, hard-hitting words. "Stay put young man," he said with a glint in his eye. He reminded me that I was more than half way through a five-year apprenticeship and to leave now would be throwing a qualification down the drain. He advised me to secure my 'papers' (a statutory apprenticeship in those days consisted of a long hand-scribed contract, which I am still in possession of) and if I still had the same enthusiasm when I became 21 I should then apply.

I came away from that meeting feeling somewhat

dejected and forlorn. But goodness me, wasn't he right. With Shel giving me loads of encouragement, I soon got over my initial disappointment and settled down to my role in the workshops, thinking quite light-heartedly that it would only be just over two years anyway.

The relationship Shel and I shared was blossoming. I knew without doubt, and so did she, that we were slowly falling deeper in love as time went by and what's more, we kept telling each other so. We were just like those two lovebirds that Donny and Marie Osmond sang about – 'but he lived on the morning side of the mountain, and she lived on the twilight side of the hill'. That's exactly where our respective homes were, but the beauty was, unlike the song lyrics, fate had allowed us to meet.

We were slowly being introduced to each other's families and after only about four months we both went on holiday with her mum and dad to Clacton-on-Sea. I reciprocated by taking her away for a few nights to visit members of my family at Eastbourne and Winscombe in Somerset. It was shortly afterwards that Shel, snuggled into my left shoulder, sat in an Austin A60 on top of Caerphilly mountain, answered quietly and lovingly "yes" when I asked her to marry me.

Some big things were also happening at work. The group's management had decided to introduce a bonus scheme for the mechanics throughout all the workshops. The scheme did not apply to apprentices, but it gave the qualified staff the opportunity to increase their weekly take home pay quite considerably. The nuts and bolts of the scheme meant that every repair or servicing task allocated to a mechanic was given a specific cost, and on successful completion that amount would be allotted to the mechanic's weekly pay.

The daily administration of this scheme involved extra clerical work in the workshop office, and they selected a man called Maldwyn Hope to undertake the role. Mal was the oldest mechanic, nearing retirement at the time, and his role for the past few years had been to carry out all mechanical and electrical work on vehicles that had undergone bodywork repairs after accidents. Mal welcomed this move to a desk job in his advancing years and you'll probably never guess who was to replace him. Yes, me!

The service manager called me to his office late one afternoon and asked me if I would like to take on the role. He explained that he was of the view that I was capable of working on my own and that I had the necessary knowledge. Furthermore, the general manager was also happy for me to take part in the bonus scheme, even though I still had 12 months of my apprenticeship to complete. I absolutely jumped at the chance.

The bonus scheme was a resounding success. Most of the mechanics were married men with families and it was regularly possible for them to earn around £20 per week. Now this increase in pay wasn't going to be handed out on a plate, it really had to be earned by the employee giving his full cooperation and working in an industrious manner with full effort. We all know that in life not everything goes to plan, and often jobs would present themselves on which two, three or even more attempts were necessary to complete the task. The mechanic would obviously take longer and therefore lose money on his day's work, but everyone realised that you had to take the bad with the good. If the service manager wanted to assist men with jobs that they knew were going to be awkward from the start, he gave them to me. I really didn't mind because in reality, I should have been on the basic apprentice's pay anyway, so I was still quids in.

The early 1970s were a somewhat turbulent time in Britain for blue-collar workers. The larger unions were flexing their muscles on the industrial scene, and nowhere more so than in the heartland of manufacturing in Birmingham. The city was the capital of the British motor industry and Derek Robinson, a member of the Communist Party of Great Britain, who was a convenor and shop steward at British Leyland, was starting to organise widespread strikes in support of higher wages and better working conditions. He was known as 'Red Robbo' and some say that his ultra-militant style was partly responsible for the complete demise of this country's motor vehicle manufacturing capability at that time. I clearly remember that in Red Robbo's heyday there were newspaper headlines proclaiming that he had secured £1000 per annum as the basic wage for his members. I could have told them all that there was a group of vehicle mechanics in South Wales who had been achieving that some eight years previously, without all the hardship and strife.

It was at about this time that something of a bombshell suddenly exploded at the garage. One morning, just after tea break, one of the lads returned to the workshop having visited the stores counter to collect various parts and told his mate that he had seen a swarm of police officers walking around the stores complex. To describe them as a 'swarm' was perhaps a little overstated, but the crux of the message was correct. In fact, I later learned that there had been two uniformed constables and a detective sergeant. Well, you can imagine how the rumours circulated, and as the initial snippet of information was passed from one to another, as is usually the case, it was exaggerated until it grew and grew. It wasn't until the following day that we started to glean the information that the police had been called in by management after the stores manager, in a routine stocktake, had discovered a fairly sizeable number of parts missing. The police presence continued for three or four days, and then one of the apprentices, who I seem to recall was one of my closer mates, Rhys Davies, was called to the workshop office and instructed that he should report immediately to the town's police station, which was only a 10-minute walk away. The whole garage complex was instantly abuzz with speculation, and the apprentices, including me, were quivering with trepidation. Had Rhys been involved in the mysterious goings-on in the stores? Would we all have to go to the police station? Were they going to accuse us of taking the stock?

It must have been a worry for every lad employed at the garage, but I was petrified. If they were going to implicate me in this enquiry, then I was lost. Shel and I had our hearts set on me joining the police service and my application was imminent. I knew that I had done absolutely nothing wrong, but my heart was pounding as we all waited for Rhys to return, assuming he was ever going to return. We passed a terrible few hours until Rhys arrived and told us that our mate working in the stores, Mike Davies, was being investigated for various allegations of theft over a fairly long-term period.

Being in the motor trade, it was natural that we all undertook servicing and repair work on our own cars and those of friends and family. In fact, the general manager had no objection to us having access to the workshops on a Sunday morning to utilise the facilities and furthermore, all staff were given generous discounts on the parts and accessories we purchased from the stores. All purchases would have been in cash and as there were only two people manning the stores counters, Mike Davies would have been dealing with the various sales a large percentage of the time. I had purchased various fittings, oil, filters, hoses, bulbs and the like from him personally over a period of two to three years and on each occasion I had handed him the payment, always in cash.

Several more members of staff were called to the police station over the following days, including me, and I explained my situation clearly to the detective sergeant who interviewed me. He was quite straight with me, easing my mind, and explained that we lads had paid for the goods as bona fide purchases and were not guilty of handling stolen property. However, he required statements to complete his case file. Every employee at the garage was shell-shocked for the next few weeks while the police concluded their investigation and we apprentices, together with quite a few of the mechanics, who had also been hoodwinked, could not really come to terms with the fact that one of our colleagues was not only taking goods from our employer, but was taking and keeping money from us too.

Mike Davies was a silly young man and at the conclusion of the case was, in my view, a very fortunate one.

The final outcome was, of course, decided behind closed doors, but there was no court case. He left the employ of Chaston's forthwith and to avoid widespread publicity, the garage management requested the police to take the matter no further. There is no doubt that if the matter had been aired in the local Magistrate's Court, bearing in mind the large amount of stock involved and that the theft was against an employer, then any culprit would have very probably been facing a prison term. Mike went to work at a garage in Pengam, which was less than three miles away and to my knowledge, he spent the rest of his working life in the motor trade.

CHAPTER 4

During the last few summer months of 1965, I was still employed at Chaston's, fulfilling the contractual requirement to complete my five-year apprenticeship. During working hours I was there in body and soul, but my mind was very often otherwise engaged with the application and selection process I had embarked on. At that time, there was nothing that I wanted to do other than become a police officer, but I do not wish to detract in any way from the enjoyment and fulfilment I had from working at the garage. It was a part of my life that I would not want to put aside.

However, at that time, as many others would have been, I was completely enthralled by the excitement of the whole process. This was going to be a challenge, a completely different way of life from that I had experienced to date. I wondered constantly about a myriad of things. Would I still socialise with my present friends? Would they in fact want me to? What would I look like in uniform with that ridiculously big helmet?

I seemed to answer all my own thoughts to my satisfaction. The one thought that was constantly with me was that Shel, the girl I loved, made me feel special and I wanted to make her proud.

My selection process went well and I was called for interview at Monmouthshire Constabulary's Headquarters in Abergavenny. My interview board consisted of the Chief Constable and the administrative Chief Superintendent together with a Mr Smeed. Now, from a police point of view this was most unusual, because Mr Smeed was the Chief Constable of the Newport Borough Force. I only learned afterwards that his presence was due to a cordial invitation by Mr Farley, the Chief Constable of Monmouthshire. The Police Act of 1964 gave the then Home Secretary power to force the compulsory amalgamations of police forces throughout the United Kingdom; in fact, they were to reduce from 117 to 49. Although these two forces did not amalgamate until April 1967, the two Chief Constables must have known that something was on the cards at the time of my application so they were working hand in hand. Actually, on amalgamation, Mr Farley continued as Chief and Mr Smeed became his Deputy. Mr Sneed retired soon afterwards, but in later years, I got to know Mr Farley very well.

So that tells you that my interview was successful. A week or two later I had an official letter offering me the position of police constable in the Monmouthshire Constabulary as and from Monday 13 September 1965. On that morning I attended promptly with two other successful candidates, when we were afforded an in-depth tour of the building with an explanatory talk on the roles of the various departments housed there. I have no idea why, but a small snippet of spurious information embedded itself in my mind during one session and remained there for years to come. It was that the Monmouthshire Constabulary had an authorised establishment of 465 officers. It also had an actual strength of 465 officers, which made it the only force in England and Wales to be fully manned at that time. It's annoyed me ever since that no one has ever asked me a question which would have allowed me to impress them with such detailed knowledge!

Back to my first day in the force, and the moment that all three of us were waiting for eventually arrived. We were taken to the stores for the uniform issue. It was probably the same as any quartermaster's stores in the army, only ours was a fraction of the size and had one employee who controlled everything. He was a retired policeman, about six feet four inches tall and named Jack. By this time, it was late afternoon and we new recruits were about to experience a life-changing event, although to Jack it was just another tedious exercise in between issuing toilet rolls and light bulbs. He made it clear that he was due to finish in 30 minutes and he had no intention of staying any longer. We were issued with uniform and appointments, most of which were second-hand, apart from the blue shirts with detachable collars that gave me a sore neck on quite a few occasions over the following years, due to the constant starching. When we tried the trousers and tunics on, it must have looked abundantly clear to Jack that we hadn't walked straight out of Savile Row, otherwise he would not have advised us with total confidence that we would 'grow into them'.

In addition to our appointments, which included the universal whistle and chain, handcuffs and the shaft of wood mechanically turned into our truncheon, or 'staff' as we were told to call it, we were also given an antiquated-looking torch, which had a set of small levers on one side which operated sliding glass panels of red and green glass. Apparently, it was the latest invention to assist an officer in directing traffic at night, but even back in 1965, we three recruits could not help but snigger. Jack was not impressed as he watched the clock tick closer to five o'clock. I never ever used that torch. In fact, I really should have tried to hold on to it, as it would be a collector's item now.

Out of interest, I never had need to blow my whistle in anger, and I drew my staff with purpose from its retention pocket sewn inside my right trouser leg on just one occasion, when I had to smash a rear passenger window in a Vauxhall Viva in order to force the door open to gain access to an injured passenger after a road traffic accident.

We were also issued with several sets of small chrome numbers which had Shel and me spending a few laborious hours that evening attaching them to all my epaulettes. I was to be known henceforth as Constable 140.

During my first day's induction at Abergavenny, I was told to report the following morning to Blackwood Police Station, my nearest Divisional HQ, where I would spend two weeks before being posted to the Regional Police Training Centre for 13 weeks' initial training. My first task on that Tuesday morning was to present myself in front of Chief Inspector Edwin Williams, the bristly-faced gentleman who had advised me to 'go away' two and a half years earlier. He spelt out to me that although I wore the appropriate uniform of the force, I was most certainly not a police officer, not until I had been sworn in and taken the Queen's Oath, and that would not be until after my initial training. He reminded me I had no more powers than Mr Joe Public and that I should remember the fact. He further told me that there were just two things he wanted me to do in the days under his command; that was to look and to listen. And that is exactly what I did.

I had eight working days left at Blackwood before my posting and seven of them were spent totally within the confines of the station building and yard. I was, of course, utilised to make copious amounts of tea each day and sat down in the corner of the enquiry office to undertake all kinds of paper sifting, box-ticking and filing. In fact, any kind of task that had been shunned by everyone for the past six months. But I didn't care two hoots, I was spending my day sat in the hub of a very busy police station, seeing and listening to everything that went on around me. I was fascinated by this new world, which had my mind spinning. I was adamant that whatever was thrown at me in the next three months, I would cope with it, because I wanted to become part of it. I would soon learn at training school that I needed to cope for two years. That was the length of the probationary period for all recruits and within that time the Chief Constable could dispense with our services for a multitude of reasons.

I arrived spick and span on the last morning at Blackwood, for I had been 'bulling' my boots and pressing my trousers each evening – a fad that passes in time – and was preparing to delve into my paperwork, when Sergeant Pratt, a man-mountain of well over six foot, told me to don my coat and helmet before introducing me to a gorgeous uniformed policewoman. "This is Jennifer, PW Jones, young man," he said, "you're going to spend today on patrol with her". I don't really know what excited me most, spending the day out facing the public or the thought of walking alongside this beautiful young lady. She was a stunner! She made quite an impression on my mind, but I have never revealed that to anyone before, not even Shel when I got home that night. The last thing I wanted to do was upset her at this early stage in proceedings.

Jennifer Jones had only been in the force herself for a short while and she turned out to be a very good police officer. She married a serving officer and resigned after starting a family some years later and tragically, was involved in a road traffic accident in which she sustained quite serious injuries. Her husband Malcolm progressed to become a superintendent, whom I supervised in later service.

However, my first day on foot patrol with his wife is something I will never forget. Not because of what happened, but for the totally confused and disorientated state of my mind. Jennifer was first class; she understood my nervousness and did her utmost to make my day as instructive as possible. Inside, I was in a hell of a state. What if someone were to stop and ask me something? It could be anything. What would I say? What if there was a road accident? What if someone reports a crime?

My whole body gave a sigh of relief later that day as we took our last few steps towards the sanctuary of the police station, but not before a dear old lady approached us in William Street. She came towards me and not Jen, possibly because I was taller and, well, bigger. I could not avoid her path; my heart started to pound and I made some idle conversation with Jen, hoping that the lady would disappear. This elderly member of the public walked straight up to me, held a small purse up to my face and said "I found this outside Woolworth's, officer". I wanted the pavement to open up and swallow me, and as far as I recall I didn't even answer the lady. Jennifer looked at me and simultaneously read the situation. She responded immediately and took over, dealing with it in a textbook manner. Full details were entered in her pocket book, including a list of items in the purse, which was signed by the finder, and on our return to the station the purse was placed into 'found property'. Seemed simple enough. What on earth had been the matter with me? I needed to pull myself together – fast.

I had settled in quite well at Blackwood during my two-week attachment. I had got to know some faces and I was known well enough by several of the day staff to receive a greeting most mornings, which makes you feel good in strange, unnerving surroundings. However, as I left on that second Friday afternoon I felt a degree of trepidation as I was only too aware that I was to leave the security of my home surroundings two days later, on a Sunday, to embark on a 13-week intensive training programme. Still, I had Shel to spend the weekend with, and I recall that we spent most of the time talking about the coming three months and packing two fairly large suitcases. I not only had to take my civilian clothes but every item of uniform I had been issued with.

My course was being held at the No. 8 District Police training Centre in Bridgend, which consisted of a group of classrooms housed in several prefabricated buildings and miscellaneous huts within the site surrounding the Glamorgan Police HQ. Also based within the compound were the Home Office technicians who installed and repaired police vehicle radios and the No. 8 District Police Driving School. The Home Office, for administrative reasons, had split the polices forces of England and Wales into groups, and number eight had been allocated to the one comprising all the forces in Wales. Our dormitories and ablutions were actually in a corner of the main building, which did afford us the luxury of central heating.

By this time, I was the proud owner of a third-hand A40 Farina, painted bright red with a black roof. Very suave! I'd bought it approximately six months earlier at Chaston's and Elwyn had helped me recondition it by fitting new pistons to the engine and overhauling the suspension. It really was a great little runner. I used it for my expedition to Bridgend on that Sunday afternoon, 26 September, where I, together with the other 21 apprehensive guests, were introduced to the two training sergeants who would be looking after us until Christmas.

We all had to report to the temporary reception area (everything in the whole centre looked temporary), for which one of the classrooms had been designated, and there we met Sergeant DR Evans and Sergeant M Thomas, both from the host Glamorgan force, identified by regimented labels above their breast pockets. They were from their own force's training department, but because they were technically on attachment to the Home Office to instruct us new recruits, they, and in particular Sergeant Thomas, attempted to impress on everyone that they were hard-headed Sergeant Majors straight off the parade ground. And boy, did Sergeant Thomas try to impress me!

I have mentioned that I had needed two suitcases to hold my gear, but in addition I had taken a small grey plaid duffle bag with a pull cord around the top (I can see it now). I was using it to hold my toiletries and it was a handy place to carry my police appointments and training booklets which had been issued to me on induction day. I was saying my last goodbyes to the family when my mother, who no doubt thought I was going to be starved for three months, slipped an apple and a large orange into the top of the bag.

The drive to Bridgend went well and with the light Sunday traffic it took some two and a half hours. It would have taken much longer during the working week because the M4 motorway was still under construction, and the A48 in those days was one of the busiest and most dangerous four-lane roads in the country.

I entered the reception room with some nervousness and Sergeant Thomas instructed me to place my bags in the area which was clearly identified and take a seat. As I slipped the duffle bag off my shoulder, the fruit escaped through the drawstring and went rolling quietly and sedately across the room. Sergeant Thomas made some light-hearted comment which I cannot recall, but was certainly embarrassing. Luckily, only one or two recruits had arrived before me but I was as red as a beetroot. Politely, but with the familiarity of someone who has worked for two weeks at a busy station, I said "sorry Sarge". Sergeant Thomas, who was some 20 feet away from me, strode across and with his face no more than six inches from mine, pointed to his stripes and said, "See these? They tell the world I'm a Sergeant and not a bloody sarge! Do you understand?"

"Yes Sergeant," I said meekly.

When all 22 of us had arrived, we were given the basic dos and don'ts of our accommodation and advised that as a group we would be known for eternity as 'Class Six'. However, for day-to-day activities we were split into two syndicates and I was allocated to Sergeant Evans. Thank God!

The three months training at Bridgend was something akin to basic training for the armed forces I would imagine, with less emphasis on the physical requirements and much more on the academic. Our physical activities involved a three-mile cross-country run every week and swimming sessions twice a week, which took place at RAF St Athan, a round trip of some 20 miles which was made in an ex-military bus. To use the term 'coach' would be misleading because it was just a green-painted metal box with one-inch wide battened seating throughout. I recall that the driver was provided with one of partial fabric. Good gosh, it was a battered old thing, not capable of much more than 30mph on a downward slope with a following wind.

The swimming pool was no grander, just a large oblong pit of water with a deep end and a shallow end, and I can vividly recall that the changing rooms were as cold as the water we swam in. We had no life-saving instruction and Sergeant Anderson, our fitness instructor, was totally happy if we could demonstrate half a dozen strokes in the water whilst staying afloat. With the weather now quite autumnal, the experience every week was like a polar expedition, which not one of us looked forward to. The only bright spot was the mug of tea we had on re-entering the bus before the trip back, and even that was poured from Thermos flasks that our canteen had provided before we left.

On a par with the armed forces, we were given a surprisingly high percentage of drill instruction. Well, I thought so anyway. Not that I was averse to marching, and I suppose it did instil in us 'civvies' a degree of pride, discipline and team spirit. In addition to three or four periods of drill each week, we would have to form up on parade at eight-thirty each morning to be inspected by Sergeant Jackson, the drill instructor, and on a Friday morning by the Commandant. This morning muster took place on the large car park at the front of Police HQ, and ran alongside the main road heading into Bridgend. We must have provided an amusing sight each morning for the local population as they passed by on their way to work.

The remainder of our time was spent learning, digesting and putting into practice all aspects of criminal law and its enforcement. We literally spent hours in the classroom being lectured on every type of misdemeanour and we were expected to learn definitions verbatim. They really had to be word-perfect to gain any marks in the weekly tests.

The hands-on instruction in how to put all this law enforcement into practice took place in 'beat occs'. This was our everyday slang for 'beat occurrences', which were the day-to day happenings which police officers would possibly be confronted with during their working lives. They were enacted by the instructors, who always made the issues far more complicated and serious than they would have been in reality, and we recruits were selected randomly in ones and twos to deal with them. After the first few days we had all bonded and were, generally speaking, good mates, but having to put yourself on a stage as it were, in front of everyone and deal with whatever confronted you was really daunting. However, no one really 'took the mick' because we all knew that we would probably be picked next.

I must admit, we had very little time for socialising and very few of the lads left the centre of an evening, which you were allowed to do for an hour or two. The amount of studying was considerable. We were supplied with a small bar at the centre for our exclusive use, which was open between eight and ten and was staffed by us recruits from a rota which was announced each Friday. It wasn't too onerous, as there were in total some 60 young men in training. The centre took on a new class of recruits each month, so during my three-month period with Class Six there were two other groups at their own stages of training.

Our working day ended at five o'clock apart from Wednesdays, when it was three-thirty. This gave the local force recruits time to travel home for an hour or so, but for me it was a little tight. I do recall that during the last month of my training I jumped into my little red bomb one Wednesday and made it home in double quick time to surprise Shel for an hour's visit. I was able, however, to get home most weekends, apart from, I believe, two, when we were detailed to be part of a security team that had to remain on site. None of us could fathom the need for it because there were scores of police officers working 24 hours a day in Police HQ. All part of the 'team building' I suppose.

As I've tried to point out, these weeks of basic training really kept us busy and the only time for personal thoughts was that hour or so, late evening, when you were either ironing trousers or bulling boots. There were no 'lights out'; they gave us credit for being adult and fairly sensible and in any event, I think that we were all ready to hit those pillows by 11 at the latest. That was when most of us, certainly me, reflected on our personal thoughts. Had I done the right thing by joining and moving away from home? Was Shelby going to go along with this or be snapped up by someone else? Was the money going to be sufficient? I'd left the garage taking a substantial pay cut.

These thoughts drifted through my mind more than once, but subconsciously I must have been happy with my answers, because I battled on.

Christmas 1965, and the end of my training was fast approaching. Although we had weekly tests to monitor our progress, there was no final examination or definitive assessment to say that we had passed. The Commandant would be preparing a lengthy report for each of our Chief Constables and they would be the ones who would determine our future.

Two weeks before we left Bridgend, one question was sending ripples of expectation and apprehension through the class – where were we all being posted? We had been discussing the pros and cons and the ifs and buts between ourselves at every opportunity, particularly those recruits from the same constabulary. Back in the Force, at police stations throughout the county, any officer being transferred to another station would be afforded an interview with their Divisional or Sub-Divisional Commander to be told face to face of their fate and usually the reasons, but all officers undergoing training outside the

Force area would be advised in writing, and very publicly. Details of their postings would be published in the Force General Orders, which was a multiple-page pamphlet issued on a weekly basis. Even this important information arrived late because we had to wait for the GPO (General Post Office, later to become the Royal Mail) to transport it to us. At that time, General Orders were issued on a Thursday in the Monmouthshire Constabulary and the 'powers that be' did not decide to commit our important information to print until 16 December. The three recruits from Monmouthshire in Class 6 were therefore notified on Monday 20 December, three days before we left Bridgend at the conclusion of our training.

I have no recollection as to where my two colleagues were heading, but I was destined for 'B' Division, Abersychan. Abersychan? I'd never heard of it and neither of my mates could assist. I was 21 years of age; I had been employed within the automotive industry for five years and I thought I was pretty knowledgeable about my own county.

Before packing all my kit back into the A40 Farina and heading east back up the A48, I had ascertained that my new home would be, for the foreseeable future, in a village lying some four miles north of Pontypool in the Eastern Valley. I arrived home on 23 December, and that afternoon made contact with my new station by telephone. The Sergeant, who was out on some mission at the time, rang back and told me that he had not yet fitted me into the duty rota. He told me to enjoy my Christmas and report for duty on 28 December. That was the last Christmas day I would have off for the next four years.

CHAPTER 5

Shel and I drove to Abersychan on Christmas Eve and spent an hour or so touring the area to take in what was to be my new environment. I would get to know it in far more detail during the coming months, and at a much slower pace. The police station was an austere red brick building which was standing just a pavement's width away from the main valley road. Constructed in the Victorian age, it had the then-familiar blue lamp suspended over the main door for all to see.

That first morning of duty saw me full of anxiety, but I was soon put at ease by one of the two sergeants who were stationed there, Sergeant Sid Davies. He was an old stalwart of the Force and he epitomised the typical police sergeant, someone who you knew could deal with any situation that arose. Well, he certainly did to me anyway. He was not that tall, but rotund. He stood in the charge office like an oak tree that defied to be moved. His upper arms were like tree trunks and as he entered through the door after collecting his mug of tea from the kitchen, which was his wont, you would glance up and the wide chevrons stitched to his sleeve would appear like a squadron of Spitfires descending from the clouds.

In describing Sergeant Davies in this manner, I in no way wish to detract from his character or abilities, because he was a gent, and more so for me, he was a damn good policeman. He won my respect within the first week and I would have done anything the man asked me to do. He was the exact opposite of his colleague, Sergeant Doug Moon. But more of him later.

Sergeant Davies gave me a tour of the building, which took no more than five minutes, as the whole station environment consisted of simply an enquiry-cum-charge office, an interview room and a small kitchen. He then took me out into the small station yard, which was just big enough to hold the brand new Commer Cob van parked there. He proudly informed me that it had been delivered from HQ just a week previously and that I was to have responsibility for looking after it. He'd ascertained that I was a qualified mechanic and he'd also arranged for me to take my force driving test the following week. Sergeant Davies was certainly on the ball and methodical.

He now turned his attention to the subject I was dreading; my lodgings. It was the practice at that time (and still could be, though I doubt it very much) for all new probationers to be initially posted away from their home surroundings and allocated lodgings in their work area, which would help them to bond with the locality. Each station's records held a list of locals who had indicated their willingness to become temporary landlords or ladies, and mine turned out to be Mrs Hutchins. The sergeant described her as a dear old lady, a widow, who was living on her own just 500 yards from the Police Station. His last task with me just before I finished duty on that first day was to take me on foot patrol along Snatchwood Road to introduce me.

He was right, she seemed very pleasant. She lived in a quite small two up, two down terraced cottage running right alongside the main road. I recall that her small home was directly opposite a large Victorian terraced property which was the birthplace of one of our former Home Secretaries, the Right Honourable Roy Jenkins. Before leaving Mrs Hutchins I arranged, with the approval of Sergeant Davies, to move in on the following Monday, which was to be my first night shift.

The authorised strength at Abersychan police station, in addition to the two sergeants, was 10 constables, which included two outstation officers at Garndiffaith. This may appear to be a rather large contingent for what I have described as a village, but our 'patch' covered an area traversing down the valley over a mile to encompass the village of Pontnewynydd, and north up the valley some five miles towards Blaenavon. It also covered several square miles of sprawling habitation which, to us law enforcers, was one large conurbation, although to the locals living there, they were defined communities with their own identities.

The colleagues I worked with were as mixed a bunch as you'd find anywhere and I can honestly say that during the following nine months there was no one I had a problem with. We had Tony, who had come out of training centre only six months before me, so we saw life through the same set of eyes. We had Bill; he was the plodder who did everything at the same speed – but he did it. Whatever the weather, Bill would religiously have his cape folded and slung over his left shoulder, which gave a clear view of the fag ash spread down the right-hand side of his tunic. There was Mel, who nobody could really dislike, but you felt like throttling him very often because of his non-stop hyperactive personality. I breathed a small sigh of relief when I did leave Mel at Abersychan, but I was to jump from the frying pan into the fire quicker than I had thought.

Then there was Adrian. He was one of those useless uniform carriers who would expend copious amounts of energy every day trying to avoid work. The one attribute he did possess was the ability to play golf to a reasonable standard. So did the Chief Constable, who was the captain of the force golf team, so it followed that Adrian was always picked to play each week and after each duty roster was formulated, it was altered and amended as often as necessary to accommodate Adrian's attendance. We were mere mortals who had to endure it and although it made the hairs on the back of Sergeant Davies' neck stand up, he knew he was on a loser because if he did attempt to involve Adrian in some work, the telephone would ring on the morning of a match day with an instruction from HQ that the Chief would like Adrian to be made available.

I will now just mention Sergeant Moon, who had joined the station not long before me. It became obvious within days that Sergeant Davies did not get along with him, and did not want to. Nor did any of the lads. Sergeant Davies did not in fact have to work with him; they were always providing supervision on opposing shifts. Not one of us constables within the section had anything good to say about Sergeant Moon. Within the first few weeks I could see not only that he had an overbearing attitude to us men, but that he was the same with the public. When you're working with someone for eight hours a day, seven days a week, non-stop, you fairly quickly spot when they have an ulterior motive. Sergeant Moon's was to gain any pecuniary advantage that he could and his uniform and vested authority were the means by which he achieved it. His professional skills, bearing and diplomacy would have all been marked on the minus scale. To be brutally frank and honest, I felt ashamed on the odd occasion when he would accompany me on foot patrol.

There are many experiences which stick in your memory after a working career, but a few do so more than most, and one such started at about 11.30 one Friday night. I had commenced work at 10pm and Sergeant Davies was the supervisor between 5 pm and 1 am. I received a call from Divisional HQ informing us that there had been an accident reported on the main A4043 at Cwmavon. They told me that the nearest traffic car was some 20 miles away and that we should attend. There were two of us in the station at that time with the Sergeant, and as soon as he had digested my news, he said to me "Get the van, I'll come with you".

Although it was a main 'A' class road, the traffic was relatively quiet at that time of night, but I was still tense because the only other accident I had dealt with previously had occurred in abundant sunlight, on a minor side street, and had involved no more than a broken light lens and one terribly frightened sheep.

The scene on arrival was pitch black with only the moon and stars to assist, but we soon ascertained that there was only one vehicle involved, which appeared to have lost control after colliding with a boundary wall. Sergeant Davies instructed me to place a warning sign on both approaches and I remember looking back towards him as he approached the vehicle. It was on its side, a Bedford van, the type which used to help me deliver milk. As I rejoined Sergeant Davies, I could tell by his demeanour that there was something seriously amiss. He said quite slowly but clearly "We've got a bad one here lad. There's two male bodies inside and one on the bank". I don't think I replied; I just felt sick. My head spun like a top for the next few moments, my mind raced and the scene just seemed to spin by in seconds. I became aware of bystanders who had appeared from cars that had stopped at the scene and as I tried to think what to do, I was asking myself, "God, is this what I joined the police for?"

Then I felt a slight sense of relief as I saw a blue light some 500 yards away, a traffic car speeding towards us. I was to get to know it in the coming months; a black Zephyr 6, call sign Tango 162. I continued to search the scene for property and possible evidence whilst the two traffic officers conferred with Sergeant Davies and assisted the ambulance personnel, who had by now arrived to remove the van's occupants. Sergeant Davies had informed me that all three victims appeared to be young lads, and although he was of the firm opinion that they were all deceased, I had learned that only a qualified doctor could pronounce life extinct.

Sergeant Davies instructed the traffic crew to escort the ambulances – the second one required had arrived by now – and to provide continuity in identification. As we stood together and gathered our thoughts, I enquired if he was going to remain with me at the scene until the traffic officers returned. He calmly replied "Oh, we don't need those lads. You can deal with this." *Me?* I said to myself. I had only been there for two months and this was a fatal, a triple fatal! However, I didn't and wouldn't have said a word in reply. If he trusted me, then I certainly trusted him.

I followed through with the enquiry, arranging all that was needed and pulling things together before compiling the report, and every step of the way I was under the guidance of Sergeant Davies. The only two things that the traffic department undertook was taking photographs of the scene and the mechanical examination of the vehicle. That was the first and last time that it was done on my behalf, as I had not yet been authorised in writing by the Chief Constable, a statutory requirement.

I eventually presented my verbal evidence to the Coroner, explaining that the three lads had left Blaenavon after providing music at a social event. The van was travelling on a dry road with no evidence of driver impairment. There was no apparent evidence of speed or vehicle defects, but for some unexplained reason the vehicle had drifted to the offside of the road and collided with a substantial boundary wall, when the driver had lost control. The three occupants had been pronounced dead at the Royal Gwent Hospital. My personal conclusion, when asked by the Coroner, although there was no direct evidence to substantiate it, was that the van was travelling faster than it should have been for the nature of the road. The driver had drifted to his right on a fairly long, slight left-hand bend and clipped the boundary wall, losing control. The Coroner recorded verdicts of 'accidental death'.

Although this was a total and utter tragedy for the three lads and their families and the scene on that late Friday night was full of carnage and horror, Sergeant Davies knew that in the cool light of day we would not be forensically pursuing a horrific crime but dealing with a sudden death, something officers up and down the country deal with every day. I guess that's the reason he sent the traffic officers on their way, content in the knowledge that I would gain an enormous amount of valuable experience.

I had now been stationed at Abersychan for some four months and the only thing I was not really happy about was my lodgings. Oh, they were clean and tidy and Mrs Hutchins, as I've said, was a most pleasant lady. I seem to recall that she and her late husband had not been blessed with children, and it really did come through in the manner in which she conducted her landlady duties. I was now a strapping youth of 22, and on a cold dark evening after working an afternoon shift, I would be presented with a fairly small plate of cold tinned meat and pickle, with bread and butter for my meal. It was probably what she had eaten and enjoyed and I'm quite convinced she thought she was doing her best, but it certainly didn't suit me. After a few days, I learnt to fill myself up from the local takeaway at every opportunity during my duty meal breaks. I spent as little time with my landlady as possible and Sergeant Davies could no doubt see the signs. I would travel home for all rest days and long changes of shift, and my constant thoughts of Shel didn't ease the situation. Our relationship, by this time, had become serious. We were engaged, and our planned marriage was only three months away.

As I've mentioned, HQ general guidelines provided for single men to lodge near their stations, but I took every opportunity that presented itself to badger Sergeant Davies, asking if I could live at home and travel each day. He would not relent. Well, not until the morning he told me that our inspector was to visit the station later in the day, and if I felt so strongly about my lodgings then I should take the matter up with him.

Inspector Mike Keohane duly arrived and as he had done on previous occasions, took me out on foot patrol. He used this opportunity, I assumed, with all other officers under his command, to discuss progress and issue advice and encouragement, but I found out over the coming months that at our station, I was the only officer he accompanied around the patch. Now, it could have been that I was the only officer there who he thought needed advice and encouragement, but I remained a working colleague of Mike for the rest of my service and some years later, when we were both of higher rank, he told me that he used to try and push me because he could see potential in my ability.

As Sergeant Davies had suggested, I broached the subject of my lodgings with the Inspector and received a very favourable reply. He advised me that he would allow me to travel as long as it did not 'interfere with the discharge of my duties', a police phrase which I got to know was a catch-all piece of terminology. I was savvy enough to realise, even at my relatively short period of service, that the Inspector's response to my request had not been given without Sergeant Davies briefing him beforehand. I was cock-a-hoop with his answer and felt as if I was working on cloud nine.

There was one other subject that he discussed at length with me on that momentous walk, during which he questioned my ambitions and asked where I saw myself going. He was fully aware of my background and showed no surprise when I explained that my aim was to apply for the Traffic Department when my probationary period had been completed. The probationary period of a constable was the first two years of service and it was, like the lodgings, an unwritten rule that no one was selected for a specialist department until that probationary period had been completed satisfactorily. Inspector Keohane explained that he fully understood why I should be keen on traffic and went on further to say that guidelines are sometimes made to be broken. He advised me that if I were to submit an application asking to be considered for the Traffic Department then he would recommend it and forward it to HQ. I went from duty to my lodgings later that evening in a state of euphoria, so much so that I can't even remember what I was given to eat!

My next morning shift would have been over a week later as we were working a three-shift pattern, a week about, and after completing the morning cleaning ritual, which included a general sweep through, re-banking of the fire and coal bucket replenishment, together with, if it was a Friday, polishing the enquiry office's brown linoleum floor and scrubbing the steps outside the front door, I settled down to compose my application as the Inspector had suggested. I would have made sure it was on a shift when Sergeant Davies was on duty as I would not approach Sergeant Moon for anything if at all possible. I took some ribbing from my station colleagues over my request because all, without exception, thought HQ would veto its implementation. This was not the only report I had to submit that day because Sergeant Davies reminded me that as I had been telling all and sundry over the past few weeks that I was about to be married, he thought it was time I sought permission from the Chief Constable. Our politically-correct present-day thinkers would shriek in horror at this, but it was a necessity for all serving officers at that time. I duly committed to paper, via my laborious two-fingered typing, the request which included the compulsory word – respectfully – that I be allowed to marry:

MISS SHELBY DORCAS JONES
of 8 SCHOOL STREET
ABERBARGOED

I omit my lady's date of birth here, but it had to be included in my typewritten script for all to see. In fact, Shel was seven weeks younger than me.

The written answers to both of my requests came back in the fullness of time. Nothing, but nothing rushed HQ in those days and I would assume that nothing has changed since. To my first request, I was told that a suitability driving test would be arranged and to my second I was told that the Chief Constable had noted my intention and that after my marriage I would be allocated the police house at number 13, Wainfelin Avenue, Pontypool. My goodness, to keep this script polite and within the realms of acceptability, I will just say that I was extremely pleased! Sergeant Davies interpreted the answer from Traffic as 'yes', dependent on me having the ability to be taught to drive to the required standard and the answer concerning my marriage – I could understand that well enough myself. Shel was going to be over the moon. There were scores of police officers asking for housing within the Force, even after their marriages, but I had been allocated one two months before mine. I wasn't complaining – mine was not to reason why!

The next available weekend, Shel and I drove over to view our prospective accommodation, which in fact was still occupied by a serving officer. He was another Sergeant Davies, and he was about to complete his 30 years' service and retire to Bournemouth with his wife. He was more than willing to show us around the house, which exceeded our expectations. Wainfelin Avenue was some 600 yards long and consisted of large three-bedroomed Victorian terraced houses, but the Police Authority, which actually owned this one, had made several improvements over recent years, by converting the small rear bedroom into what was a relatively large bathroom and adding a small kitchen on the rear ground floor. The other two bedrooms were of adequate size and downstairs, both Shel and I joked that we would have enough room to entertain the whole avenue. There was a large bay-windowed front reception room, a large central living room and quite an adequate rear kitchen. A small extension which had been built at the back housed the cooker and sink, and was exclusively used for food preparation and cooking. There was no central heating installed in any part of the house, which was not unusual at all for 1966, but the downstairs rooms each had fairly modern fireplaces, with the kitchen's supplying the domestic hot water.

Generally speaking, police officers did not expend any money on the houses with which they were provided as part of their financial recompense, so the décor was plain and simple, but Sergeant Davies and his wife had kept it spotless. To say that I wouldn't have cared what it was like would perhaps be an overstatement, but Shel, far more importantly, was over the moon. She was like a dog with 15 tails for the next few weeks, quietly boasting, quite naturally, to all the family, and whenever we were quietly on our own, she would explain to me exactly what she had in mind for every nook and cranny. Our wedding, which was fast approaching, with all the arrangements that involved, just slipped into second place for a while.

As far as I was concerned, Shel took complete control of the wedding arrangements, but I was fully aware that she was keeping both sets of parents involved and rightly so, as they were more or less paying. I had been saving all I could for the previous two years for the continental motoring holiday that we had planned for our honeymoon.

When she left school, I think it's fair to say that Shel was no more of an academic than I was, but her parents paid for her to go to a private secretarial college in Cardiff on a full-time basis for 12 months, and when I came into her life she was employed as secretary to the Estates Manager at the head office of Rhymney Breweries. The firm was bought out in the early 1970s by Whitbread, but at the time it was one of the leading brewers in South Wales, with a very large portfolio of public houses. In organising the reception, Shel used her influence and secured the catering facilities of the Argoed Arms, an outlet owned by the brewery, with a very large first-floor function room, at a very discounted price, and the brewery, as a gift, gave us two dozen bottles of champagne for the toast. Our reception was held at this venue with some 90 members of family and friends after the ceremony on Saturday 25 June 1966 at St Sannan's church in Bedwellty. It was the parish church for both our villages and dates back to the 13th century in the Gothic style.

Two days previously, I had hosted and as far as I remember, enjoyed my stag evening, which was held at the Church Inn, the hostelry where Shel and I first met, which stands directly opposite the heavenly blessed building where we were to exchange our solemn vows. Those attending consisted mainly of my old garage colleagues and a few friends, with one or two male members of Shel's family. A significant unwelcome guest that evening was Sergeant Moon, who had made his way some 20 miles across the county to attend, uninvited, I would add. Some weeks later, when I was discussing the event with my brother-in-law, I was informed that my supervising officer had not been seen to put his hand in his pocket all evening. What a surprise that was!

There was no evening function with a knees-up after our reception as is the general custom today, so after the meal we drove off into the setting sun with everyone waving, shouting and wishing us all good blessings (I hope), after secretly tying several lengths of string, which were in turn attached to a number of assorted tin cans, to the rear bumper of the car. We travelled to Westcliff-on-Sea, our destination for that evening, where we had a hotel prebooked, and spent a peaceful night…

The following morning, we made for Southend airport, where we were booked on an air ferry to fly with the car to Ostend. The service was operated by British United Air Ferries, which had a small fleet of ATL98 Carvair aeroplanes. They were designed as dual-purpose cargo/passenger transport and had a large bulbous nose (very similar to the modern 747 jumbo), which accommodated six to eight saloon cars on twin decks, with basic seating accommodation at the rear. Both Shel and I were about to fly for the first time, and as we stood in what appeared to be a glorified shed, which was the departure building, and watched my car being loaded into the front of the aircraft, I could feel my apprehension about flying rising up through my body as though I had stepped into a hot bath.

Twenty minutes later, sitting in our seats as the pilot built up engine speed at the end of the runway, the whole body of the plane started to vibrate. Shel and I looked worriedly at each other. Glancing around the small cabin area I could see the structural rivets holding the body panels together actually moving under the stress to which they were being subjected. At that moment, my apprehension about flying went off the Richter Scale and has stayed with me to this day. I have very rarely flown since, and only with extreme reluctance. Shel was another kettle of fish, with a slightly different outlook on life. I could see a little concern in her smile as we held hands just prior to take-off, but once airborne, she was as cool as the proverbial cucumber and enjoyed every second of the flight.

Our honeymoon was to be the trip of a lifetime. We motored through Belgium, Luxembourg and Switzerland to our final destination, Innsbruck, the capital of Tyrol in Austria. For the first few days it took to travel down, we stopped on spec at various hostelries that took our fancy, and one of them was a very well-appointed farm which was offering accommodation. Our instincts were proved pleasantly correct when we sampled the family's fare and hospitality, but when we were directed to our room at bedtime, we had a surprise. We discovered that our bedroom, which was palatial in size, was directly over the cowshed, which gave off the most pungent country aroma all night. Shel and I stood and looked at each other and the smiles on our faces quickly turned into hilarious (if controlled) laughter.

Our arrival in Innsbruck proved to be another scene altogether. We had booked the equivalent to our country's 'Railway Hotel', a four-star luxury establishment in the centre of the city directly opposite the train station, with all the international activity generated by it. We spent a glorious 10 days exploring Tyrol with not a moment's regret, and for years to come we both shared the view that Austria was one of the nicest countries on Earth.

We toured back to Ostend via a slightly different route with the overnight stops not quite as exciting as our earlier unique bedroom, but it was all just as pleasant. As the last few days of our return journey through Europe ticked by, my mind started to wander on the odd occasion to the thought of that flight home. Still, it had to be endured; I had a night shift to start the following Monday.

Our arrival home was something of a bittersweet occasion. We were in love and the world appeared to be our oyster.

We were looking forward to occupying what we thought in 1966 was the home of our dreams and I had that masterful feeling, which I'm sure all young men have when they cut the apron strings of living with parents, of being in total control of my life. Things would happen if I deemed to say so or say not. I only too soon realised that it doesn't work like that in the real world, but every young man has, or should be allowed to have, that feeling for a short time in his life. Oh dear, I must apologise; in this modern era I should attribute my comments to all genders and not just young men.

My wife – that's another feeling of warmth and security I had, publicly declaring that Shel was my wife – well, she was busy organising our move into the police house, and although we didn't have a vast amount of furniture we had bought, begged and borrowed enough items to make our first home comfortable. I clearly remember that Shel wasn't too happy with the anaglypta wallpaper, which had been painted a bright yellow all through the landing, stairs and front passage, but she must have had a few sweet and gentle words with Mr Johns, the Police Authority's Clerk of Works, because on his visit to examine the house on change of tenant, he agreed to redecorate the whole area to her complete satisfaction.

Since returning from our honeymoon, I've explained the sweet things that faced us, but the one further issue was that Shel was forced to relinquish her job at the brewery. Although it would affect me indirectly, as I was now the only one earning a wage, it must have been quite a wrench for her. The travelling distance prevented her from realistically retaining her position, which she had enjoyed since leaving school, and I know that she had many friends and colleagues who she was sorry to leave behind. However, as she said, "A new day, a new challenge".

As a couple, we had decided to wait a year or two, if the stars were with us, before starting a family, and in the meantime she was intent on looking for other employment. In her own secretarial field she was well qualified; she had very good typing skills and could take down Pitman's shorthand faster that I could get words out of my mouth – a task which she quietly enjoyed being tested on by me as my career progressed. Although the police service had adequate admin support, Shel would very often take dictation from me and type out that contentious or urgent report during an evening or weekend. It was only a matter of weeks, once we got the house sorted to our liking, before she secured a post, copytyping with the children's department of the local authority in Caerleon, a 30-minute bus ride away.

I soon settled back into the routine of work at the station, having caught up with all the crime bulletins, back issues of General Orders and, perhaps more importantly, the gossip. In my document tray I found a small piece of paper which had the force crest stamped clearly in the top left-hand corner. It was a report from the Chief Superintendent at HQ Traffic Department to my Divisional Commander advising that I would be allocated a driving assessment as soon as could be arranged, and I had been instructed to 'note it'. Because of our shift patterns it was some 10 days later, whilst working 6am to 2pm, that Sergeant Davies informed me that a member of the Force Driving School would be arriving the following morning for my assessment. It was Police Constable Thompson, who sat beside me for some two hours and observed me driving the Hillman Hunter unmarked vehicle around the highways and byways of the county. Before he left our station for his return to HQ he advised me that he would recommend that I was suitable for training.

Sergeant Davies gave me a quiet nod and wink with the clear message beaming from his face that he was proud that one of his lads had reached the required standard. He did however tell me in an honest and open manner later in the shift that everything was now 'in the lap of the gods'. He didn't want to lose me, but would not do or say anything to stand in my way. At this point in time I had only just over one year's service, and realistically I knew that a move to Traffic was a forlorn hope for the foreseeable future.

We settled well into our new abode. I secured the use of a garage for our car at a very reasonable cost, from someone living close by who seemed to be over the moon, not so much because of the rent he received, but because of his association with a local policeman. The garage was a boon to me because the road at the front of the house was typical of the Welsh valleys. Built pre-war just as a means of access and no more than 15 feet wide, it made parking at the front of your house a nightmare. Perhaps just as importantly, the garage allowed me to service and repair my car, along with those of family, friends and colleagues. I very often wondered how we had so many!

Our avenue was situated on a gradient, either up or down depending which end you stood, and our house was only four from the bottom. It was about a quarter of a mile in length, so you can imagine how many terraced houses there were on each side and when constructed, the Police

Authority purchased quite a number of them to cater for the town's police establishment. Police officers were not allowed to purchase or live in their own accommodation in those days, which meant that the Chief Constable had total control over where you would work. Police Regulations were amended within the following 12 months to allow police officers to purchase their own properties <u>with</u> the permission of the Chief and receive an appropriate allowance in lieu. To my recollection, there were about eight police families living in the avenue, but there were two quite close which we associated with socially. The problem for Shel and me was that both husbands were named John Williams; the confusion in our domestic conversations was annoying! So the Mr Williams who lived to our right and was 5' 9" tall was called 'Little John', and the Mr Williams living to our left and was 6' 1" tall we called 'Big John'. Both gentlemen retained these identities throughout their lives, until they passed away in recent years.

CHAPTER 6

I had the satisfactory feeling at this time that I had settled well into police life. I had no problems accepting the discipline and, very often, the bullshit, and at this early stage of my career I was quite happy to listen and respond with a 'Yes sir' or 'No sir'. My Divisional Inspector would visit our station at least once a week and I noticed that more often than not, he would arrive when I was on duty and spend at least an hour walking the local area with me. While strolling along, and in between chatting to various locals, he would question my workload, advise me on procedures and generally encourage me to try and stand a little higher than my peers. He gave me his view that the majority of police officers were happy with their lot, complaining quite often that things could be better, but plodding along to retirement and pension. He would always conclude that he didn't see me as one of those. To many of his subordinates, Mr Keohane was considered to be a 'stickler' and someone to be avoided, but to me, as I progressed through my service, he was a 'copper's copper', with qualities the modern service is desperately lacking.

There was little I wouldn't turn my hand to in the station without relish – I would rather get stuck in than argue whose turn it was, but the two things at Abersychan that I would have ditched if ever I had the chance would have been the night shift and attending post mortems. The night shift, not because I was in any way afraid of the dark – don't forget, I had a torch with three colours – but because it was just totally boring. There were two constables rostered on nights (10pm to 6am) and the section had two night beats, north and south. Both were approximately four to five miles in length and in the winter months it was very dark without street lighting, and you were often wet and solitary. Whilst strolling along you never saw a moving thing apart from the nocturnal wildlife. I did note from a lecture on one of my early courses that the chance of a patrolling policeman detecting a burglar in the act was once in every 14 years. I changed my mind when I transferred to the Traffic Department, but at my first posting I hated the night shift. It was made even worse when you were constantly thinking of your young bride tucked up in bed.

I suppose post mortems speak for themselves, well, for the majority of us anyway. We would have constant calls from the coroner's office to attend our local mortuary, because if any deceased male had been an employee of the National Coal Board, and in South Wales thousands were, it was necessary to determine whether the death was caused by the lung disease pneumoconiosis. If this was the case, then payment of compensation was a major factor. It was evidentially necessary for someone to attend a post mortem when serious crime was an issue, to prove identification and continuity, but with the miners we were really representing the deceased's family. Our role was not just to have a quick tête à tête with the pathologist; we were expected to be with him as he delved into his work and complete the necessary forms as his findings were revealed. I attended two during my short time at Abersychan, but although I dealt with numerous fatalities in later years, I attended no more pathologists' investigations. There were two officers at my first station who would actually volunteer for such duties, and that was because the pathologist always gave the police officer five shillings for completing the paperwork. I preferred to earn some extra pennies servicing someone's car on my day off!

Only about three weeks after my driving assessment I received a short memo, followed two days later by a force-wide announcement in General Orders that Police Constable 140 FA Thorne would transfer from Abersychan 'B' Division to Traffic and Communications Department, to be stationed at Pontypool. Well, it was either that someone, somewhere thought I had something special or that they were desperately short of applicants for the Traffic Department. Modesty made me think the latter.

In those early days, the Traffic Department and all its ancillary operations were based at force HQ, but to give adequate cover to the county there were two 'satellite' bases, one at Blackwood, the other at Pontypool. Each was manned by eight traffic officers to cover the three continental shifts, and when I started my new duties my whole body had problems adjusting to the new hours. We worked three eight-hour shifts covering the 24, all in the same week, with the Friday shift being worked on Saturday and Sunday. For several weeks I didn't know when to sleep, wake up, eat or go to work. Shel pulled me through.

I found these new duties exciting because, apart from a brief telephone conversation with the relief sergeant at the commencement of the shift, you were left to your own devices to police your patch. The fact that initially I was not allowed to drive the patrol car as I had not attended the appropriate driving course did not deter me; I was the proverbial 'pig in poo'. The colleague I worked with, who was a Class I driver and quite advanced in service, was Constable Bryn Williams, and I had reservations about him from day one. To say he was a sombre type would be an understatement. He was just devoid of any personality. However, at this very early stage in my progression within the department I dared not voice my discontentment.

I had been working out of Pontypool police station for only about eight weeks when our section was evicted from our small office and rehoused at Cwmbran, some five miles down the valley. Although in recent years Pontypool has been given a facelift with extensive redevelopment, the town in the late 60s and 70s was a depressing area. It was one of the coal and iron works communities of the South Wales valleys dating back to the mid-19th century, moulded by the hands of workers who helped pull our country through the Industrial Revolution. No one on our small section had any argument about our move; we were given a slightly larger office in a more modern building and a yard which had more than ample space for our two patrol cars.

Cwmbran was planned under the New Towns Act 1946 to enable the government to relocate populations who had been bombed out of housing following the Second World War. The English translation is 'Valley of the Crow' and it was set, as the name suggests, on green secluded pasture land alongside the banks of the river Llwydd. It soon swallowed up several outlying villages and has, over the years, become one of the major towns in South Wales. An interesting point is that these new towns, which were planned on sites running the length of the United Kingdom, were removed from local authority control, I should think much to the disagreement and disgust of local councillors, and placed under the supervision of a development corporation. I can't speak for others, but at Cwmbran, where Lord Raglan held the chair of the corporation for some time, they stipulated that all car parks built around the retail area would be free of charge to all users. This simple issue was not insignificant in its success through the following decades and when the corporation was disbanded some 30 years later, the local authority was forced by public pressure to continue the practice, which is still in force today.

Within weeks of our move to Cwmbran I was placed on a standard driving course and successfully became what we termed a Class III patrol car driver (Class I and II could only be awarded at an advanced regional level). I was delighted obviously, but it meant that when driving unsupervised by an advanced driver I was restricted to a speed of 50mph.

The next few months saw me settle down to some good old fashioned 'bread and butter' policing, from a traffic aspect. The variety of work, which included ambulance and wide-load escorts, radar checks for speeding vehicles (speed cameras were years away), accident investigation, traffic control and quite importantly, crime detection, just made the working day fly by.

I was soon singled out, quite naturally I suppose, for the specialist role of vehicle examination. All traffic officers were trained to detect vehicle defects at the roadside, but it took a degree of mechanical knowledge to fully examine a motor vehicle, to determine if any defect was a primary or contributory cause of an accident. The Ministry of Transport would undertake the examination of all goods vehicles and PSVs, but it was our role to deal with private cars, dual purpose vehicles and light vans.

In early 1966, it was a requirement for owners to have a new test certificate for their vehicles every 10 years, but due to the high failure rate, this was reduced to seven in August of that year. Vehicle maintenance was not a priority for most motorists, so far too many accidents were being caused by vehicle defects. Most of my colleagues undertook examinations, but I was nominated for the vehicles involved in accidents causing the most serious injury. There were times when I would be required to carry out an examination on a daily basis for weeks on end throughout the force area. The knowledge required to undertake this task was no problem to me; the difficulty came in the actual physical procedure. There is a substantial difference between examining a vehicle in a well-appointed workshop with all up-to-date facilities, and carrying out an examination on a mangled heap of metal in a back street lock-up with a small tool box of basic implements. Still, somehow, we managed.

Shel had been beavering away at her job in the county's Children's Department for about three months when she arrived home one evening to announce that she had seen a vacancy advertised in the magistrate's clerk's office, and asked if it was worth her applying. I need to stress that she wouldn't have had to ask my permission to do anything, we would just discuss an issue, but this office was in Pontypool and responsible for the petty sessional area that I policed, and she wondered if the powers that be would consider it a conflict of interest. I didn't see why, so she applied.

She secured the post and within weeks was walking the five minutes to work from our abode. She must have impressed Des Jones, the magistrate's clerk, as it seemed no time at all before he took her into court to assist him with his duties. There was one instance I remember only too well when I was giving evidence at Pontypool Court in a contested case of 'defective brakes'. I was addressing the magistrates with my evidence, in what I thought was an exemplary manner, when Mr Jones suddenly stopped proceedings, looked directly at me, and with a twinkle in his eye said, "Officer, could you possibly slow down a little? My clerk is having difficulty taking down your evidence". I simply replied "Certainly sir". The magistrates had no idea that his clerk was my wife and that he was taking a rise out of me! I could see that Shel didn't dare look up or she would have burst out laughing.

Early one weekday evening, Shel and I were watching television in the middle room – it was the cosiest and easiest to keep warm – when I went to answer a loud rap on the front door. Standing there was Police Sergeant 35, an officer I recognised but had never met. It was Len Reynolds, who, I found out the following day, was in the traffic department running the motorcycle section, and was attached to the driving school with Ministry of Transport qualifications as a driving examiner. Len remained in that rank and post all his service and in later years, I would get to know him quite well. He was one of the few police officers I found I could respect. He was totally unbiased in his work, and what he didn't know about road traffic law wasn't worth knowing.

Len joined us for the obligatory cup of tea and told me that I was to report at nine the following morning to the Chief Superintendent of the traffic department in Abergavenny. I naturally quizzed him about the reason, but nothing more was forthcoming. I later became convinced that Len knew exactly what was on the cards, but he was following the official line out of loyalty to his boss. I got to know the personnel and workings of police HQ during the following few months, and if anyone knew any snippet of information which was supposed to be confidential, it was Harry, the driver/handyman, or Sergeant Reynolds. However, as he closed the gate outside my front door, he turned and said "Whatever Mr Walby says tomorrow, don't you say no". I might as well have been working that night, because I spent some hours speculating with Shel before going to bed late and getting very little sleep.

The police HQ at Abergavenny was a very small building for the purpose for which it was being used. The photography and fingerprint departments were crammed into areas no larger than a store cupboard. CID were housed in Portakabins in the corner of the traffic yard and the operations room, the controlling hub of any well-organised law enforcement body, was set out in an area no bigger than the average modern bedroom. To say my interview with Mr

Jim Walby, the Head of Traffic, was somewhat intimate would be an understatement. His office was an anteroom off his administration department and because of the lack of space, I had a little difficulty easing myself into the chair opposite him.

He explained to me that the sergeant in charge of workshops had been assigned, in an emergency, to other duties on a temporary basis and offered me the opportunity to run the workshops in his absence. The Chief Constable would not be prepared in the circumstances to give me any extra payment or temporary rank, and I should look on this opportunity as a challenge. He did offer me the casual mileage allowance, which was really a pittance, and would just about cover my daily petrol costs for travelling to work. I thought long and hard – for about two seconds, until Sergeant Reynolds' comments flashed through my mind. "Yes sir, I'd be happy to" was my response.

Ironically, my temporary move to Abergavenny was triggered by a catastrophe; the disaster of Aberfan, in which 144 lives were lost. At 9.15 am on Friday 21 October 1966, after several days of heavy rain, part of a colliery waste tip, which had been slowly created over 50 years or so, began to slide. The front part of this mass became liquefied and more than 40,000 cubic metres of debris smashed into the village nestled below, covering it to a depth of up to 12 metres. It destroyed a farm and 20 terraced houses before engulfing the northern side of Pantglas Junior School. The lives of 116 children and 28 adults were lost. It was the last day before the half-term holiday and at the time of the tragedy, the school was just coming to the end of morning assembly. The communities of South Wales were stunned by the enormity of this sudden, and in the immediate aftermath, unexplainable loss, and the whole of the United Kingdom and many parts of the world offered their heartfelt grief.

The Merthyr Tydfil Constabulary responded as best it could, but national action was required for a civil disaster of this scale, so the powers that be made the decision to summon together the Police Mobile Column. This comprised some 50 officers with supporting transport and equipment and was formed in the 1950s to counter the threat of a nuclear strike on this country, or any other similar disaster. The 'column', on anticipation of such a threat, would form up and encamp in some sparsely-inhabited area where they would be able to assimilate, coordinate and direct assistance to any affected area of population. There was such a column planned for each of the eight police regions in England and Wales and they were brought together every two years or so for training exercises. When the enormity of Aberfan struck home, within hours the Welsh Police Mobile Column was activated, and Sergeant Ken Pritchard, whose role I was to take on in the force workshops, was an active member.

CHAPTER 7

It was a dark and wet morning on 28 October 1966 when I drove the twelve and a half miles to police HQ to take up my temporary role. Not a bit like that bright sunny afternoon about a year later when Marty Wilde was heading to the same town, albeit from a slightly different direction. The police HQ social section had organised a charity dance and the then Deputy Chief Constable, John Woodcock, had secured the attendance of Mr Wilde, who was at his professional peak. As he drove along the A40, approaching his destination, he composed the basic words in his mind of 'Taking a Trip up to Abergavenny'. The song didn't make the top ten, but I warrant Marty made enough money to remember his trip into Wales. I can advise all those who were taken by the record that Marty Wilde didn't really see that 'red dog running free'. The words just fitted in nicely.

I digress. I had given a lot of thought to my role in

workshops since being asked and realised I would have to muster all my diplomatic skills to supervise the totally civilian workforce that was employed there. With the brief I had been given to hold the fort, I would not be contemplating the introduction of any new working practices and there were probably several mechanics who were older and a lot more experienced than me. I knew most of them quite well from the visits I had made as part of my traffic duties, but I was worried that Tom, the foreman, would be particularly annoyed that he hadn't been offered the temporary role. Thankfully, I was wrong.

In the police service as a whole, there were very few civilians employed, particularly in an operational role, outside the Metropolitan force. Because of its size and unique problems, the 'Met' had its own structure and peculiarities, to which I would be introduced within a short period of time. All other provincial forces in England and Wales were headed by chief constables, many of whom, like ours, had a military background, and I believe they thought it wise to keep a tight control on discipline under the 'code' contained in Police Regulations to which all serving officers were subjected. Civilian members of staff could not be ordered to do anything, no matter how lawful. To my recollection, the only civilian staff employed at that time in the Monmouthshire Constabulary were a few radio and telephone operators, a driver/handyman, two matrons, a handful of cleaners between the larger stations and my seven mechanics at the force workshops.

All my lads (as they were referred to by most people) were time-served engineers who had come from private retail businesses in the surrounding area and had taken up employment with the Police Authority with their eyes wide open. They knew there was ongoing finance to provide the best of working conditions and the vehicles, though heavily used, were always the latest models and generally no more than three years old. Although the pay perhaps was not the highest that could be found, it was guaranteed. There was good job security and a fairly adequate pension. All in all, they, including Tom, were quite prepared to accept a police officer to supervise the unit, as long as he was not some bombastic idiot.

As with all new roles, things are strange at first and it takes a little while to find your feet, but in all honesty, I was more than happy with the way I settled in. The lads were satisfied that I wasn't that idiot and apart from one or two, who would often prefer to talk and voice their opinion instead of getting on with it, I had a good set of lads under me whose respect and loyalty would hopefully grow.

When I took on this temporary role, the vehicle fleet which I was responsible for numbered 147. It included a mixture of small vans, outstation and traffic motorcycles, several miscellaneous emergency vehicles, Austin Westminster and Ford Zephyr patrol cars and a boat. I know not how or when this boat came into the ownership of the Force, but it seemed to have been an integral part of the fixtures for decades. It was of metal construction, some 15 feet in length and eight feet wide with a draught of about four feet, painted in the obligatory police blue. Whoever initially purchased this monstrosity, which was to be used for rescue purposes, had no idea whatsoever about the physics of buoyancy. It was like a huge oversized coracle. I can actually remember it being used; it was launched in

1967 in the town of Usk, which was regularly flooded by its namesake river. I was one of several officers who pushed it from its trailer for what was no more than a public relations exercise, because it could never be manoeuvred to rescue any marooned person.

The Mobile Column was still deployed at Aberfan helping to coordinate the clean-up operations, which I thought would determine the length of time I remained at workshops, but when it was eventually 'stood down' some weeks later, I was informed by the Chief Superintendent that I was to stay in my position because the sergeant was going to take on the role of temporary inspector in the Operations Room. Chief Superintendent Walby reminded me that my stint at workshops would be valuable experience and I knew that during my period there so far, he had not voiced any displeasure. Well, not to me anyhow. So I kept my head down and moved forward. I could read the situation – Sergeant Ken Pritchard had been in workshops for about six years, he mixed with the right company at HQ and it was pretty clear that his substantive promotion was not too far away.

As I've outlined, I was, and still am, an easy-going person, but Sergeant Pritchard was ex-RAF and more of an 'act now and ask later' sort of chap. His military background could rub some folk up the wrong way and I knew that when running the workshops, staff had to do as he said, which was not always received with good grace (I am trying to be diplomatic here). I was sure that Tom would react to the benefit of all if I encouraged him a little more than he was used to; after all, he was the foreman and I was not at hand eight hours a day for numerous reasons. Tom was a keen road runner who would think nothing of running seven or eight miles each evening and a marathon every weekend. He was from a large family hailing from Brynmawr and one of eight siblings. He was an extrovert and often said that he would have liked to have been a stand-up comic. In relation to his large family, he used to tell me that whenever he took a taxi for some social or domestic reason and the driver asked "where to?" he would reply "anywhere, I've got family all over the place".

One dismal November afternoon I was sitting in my office attending to paperwork, submitting a file of administrative forms that each employee had been required to sign, when I saw that Tom Aylett's first name was listed quite clearly as Adrian. I summoned him from the workshop floor and just like Trigger in the BBC's *Only Fools and Horses* asked him "Why does everybody call you Tom?" He replied "Oh, my name's Adrian, but it's Tom for short". I couldn't respond. We both returned to our work and he's remained Tom to this day.

I did encourage him over the following few months; he took on more of a supervisory role and I gave him specific areas of responsibility, with far more interaction with operational officers at police stations. At this time, I started to wear a white coat to enhance my authority within the traffic complex instead of the mundane light brown storeman's type I inherited from my predecessor, and I invited Tom to do the same. It's surprising what a lift that gave him. Tom got married to a devoted Jennifer a few years later and they were blessed with a son, Justin. As I write, they live in a picturesque cottage on the edge of the Brecon Beacons. I took a drive there several months ago and we spent an hour or two reminiscing.

From the early 1960s the Research and Planning Branch of the Home Office had been carrying out research into Unit Beat Policing and in 1966, along with a few other areas in England, they chose Pontypool as a suitable location to base an experiment, so the Home Office gave us six brand new Triumph Heralds. They were already decked out with police insignia; all we had to do at workshops after their delivery by transporter was to give them a quick once over before they started to earn their keep over the bumps and potholes of the valleys.

I was still gaining experience in my new role, as my supervisors kept reminding me, as 1967 dawned upon us, and literally everyone in our force and the adjoining Newport Borough was aware that we were to take them over – oh, sorry, amalgamate – on April 1. The two forces hadn't really got on for many years, with operational officers from both camps being loath to give assistance to each other, unless specifically ordered to from above. Borough officers thought of us as a load of country bumpkins and we thought that they were a bunch of scruffy, ill-mannered yobs whose working practices quite often crossed onto the wrong side of the law. Our force, numerically and geographically, was over four times larger than theirs and we could not resist, at every opportunity, reminding them that it was a takeover. It really didn't bode well for a harmonious start.

Well, under directions from the Home Office, who were moulding the future of the British Police Service, the chief officers of the forces involved were duty bound to make the transition as smooth as possible and to promote harmony, so in our little corner of South East Wales they decided to have a dance. The headquarters of the Newport Force was housed within the office complex of the Borough Council and they were fortunate enough to have a fairly large gymnasium on the first floor. Coincidentally, that April 1 fell on a Saturday, so shifts were rearranged to allow as many as possible to attend and the Newport social committee organised it at their venue. Shel and I attended with a few of my working colleagues and their wives, and the night was a total disaster. We 'country bumpkins' were ostracised in one corner of the room and made to feel most unwelcome. Both chief constables made an appearance with the intention of welcoming everyone to our 'new large family' and when Mr Farley spoke first for the county, he was openly and loudly booed, which clearly indicated to us that our long-held view of our new partners had been perfectly correct. Mr Smeed spoke briefly to reciprocate, to the sound of claps and cheers. We left immediately, the whole evening having been a complete failure and an embarrassment. This deep-seated resentment stayed with Newport officers for several years until it fizzled out with retirements.

They say all good things come to an end – and so it was. The inspector returned to Operations Room after extended sick leave; Temporary Inspector Pritchard returned to his workshops and PC Thorne was reunited with his colleagues at Cwmbran to resume traffic patrol duties. It was no let-down really; I had enjoyed my stint in workshops and was returning to work that I thoroughly enjoyed. Importantly, I was not going to lose any recompense because I was not given any to start with. Mr Walby had been right, I had gained experience, not that I had been noticing it day by day, but when I sat and reflected I had been involved in decision making and holding responsibility. I had learned a lot about human behaviour and man-management and perhaps surreptitiously, but quite importantly, I had observed and noticed how the headquarters 'bubble' worked. I had not only been in daily personal dialogue, giving briefings to my Chief Superintendent about the workshop's activities, which were under his overall command, but was on daily acknowledgement terms with the heads of all other departments, including the Detective Chief Superintendent, head of the force CID. To cap it all, the Chief Constable would alight from his chauffeur-driven car most mornings, just outside my office window, and pop his head around the door to enquire about the state of the fleet. After several weeks at Abergavenny he was addressing me as 'Alan'. What about that!

I had settled back into my routine of shifts, still working with PC Williams, who as I have mentioned needed an injection of charisma, and after three or four weeks I discussed the issue with Shel and decided that I had to do something. He would arrive for each shift with a minute to spare and announce his presence to me and the colleagues we were relieving with a grunt. No problem there, if that's how he felt. I've known many that are not happy about starting work each day. It was his behaviour and attitude for the remaining eight hours that upset me. He would sit in the patrol car, whether driving or not, in total silence, and any conversation I would try to instigate would be given short shrift with a one-word response. He had not altered one iota in the months we'd been apart. It wouldn't have been a problem if we had been on foot patrol because a street has two directions and I would have a choice as to which way I walked, but to me, shut up in that tin box for almost eight hours, it was becoming purgatory.

Before I acted I made sure it wasn't just me looking through a pair of distorted glasses, and found that everyone I made discreet enquiries with agreed that he was strange. The only problem I would have was from an operational point of view; PC Williams was a worker; he had the highest process rate in our section. To coin a phrase, 'he would book his own grandmother'! I took the bull by the horns within days, when I found myself working single crew on a night shift, and during a routine conference with my sergeant, I opened my soul and let it all come out. I explained the problem to Sergeant Gardner, pointing out that it was beginning to affect my duties. Within 10 days PC Williams and I said goodbye to each other. Not literally, as it wasn't PC Williams' style. He continued on traffic until his retirement a few years later.

Whilst I was helping out at workshops, the remainder of the force had kept ticking along and one of my colleagues who I had worked with at Abersychan had been successful on a driving assessment course. The man I was to share an Austin 110 Westminster with for the foreseeable future was Melvyn Hartree. Mel had not changed one bit since I left him at Abersychan; he was still like a bottle of pop, always on the go. He dashed around everywhere, he talked non-stop and to solve a problem, he thought just as quickly. It was a difficult job explaining to him that thoughts at that speed don't always come up with the right answers.

However, he was a breath of fresh air and we got on really well, even if I was exhausted at the end of most shifts.

I found myself laughing once more during our conversations as we drove along and that couldn't be bad. He was really keen to learn more about the mechanics of vehicle examinations, and it was a pleasure to impart what knowledge I could over the following months. He was a relatively young married man with two small boys, and Shel warmed to him during the visits he made to our house. We became friendly and he and his wife would make up a foursome to attend the occasional social function together. That was another car I had to fit in for service on my days off!

I was soon informed that I was to attend an advanced driving course at the regional school in Bridgend. It was for six weeks and situated within the police HQ complex where I had undergone my initial training almost two years previously. It wasn't only me; the other five, who were from North and West Wales, found it the most stressful time of their lives to date. We were driving 3.4 litre Jaguars and the concentration producing adrenalin within your body when it was your turn at the wheel was unbelievable. One of our number found it too much after the first week and returned to his force. On the whole, I thoroughly enjoyed it and considered it the experience of a lifetime, but I nearly came unstuck on my final drive. This one-and-a-half-hour session was the culmination and deciding factor of your six weeks' sweat and toil. Sitting beside you was the Chief Superintendent, who had ultimate charge of the school and was the person who would decide on pass or fail. Eighty-eight marks and above secured you a first-class pass, 85 to 87 gave a second class and below 85 you returned to your force with no more qualification than when you arrived.

I was driving west along the A48 in the general area of Port Talbot and passing, on my left, the large country estate of Margam Park. Traffic was fairly light and I could see way up ahead, travelling in the same direction as myself, the rear of two horses being ridden, quite properly, in the nearside kerb. I was not on the section where I had been asked to give a driving commentary and there was total silence in the vehicle apart from the roar of the engine. I was approximately 100 yards from the animals when the Chief Superintendent, sat sedately to my left, said, quite loudly, "Don't sound your horn, will you?" My whole body was one mass of concentration. My right hand lifted from the wheel and I subconsciously pushed the horn-ring, giving one clear blast. Nobody said a word, not even my aghast instructor. I was by this time some 200 yards past the horses, who seemed fine in my rear-view mirror, but I could have died. What the hell had I done? I'd bloody well blown my chances of a pass, that's what I'd done. To make matters worse, I could see in the mirror one of my colleagues smirking in the back seat.

I took my place in the rear of the vehicle when my run was finished and spent the rest of the journey in silence and dejection. As we all left the vehicle late afternoon, Chief Superintendent Robinson came up to me and said "Don't fret lad. You were concentrating so hard I had no business saying a word". The following morning before returning home, I was presented with a Class I certificate, having been awarded 91 marks. Phew!

Police work isn't the exciting, glamorous lifestyle portrayed in films and soap operas all the time; in fact, it can be boring, repetitive and tedious, and if you're not prepared to put up with the more mundane tasks you should never contemplate joining. However, if you have the instinctive urge to help, assist or support other people, as I did when I was draining oil from an engine's sump, then every day being a 'bobby' will give you a buzz and a sense of adventure. Every time a police officer takes one step outside the station, he or she can expect anything to happen, and it is to you that everyone looks. The big redeeming factor is that thankfully the vast majority of the British public are grateful and full of appreciation for your efforts.

The memory of one incident from my early career has stayed with me. It was the result of Mel and me being directed to attend a road traffic accident late one night on a nasty section of two-lane carriageway just north of the M4. It was quite obvious on arrival that it was serious; in fact both occupants, one male and one female, were conveyed to hospital, with the elderly lady being pronounced dead on arrival and the male driver unconscious and in a critical condition. There was no other vehicle involved and with that scenario we commenced our enquiries. We had no idea who the occupants were, but the vehicle's registration number led us to The Greenhouse, an old coaching inn only half a mile from the scene in Llantarnam. Actually the inn was, and still is, a renowned and popular public house which is documented as having provided refreshments to the Chartist marchers on their way to the fatal battle in Westgate Square, Newport in 1839.

We soon established that it was the licensee's mother who had died and his brother was the driver. You can imagine the stress and emotion that this poor chap was faced with when he heard our news and furthermore, we needed his assistance at the mortuary for identification purposes. The following day he asked if we would take him to view the scene before we signed over the personal property found in the vehicle. It was at times like this that I felt quite humble and somewhat privileged that I could help. It was my opinion that the driver had lost control, inadvertently clipped the kerb and ended up in the hedgerow, but after lengthy deliberations by the Divisional Commander and the County Prosecuting Solicitor (no Crown Prosecution Service in those days), it was decided that court proceedings would not be in anyone's interest. The family, of course, still had to face the trauma of the inquest in the fullness of time, which was some two months after the initial accident.

We bade our farewells to the licensee and his family on the steps of the Coroner's Court, but the following day I received a telephone call from him asking if we could call in when passing as there was just one more issue he wished to sort out. Mel and I duly obliged and were subjected to overwhelming thanks for all our assistance during what must have been a very trying time for the whole family. He also invited us, along with our wives, to a meal at his restaurant, which, on the spur of the moment we both accepted, but over the next 24 hours we thought deep and hard as to whether we should have. There were one or two senior officers in the force, even at that time, who although they could not interpret it as a bribe, would have loved to suggest that we were taking advantage of our positions in public office. Mel and I didn't need to contemplate this gesture any longer. We went with our wives and were presented with a sumptuous meal in his private quarters along with him and his good lady. It was obvious that they were genuinely most grateful for the delicate way we had handled the whole episode, proving that the grateful appreciation of someone who you try to help stays with you a long time.

Another incident which occurred at roughly the same time in my role as a constable on traffic patrol came to light as a result of a road traffic accident. It happened on a section of dual carriageway, which had recently been constructed to bypass the ancient hamlet of Croesyceiliog. Drivers were prone to get a little over-excited on this open expanse of highway and would attempt to test their vehicles' engine performance. Late one wet Saturday night a Vauxhall Viva was pushed to its limits by its middle-aged male driver, who hailed from the Heads of the Valleys area. The vehicle lost its grip, spun and rolled, I estimated at least twice, before climbing the nearside bank and badly damaging the local farmer's newly-constructed fence. It was my good self, working single crew, who was summoned to attend from near Abergavenny, about 15 miles distant. By the time of my arrival the driver, the only occupant, had been taken to hospital by the ambulance service. The traffic flow was not impeded in any way so I concentrated on recovering any property that was in the vehicle. I had ascertained via the Police National Computer that the owner lived in Blaenavon and within minutes, officers from the local 'nick' confirmed that he was known to them as a local married man and they would ensure that his wife was informed. In addition to the usual odds and ends and a couple of garage repair receipts, I recovered from the glove compartment an envelope containing several letters of a very personal and explicit nature. The lady's name, quoted in several places, was certainly not that of his wife and the contents made it clear to me that these letters were the by-product of an illicit and steamy affair.

As procedure demanded, I listed them, as inconspicuously as possible, in 'Miscellaneous Property', before terminating duty and having briefly explained to my sergeant, I was given permission to start my night shift a little early on the Sunday night. The driver, as I recall, had suffered severe concussion and a broken leg. At 8.30 pm the following evening, I visited the Royal Gwent Hospital and on speaking to the ward sister was advised that the patient's wife was still at his bedside – oops! I enjoyed a cup of coffee provided in the nurses' rest room until she left, then entered the ward and after exchanging pleasantries with the driver I informed him that I had recovered property from the vehicle and his wife had signed for it. I know I shouldn't have taken advantage, but it was comical to see his reaction. He coughed, spluttered and started to turn a colour between puce and purple, until I produced the envelope from my tunic pocket. I've never seen so much relief on a man's face; if it hadn't been for the plaster moulded around his leg I am convinced that he would have jumped out of bed and kissed me. I never did become aware of how his marriage progressed, but I hope I helped him see the error of his ways and that a long and happy family life ensued. If not, I am sure he found somewhere more secure to keep his clandestine belongings.

CHAPTER 8

I know I can speak for Shel at this point in saying that we had both settled into married life and were thoroughly enjoying it. Our first home, although very cold in the months of that first winter we shared there, seemed like a palace, and we were blessed with good neighbours. Perhaps more importantly, it made me realise the commitment I had made. Married life however, was no summer ball. There were bills to be paid – lots of bills, and they were not the responsibility of our parents any more. As I've mentioned, I had been earning quite good money at the garage after the bonus scheme was introduced, taking home about £20 each week which, matched against the £47 a month I got as a constable, left a considerable difference. We had free housing and I wore uniform each day free gratis, but things were still tight, even with Shel's income from the Magistrate's Clerk's office. But we were in love, and everyone says that's what matters.

It was May 1968 and the house was slowly warming up. I had been busy tending the six-foot square back garden and over our evening meal, which we always ate in the kitchen, Shel hit me slowly and gently with the news that she thought she was pregnant. I thought, "pregnant? WHAT?" I was bewildered for a few seconds and was just about to ask "how did that happen?" when excitement and a feeling of ecstasy took over. I couldn't tell Shel to sit down and take it easy – she already was.

That evening and for the next few weeks were taken up with all sorts of discussions and chit chat about the future. I certainly came down to earth with a thump when I again considered my responsibilities. If my future and that of my family were to be reliant on the Police Service, I had better knuckle down and study for my promotion exams; without success in those, I was going nowhere. The relatively short time I had spent at Police HQ might have been good experience, but I had to prove to the ones that mattered that I was capable.

I was looking forward to a period of quiet normality in our new home with the wonderful news Shel had announced, and without that daily trudge to HQ and back, when lo and behold, I went to work one Monday morning after a long weekend off and found that I had been nominated to attend a C10 course. This short and uninspiring title belongs to the Stolen Vehicle Squad of the Metropolitan Police and I knew that Shel was not going to like it one little bit. I made some rapid enquiries with the only other traffic officer in the Force who had attended this prestigious course, and found that although it was only two weeks long, it meant two weeks away without being able to travel home at the weekend. I would be in the 'big city' where, according to Max Boyce, there are "lots of girls with shiny beads".

I was right – when I got home that afternoon Shel was not very happy. I slowly pacified her that one, I would probably be staying a long way from central London, and two, I had been told the course involved working shifts with officers, so I'd have hardly any spare time. Both counts proved right.

The Stolen Vehicle Squad had been set up by the Met some years previously to counter the dramatic increase in stolen vehicles in the capital. They were not interested in the Ford Anglias and Minis that were being taken most nights by joyriders; they were after the well-organised gangs who were stealing the prestigious makes, changing their identities (termed 'ringing') before shipping them to the Continent and Africa for sale, very often to order. Other forces soon found that such organised crime was starting to take place in their own conurbations outside the Metropolis, so Scotland Yard invited provincial officers, four at a time, to visit them to glean an insight into their detection methods.

I travelled up by train – my car would have been no use in London – and was accommodated in a 'section house' in Leytonstone, almost as far north-east out of the city as you could travel by tube. These section houses were a purpose-built type of hostel which provided lodgings for the Met's single officers, of which there were thousands. You had a small room housing a bed and a writing table, with shared shower and toilet facilities. There was a 24-hour canteen to cater for the shifts and the whole complex was managed by a 'matron'. I can tell you that the one at Leytonstone was one of the old school and would not tolerate any nonsense or misbehaviour whatsoever. The squad was based in a large multi-storey car park in Chalk Farm, in the far north west of the City, which left me with a one and a quarter hour journey twice a day on the underground. Gosh, what an eye-opener.

We had two days' verbal instruction in one corner of an office (things were very ad hoc and basic) before we were teamed up with a double-manned investigation unit to work the same shifts that they were allocated, and the two weeks just flew by. It was mid-December, and on our last afternoon we four country bumpkins were brought into the office together with our tutors to say our fond farewells. The Chief Inspector in charge of the squad suggested we should partake of a 'snifter' before we left. I was not too enamoured by this suggestion as I wanted to be on my way back to Paddington to catch the first train I could, and I could foresee a knees-up in the local Dog and Duck. However, no sooner had these thoughts flashed through my mind when the 'boss', as he was referred to by his officers, unlocked a large three-door cupboard to reveal bottles and bottles of every alcoholic beverage you could imagine. We four visitors were invited to 'name our poison', and at that time I think I was into vodka when the pennies allowed a little more indulgence than a pint of best. A good time, well, a good three-quarters of an hour, was had by all before our hosts delivered us by squad car to our various main rail stations for our homeward journeys.

Whilst enjoying our farewell tipple in this seven-storey

car park in North London we didn't ask too much about the small brewery lodged within its walls, but from various snippets of conversation, I gathered that it had been donated by numerous grateful clients and quite an amount came from some dubious characters who hadn't felt the weight of the law as fully as they deserved. That's possibly why the Metropolitan Police had an Internal Investigation Unit in those early days.

Once I was settled back home, I decided to attend the evening study classes that the Training Department held weekly in each division, and somewhat to my surprise, I seemed to enjoy them. The more I read and learned, the more I wanted to. After several weeks Shel and I sat one evening and analysed our weekly expenditure, which helped her to agree that I should register for a home study correspondence course. There were one or two firms providing this type of service and I embarked on one which advertised that it could prepare students for the National Promotions Examinations, at a cost in the region of £70, which could be paid in instalments. Things would be tight, but we were both up for it. We really felt the pinch when Shel gave up work about three weeks before her confinement.

It was about 10.45pm on Wednesday 15 January 1969. I was the observer in our Austin Westminster traffic car, Tango 158, being driven by Mel on patrol through Llanover, a very upper-class little village just outside Abergavenny, having just conferred with our sergeant at HQ. I had taken Shel into hospital the previous afternoon at the instruction of my mother, but things, as they say, were progressing slowly. Suddenly the darkness and road noise inside the vehicle were disturbed by the loud voice of Christine, the civilian radio operator in control room.

"WO to WO158 over".

"Go ahead, over".

"Mrs Thorne gave birth to a baby boy at 10.20 pm. Both doing fine. Congratulations".

It seemed an eternity before Mel reached across and took the handset from me to acknowledge "Roger".

My pulse rate started to subside after a minute or two, but I can't remember a thing we did for the remainder of that shift – I was a dad!

I had further good news three months later. As a result of my studies and the stress to which I had subjected our monthly income, I had passed my promotion examinations and qualified for the rank of Inspector. Promotion to Chief Inspector and above was by selection only, so I had completed my career's quota of serious study. Or so I thought.

They say that good news, or otherwise, comes in threes, and it certainly did for me during 1969. After the birth of Michael, Shel became the loving mother and housewife, tending to the constant requirements of a baby and turning her attention to all those little jobs around the house she had been too busy, in work and latterly in confinement, to get around to. Me? I was happy helping to keep Michael clean at the rear end, showing him off whenever possible to all and sundry and busying myself in work doing a job that I thoroughly enjoyed.

In the third week of September I was summoned to

attend Police HQ by my Divisional Commander and in his office, I found him to be in an unusually light-hearted mood. My then boss, Chief Superintendent Jim Walby, was a serious but fair-minded individual. He told me to smarten myself up, because in 20 minutes' time at 3.30 pm, I was to be upstairs, outside the Chief Constable's office. When I was ushered into the Chief's inner sanctum, he was standing bolt upright behind his desk, in uniform as smart as a new pin. It always was; he was a retired army colonel and proud of it.

He welcomed me and without beating about the bush said, "Mr Thorne, I'd like you to come back to HQ and look after the fleet again, but this time with three stripes".

"Thank you sir," I replied.

I returned to my Commander's office, and after congratulating me he spent a good half an hour outlining the responsibilities of rank and what the future would hold. I just made it to Jack's stores to meet his 5 pm deadline. Surprised to see me back at his counter so soon, he issued me with several sets of chevrons. My promotion was to take effect the following week, so Shel had plenty of time to get hold of some black thread for her sewing needle.

I had no problem settling back into the workshops; I knew the staff, the premises and procedures, the only difference being that now I really was the boss. I would no longer be caretaking the position with the objective of keeping things on an even keel. This time it was for real. This became abundantly clear to me during the first few weeks and my eyes were opened at this early stage to the in-fighting, back-biting and pure jealousy you find among members of an organisation when it comes to promotion and advancement.

My previous relatively short period in the workshops had been fully accepted by all. I was considered a young nobody who was helping out just because he happened to be in the right department at the right time, with the necessary knowledge, but this time it was serious. The Chief had gone 'too far' and promoted me, a young twenty-something with only four years' experience, who was bound to make a total cock-up of everything. I was given the cold shoulder by quite a few individuals, mostly members of HQ CID who thought they should be in the front line for everything, although they must have realised the post required some specialist knowledge. There were a few longer-serving qualified constables on traffic who were not too pleased either.

Within several weeks, it became clear that there were some officers based at HQ who were starting to show their true colours, which I ignored without any concern. It appeared to me that a police HQ, certainly in those days, was akin to what we term now as the 'Westminster Bubble' in the heart of London, which accommodates those individuals who consider themselves to be the country's elite – a group of people who are not all infused with intelligence, who have managed to secure plum positions by wheeling and dealing, and who have no idea how the world revolves outside their own little circle. However, I was completely satisfied that my move to HQ was due entirely to my ability and that the Chief had been advised of my merit. To my knowledge, at that time, I was aware of only three people in the Force who had the necessary qualifications to maintain the fleet to the standard required. One was Sergeant

Pritchard, who had just been promoted, creating the vacancy for me, and the other was a traffic officer in 'C' Division who obviously lost out to my selection. I can reveal that he took my place on my transfer four years later.

When my Divisional Commander was welcoming me after my exit from the Chief's office he gave me two pieces of information which, although significant, did not bother me and certainly did not make me think of the additional work I would have to undertake as time progressed. The first was that the experiment involving our force and Unit Beat Policing which had commenced some 18 months earlier had been deemed a success by the Home Office, and in the not-too-distant future it was to be introduced nationwide. Gwent Constabulary, to give us our new official title on amalgamation, was to introduce it throughout the county as soon as the necessary funding could be put in place, with our police authority vying for an extra grant from Central Government and, very importantly, when the vehicles could be delivered. There would be 37, which had been decided by the Chief Constable and his senior management team.

Actually, within days of my transfer to Abergavenny, my Chief Superintendent advised me that in fact the unit beat vehicles were on order with the specification having been sent to the County Council's Supply Department, which was responsible for negotiating the purchase of all major items of equipment on behalf of the Police Authority. Our vehicles were to be Ford Anglia 105Es. The vehicles weren't delivered for several months, but when they did arrive it was in one consignment, and within two or three days we had them kitted out with roof signs, blue lights and police signage. The local vehicle registration office had kindly issued them numbers from NWO 1F to 37F which helped us in workshops when identifying vehicles for servicing and repairs; we didn't use fleet numbers.

Some political commentators over the years, and indeed some eminent senior police officers, have said that the introduction of the 'unit beat' system saw the demise of British policing as we knew it. My view was that the concept in itself was sound, but the police service itself was incapable, even with proper and adequate supervision, of bringing its advantages to fruition. The concept was drawn up by civil servants at the Home Office, being advised, I add, by senior police officers who had worked their way, on secondment, into that 'Westminster Bubble' and really had no idea how their 'vision' would be interpreted by the average bobby on the beat and their supervisors.

It must be an accepted fact that in the early 60s the Police Service and its style of policing, like all other large organisations, had to adapt to the quickly-changing life of the second half of the 20th century. Policing the community had been, for the previous 30 years, based on a foot patrol beat system with transport being slowly introduced via the odd motorcycle or van, to keep up with an advancing way of life. However, as the population increased and crime became an issue on the political agenda, the country needed more police officers to cater for this leap forward in society. But the Treasury could not afford to answer the call for extra manpower. It was just not realistic or possible to expect a police officer, donning the blue uniform, to be available on every street corner, which is, by the way, in the early 21st century, what is being called for by all political parties when they are in opposition.

So maybe Unit Beat Policing was the way forward in the larger conurbations. Foot patrol beats were bunched up into large groups termed 'units' and the officer assigned to a unit for a tour of duty would be given a small saloon car to enable him or her to cover the larger area and a UHF radio so that the station could direct them to reported incidents. Now that seemed simple; a better use of manpower, which is always the expensive commodity in any scheme. What the boffins in the Home Office and officers seconded to the Police Research and Planning Unit had not really thought through, which should have been an obvious major stumbling block, was the basic fact that police officers are drawn from the community they serve. They are not factory made on an assembly line like the Welsh rugby outside-half conveyor belt. They are human, with all normal human failings. This new policing innovation required that officers should patrol on foot with their vehicles parked in a conspicuous position as a deterrent, and be moved from locality to locality as required. However, if I were to ask a group of people if they would prefer to walk the streets on a wet, windswept afternoon or ride around in a warm little car with the heater on full blast, then nine out of ten would say the latter. Quite a lot of police officers, on the introduction of Unit Beat Policing, did just that.

Of course, there were other issues which exacerbated the situation, one of which was a total lack of pre-launch briefings to all ranks, which resulted in poor supervision of the new system by operational sergeants and inspectors. John Woodcock, our Deputy Chief Constable at the time, must have become aware of the issues I've outlined, because a good nine months after the introduction throughout

Gwent he gave a series of divisional talks, which everyone had to attend, to explain the rationale of this new system in detail. It was, however, too late. The officers who were expected to operate this new system had formulated their mindsets of what they wanted it to be, and they liked it.

The other innovation introduced as part of this new policing package was the UHF radio system, which now meant that foot patrol officers, who now had wheels, were contactable every second of their shift and not just when they rang in from a landline or conferred with their supervisor. A large section of our entire population, who firmly believe it is their right to have the complete attention of our public services, soon realised this and were demanding the attendance of a police officer for even the slightest problem they encountered in their daily lives. With the demand for figures, percentages and response times by our Civil Service statisticians throughout the 1970s, the town bobby, who should have been the 'Unit Beat Pioneer', was simply driving around responding to a host of unnecessary calls and busier than a hive of bees on a summer's afternoon. The 'bobby on the beat' was confined to history and Unit Beat Policing had proved itself a disaster.

It is of course relatively easy for me, in the cool light of day, to give you my view, formulated over a period of many months after this policing phenomenon was introduced, but at the time, in my role as fleet manager, Unit Beat Policing gave me and my foreman nothing but headaches. Up until this point in the evolution of the Police Service, mechanically-propelled transport had been a luxury not available to all, and those relatively few officers who were given access saw it as a bonus; something to be cossetted, to be treated well, looked after. The outstation officer and other rural law enforcers tended their motorcycles and small vans with the same care and enthusiasm they gave to their garden's vegetable plot, and even the larger, more urban personnel carriers and traffic patrol cars were, generally speaking, utilised by a small group of drivers who firstly, treated the vehicles as they would their own and secondly, if there were any miscreants who failed to comply with the standard set by the majority, they were quickly shown the error of their ways and if necessary their supervisors were badgered to move them to other duties. I can say quite honestly that it was a pleasure to see vehicles arrive at workshops for service or repair which were obviously being cared for to a high degree and it was a standard which had been set throughout the Force as the norm. The arrival of the 37 unit beat vehicles, or 'panda cars' as they were soon labelled, put paid to that. You must remember that Gwent was one of the smallest constabularies in the Country; our additional 37 cars were dwarfed by the numbers introduced to most other forces.

The police vehicle, integral to this new system, was labelled a necessity; these cars were accessed 24 hours a day by the vast majority of the Force. One of the mandatory courses for all officers as they concluded their probationary period was the Standard Driving Course. Familiarity breeds contempt, and that certainly applied to police transport, post Unit Beat. The standard of vehicle care became abysmal; not just the state of cleanliness of the vehicles but through the harsh use of controls and mechanical components. As time went on, the situation deteriorated, because on transfer or promotion, this uncaring attitude spread rapidly throughout the Force. Today's supervisor was yesterday's panda driver, who wouldn't or couldn't do anything to reverse the situation. I began to contact sub-divisional commanders directly and threaten to take the vehicles off the road because of wanton damage, only to be given a reply to the effect that the vehicles were 'workhorses'. Horses don't work if they are not shod and fed properly! The other issue which really exacerbated the problem was that these vehicles were not designed or built for such constant use. Ignoring individual makes and manufacturers, the automotive industry as a whole was not sufficiently advanced to produce the right vehicle at the right cost for such a tough role. These small and medium-sized saloons were designed for work commuting and the occasional family outing. The stream of defects and breakdowns was constant.

The other topic discussed at the initial meeting with my Commander was the move of our Police HQ from the ancient border town on the Welsh Marches to Croesyceiliog, primarily a residential enclave of Cwmbran. In English it means 'Cockerel's Cross' and at the heart of this small community sits the Upper Cock public house which, like its neighbour lying a few miles south, provided refreshments to John Frost and his Chartist marchers almost 200 years ago.

The Local Authority had been planning this move for quite a few years; the capital funding was in place for this multi-million-pound development, which would see a new County Hall to serve the residents of Gwent, with its Police HQ standing alongside on the same site. As we spoke in the Chief Superintendent's office I knew the building's foundations had been laid; it had been the talk of the Force for several months. He explained that he had involved my predecessor in the basic planning of the new workshops and we were at the stage when the final layout was a done deal. He was no longer able to make any significant alterations, and apart from really minor issues I had to go along with everything. Ken Pritchard, the sergeant before me, had been promoted to traffic patrol duties based at the other end of the yard, so he would be close at hand to confer with. I was quite happy with that; I got on well with him and in any event, I was in no position to argue.

This forthcoming move raised a major issue with the civilian employees, whose numbers were not large by any means, but my department had the majority in the form of mechanics. They were concerned, quite naturally, about their employment positions and the cost of travelling each day some 30 miles back and forth across the county. After lengthy discussions with the lads, I put some suggestions into the discussions with management and the union rep, and everybody seemed relatively happy with the suggestion that for at least 12 months, the Police Authority would provide a minibus (actually an old police personnel carrier) to ferry them back and forth each morning and evening. My workforce seemed content and kept beavering away keeping those temperamental panda cars mobile and looking forward to their new premises.

The architect's plans appeared fine on paper; the new building was to be provided with large easy-access front doors, four electrically-powered four-post vehicle lifts and a completely separate workshop for our fleet of motorcycles, along with all the amenities that any new workshop could be provided with. To the delight of Harry, our handyman, it included a fully-enclosed automatic vehicle wash, and the *pièce de resistance* was a separately-housed vehicle rolling-road and diagnostic bay to be supplied and fitted by Crypton, the leaders in the field of automobile diagnostics. It all seemed ideal.

However, as the months went by and the complex neared completion, I had need to visit more often and I saw the end result slowly materialising into a working environment which could pose some practical problems, most of them built in at the initial design stage and some from the specifications given to the construction firm. A few problematic threads running through this new complex were unfortunately down to Ken, who was ex-RAF and had been in post at workshops when the ball had started rolling. I never did find out if any of his service was completed at St Athan, that place where the swimming pool nearly froze me to death, but he told me later that before he decided on the day-to-day working requirements of the lads, he had visited the air station and based his suggestions on the motor transport workshops situated there. Now that Ministry of Defence establishment officially opened on September 1 1938, so I wouldn't have thought it could be viewed as modern and worthy of replicating.

I have no idea what Ken saw on his visit to our esteemed military neighbours, but as a result he decided to have all the spanners, sockets and hand tools, of which there would be hundreds to cater for eight mechanics, neatly and individually set out on racks attached to the main wall of the building. Such a display looks smart and professional and it may have looked the bee's knees in the military workshops, where, with the greatest respect, in times of peaceful coexistence, they had all the time in the world with only their commander's whim bearing down on them. In an operational workshop, maintaining a fleet of nearing 150 vehicles, our mechanics just didn't have time to replace tools between each job, and there could be 20 or more jobs a day for each lad. We tried to maintain the system for a month or two, but I found that some were spending far too much time each day walking back and forth keeping the tools looking tidy, and some just left them lying about. I issued each lad with a tool box which they carried from job to job and things flowed much more easily. Set underneath these sparkling tools on the wall was a workbench running the whole length of the workshop; it must have been 25 yards long, bespoke, with every inch crafted out of what appeared to be solid oak, with an expensive block of shock-absorbing material set in its top. It must have cost literally thousands of pounds to produce, and for any workshop fanatic, it really was a show-stopper. The one major flaw: it was constructed too high for the average mechanic. Only two inches, but for our lads it was enough to make life really awkward.

One other bright idea was implemented, and I say 'bright' because it involved bright light blue paint being applied to the whole screeded concrete floor of the workshop, which was about half the size of a hockey pitch. This special sealing paint was designed to give the area a bright appearance and keep the floor clean; spillages of oil and grease could be wiped up easily. Well, it just didn't work. It chipped and peeled and all the remnants of spillages could not be removed. However, we were stuck with it, so before anyone would come on an official visit, we were forever repainting odd patches everywhere.

The last issue I shall have a little moan about, is to do with the original design. The whole complex, including County Hall, was built on a rather shallow undulating site which, from the main entrance, sloped down slightly to the right-hand side. The workshops were built close to the right-hand edge and I was given to understand that the architect wanted to keep the roofline of the whole complex somewhat even, which meant that the roof of the workshops was higher than necessary, apart from keeping the aesthetics in balance. As I have mentioned, the workshop area housed four vehicle lifts, so the roof height needed to accommodate the likes of a Transit van held some six feet off the floor. However, even then there was still about 15 feet clearance between the lifted vehicles and the roof timbers. As you can imagine, the cubic footage of the workshop building was vast. Coupled with this, the front elevation of the building was fitted with six large sliding doors the entire height of the structure, to afford easy access, and this elevation was facing north-west. The weather predominantly, in this country, comes to us from a westerly direction, so in autumn and winter the wind would howl across the Cwmbran valley and hit the entrance doors with a force outside our control. Bearing in mind that the doors of the busy workshop were in constant use, our workplace was cold, very cold. It was necessary, just from a health and safety point of view, for us to purchase two large cylindrical paraffin space heaters within days of our first October of occupation. With hindsight, perhaps I was being somewhat pedantic, but at the time several issues were causing us extra work and inconvenience. Tom, my foreman always seemed to be in agreement with me – or was he just keeping on side?

In any event, we coped. All our official visitors, of which there were many for the first six months, including members of other local authorities and Chief Constables from other forces, were impressed with the complex. Although I, and possibly a few others, would argue that far too much money had been spent on fittings and furnishings (The Chief Constable's office had been provided with a white carpet), the basic design and construction of the building was intended to be frugal. The outside walls were pre-cast concrete blocks and all internal walls were left as plain breeze blocks with electrical switches and conduit standing proud of the surfaces. I have no idea whose ultimate decision it was to agree to this type of design and construction, but as I unfold this story to you, exactly 45 years after the official opening, the County Hall building has this year been razed to the ground, due to serious safety faults in the concrete used for the construction, and Police HQ staff are also under notice to evacuate. Can we honestly say that's prudent use of public money?

After 18 months or so of fulfilling my role in workshops, I applied and was admitted to the august organisation of the Institute of Road Transport Engineers, who are very particular about who they allow to join, so being able to use the letters AIRTE after my name gave me a lift.

Before I move on I will just add that on 12 November 1971, after being in occupation of our new premises for some 12 months, we had a very special visitor; HRH Princess Anne. I am not a devoted royalist but I do have some time for the Queen and her nearest and dearest, so in my book, the Princess was okay. She flew in by helicopter to officiate at two functions in Cwmbran, one of which was to officially open our HQ. In those days security was not such an issue as it is now, so we had no detailed searches or briefings beforehand. On the day in question, Tom and I stood at the front door of our humble abode in our best white coats while the Princess slowly meandered across the traffic yard towards us, accompanied by our Chief and the Chairman of the Police Authority.

The Chief introduced us and then, surprisingly, stood back. He remained outside while Tom and I escorted Her Royal Highness and the Chairman through our domain. There was no one else present and no one to prompt her, and we had a thoroughly pleasant 20 minutes or so during which she asked some serious questions which clearly indicated that she had been fully briefed. In the diagnostic bay, we had a traffic patrol car suitably parked on the rolling road and when I asked the Princess if she would care to drive it, she gave a little chuckle and suggested that perhaps I should. As she spoke to me, I could see by her smiling eyes that she would have loved to, but knew that her entourage, who were watching us through the large open doors, would not be too pleased. As we had planned, Tom gave us all a short demonstration before she left us to our own devices.

We had all known about the proposed royal visit some months beforehand, but as it drew nearer, all HQ staff were busy in their own little domains dotting the i's and crossing the t's, so as the Princess flew off into the sunset we all experienced something of an anti-climax. However, little old me became something of a local celebrity. Princess Anne had actually spent quite a bit longer with Tom and me in the workshops complex than had been planned, something that would not happen today with the tight security cordon placed around the royals. Apart from numerous HQ staff and County Hall officials pestering us to enquire why and who had said what and when, I had telephone calls from the press throughout South East Wales wanting to know the same, and even clandestine visits from a few reporters who were of course, all referred to the Press Office.

On the Monday morning, three days after the official opening, I was surprised to see Reg, a recently-appointed driver/handyman, waiting for me at 7.30 am as I arrived for work. Reg was a retired police sergeant who had taken on this role perhaps either to supplement his pension or to give him some continued peace away from a nagging wife. He explained that his early arrival enabled him to have a quiet word with me. To my complete surprise and astonishment, he asked me if I was interested in an introduction to the Freemasons, as he would be quite prepared to arrange one. I was somewhat taken aback, because I knew nothing about the society, apart from some non-members in the Force passing derogatory or humorous comments about various officers who they were pretty sure had joined. Well, I was now certain of one ex-officer who had. I made a light-hearted comment to Reg that he was only asking because I was now a friend of the Princess, but I did tell him that I would give it some thought. I had little to think about really; deep inside I could not accept the degree of secrecy that overshadowed the whole aspect. It was, in our force, and I'm sure countrywide, a regular topic of chit-chat in the canteen that many officers were Masons, and their belief that 'each looks after its own' was detrimental to others who trod a different path. Our Chief, Mr Over, made it clear to the Force that he was not a member, and did not agree with the secrecy surrounding what probably was good charity work. However, many thought his lifestyle did not match his verbal protestations and didn't believe him. My thoughts were clear; it wasn't for me, and I spoke with Reg later that week. It didn't alter our working relationship one little bit.

CHAPTER 9

Whilst I had been keeping myself busy organising and coordinating the move across the County, which took upwards of 18 months although it was physically carried out over one weekend, Shel had been pretty busy too. She had given birth to our second son, Brian, and this time she was allowed to have her own way. He was delivered at my mother's home, by her, and I was present, sorting out the hot water and things, as you do. Brian didn't have a universal announcement of his arrival like his brother, but I was in a position to arrange a few hours off when Shel went into labour, and fair play to the little fella, he didn't hang around.

Prior to Brian's birth and fully aware that the move to our new workshops was imminent, I took the opportunity of mentioning to my Chief Superintendent, with whom I conferred as often as three or four times a day, that Shel and I would welcome a move to Cwmbran, so that I would be 'on the spot' so to speak, and readily available for emergency callouts, if and when necessary. I had, of course, discussed this matter with Shel. Although we were both very grateful for being allocated housing to coincide with our marriage, I knew there was a mammoth logistical exercise being undertaken by the Force's admin. department which involved the relocation of personnel and resources. I also knew that the Cwmbran Development Corporation considered it a bit of a coup to have secured the operational centres of the Council and the Police Force so close to their jurisdiction, so they were only too pleased to allocate them both as much rental housing as they were asked for. Although I was only a lowly sergeant, I occupied a very influential position, from an operational point of view; I conversed daily with sub-divisional commanders and anyone who was anyone within the Force knew me, particularly at HQ, where the influence was. I not only had the odd chat with the Chief, but his wife used the parking space outside my office window whenever she popped into town for shopping. Her gratitude and our acquaintance resulted in a present to me of a bottle of her homemade orange wine each Christmas. Yes, Shel did know – she sampled it!

My family moved to Cwmbran within three months. The Development Corporation had planned the New Town to be set out in specific areas to meet the community's needs; recreational, retail and several residential estates with necessary schools and medical facilities, whilst retaining the identity of the long-standing hamlets it encompassed. We were given a fairly new four-bedroomed house on the southwestern edge of the town with warm air central heating. Good grief, central heating was going to be fantastic, but I'd never heard of 'warm air'. We didn't really get on with it because the system gave the house a very dry atmosphere which wasn't something to be enamoured by. However, the accommodation was modern, Shel was impressed with the kitchen, bathroom and room sizes and we were one contented little family. I really enjoyed the larger garden and Shel had become an accomplished mother and housewife, although I quietly knew that she was looking forward to the independent feeling of employment in the future.

We had been living in our new surroundings for 10 to 12 months when one evening Shel told me that she thought she could detect a small lump in her breast. She added that she was pretty sure there was nothing untoward, but she was going to visit the doctor as a precaution. Dr Khan, the female half of a married medical couple who practised in our local surgery, examined Shel within the next two weeks and reassured her that there was nothing to worry about; there was no treatment or medication needed. With this news, we devoted the next few weeks to discussing a subject I had mentioned some time earlier, the possibility of buying our own house. This was one hell of a step for a young married couple, which has not diminished for youngsters today, but it was all the talk for young police officers who were being advised by the Federation to plough their rent allowance, which you were entitled to if you were not provided with police accommodation, into bricks and mortar. Shel and I used to sit at the kitchen table for nights on end working out our finances and willing them to indicate that we could afford it. Well, whether we could or not, I can't honestly remember, but we went for it. There was a relatively small private estate being constructed not too far from our house by a local firm who I knew to be sound and capable. Mr Arthur Jones, a local farmer, had retired several years previously turning his 18th century farmhouse into a country club and was now selling off several of his fields. The name of the farm was Maes-y-Rhiw ('Field on the Hill' in English), which it had passed on to the club and indeed, the enclave that was to be built surrounding it. It was a nice spot, with a distant view of the Bristol Channel coast. We had no reservations about the club being so close and so the detailed procedure of negotiations with the builders, solicitors and mortgage providers went ahead. I think that fairly short busy period took Shel's mind off her personal problem somewhat, but we'd hardly moved in when she told me she was not really satisfied with the doctor's advice.

I accompanied Shel to the surgery this time and saw Dr Sharma, an Indian gentleman who had recently joined the practice, and without hesitation he suggested that Shel should see a consultant. Not long after my promotion, I had joined a private healthcare scheme being promoted by the Federation, so he referred Shel privately to a Mr Sturdy, who held clinics at a local private hospital only three miles from our home. His examination revealed something abnormal, but of course, a biopsy would be required to give a conclusive answer. He explained that he would obtain a sample of tissue under general anaesthetic and would be able to have the sample analysed in minutes. If benign, all well and good, if not, he would obviously proceed to remove the affected tissue whilst Shel was still anaesthetised. As we drove home, I was as scared as hell. I just couldn't accept that only two months ago, a doctor had said there was nothing to worry about, and it had turned out like this. Furthermore, my wife looked fine, just her normal radiant self. She was however, quite human and I knew she was concerned, but she wouldn't show it, not even to me. She knew she had to greet our two youngsters on our return without any glimmer of worry. I have never known or met anyone in my life with such a loving, caring attitude.

Shel underwent surgery within two weeks and on the day of the operation I remember pacing the floor of the visitor's lounge for some two hours. Then, click, the door handle moved and the door slowly opened. Mr Sturdy, a short, heavily-built man in his late fifties slowly walked across the room towards me, scrubbed up and out of his operating gown. He advised me, "Your wife is fine; you can go and see her in her room".

"How did it go?"

"Well, I did find a malignant tumour in her breast which I had to remove".

"Did you need to remove any of the breast?"

Mr Sturdy, without any hesitation, looked at me as if I was lacking even an ounce of common sense and replied, "All of it, of course."

I just froze; I couldn't even open my mouth, but I thought quite clearly in my mind, "You bastard".

I've relived that moment over the years more times than I care to remember. Surely a man with such intelligence and in such a caring profession could have imparted such news with a little more compassion? Or was it me? Was I just naïve?

On leaving the room, I shut the door much more harshly than I should have and made my way to Shel's room. She was awake. A little drowsy, but she knew I was there. I will always remember the little forced smile she gave with the smallest of tears running down her cheeks. I sat on the bed, held her in my arms as best I could whilst avoiding her dressings, and that's how we stayed, it seemed for hours, without saying a word. We didn't have to.

Although Shel was only kept in overnight, it took us a few weeks to regain our equilibrium; well, it did me anyway. Shel, always the pragmatic one, kept telling me not to fuss whenever I'd offer to help with the odd chore. "I've had a mastectomy" she'd say, "thousands of other women have. I'll be fine." There was no medical necessity, apparently, for her to undergo any kind of therapy; she was to visit the consultant for a check-up on the operation procedures after six weeks and unless she encountered any complications, she would be called for monitoring every five years. She was soon back to her bright, positive self and was eagerly awaiting new bras and a prosthesis, which she had ordered from catalogues the nursing staff had told her about, which, incidentally, if my memory serves me right, were very expensive.

I make mention of this not because I was in any way concerned about the cost, but for many years it has annoyed me that manufacturers who produce important aids for the disabled and chronically ill play on their misfortune and charge exorbitant prices. It's a pity our elected representatives didn't concern themselves a little more about day-to-day issues that adversely affect members of society instead of their own wellbeing – whoops, I must stop this or I'll begin to rant. Back to the story.

Our two toddlers were now both in school and were, like others, a handful, and capable of many things much more mischievous than toddling. I had been carrying out my role in workshops for almost four years and had just applied to appear before a selection board, which were held irregularly, about every two years. I was qualified for promotion, but my real purpose in applying was so that our new Chief Constable would be able to put a name to my face. He had been in post with us for about two months, arriving from Dorset. I believe he had served in the Met at some stage in his career and I knew that he had spent a couple of years on secondment in Hong Kong, a fact that he kept reminding everyone of for the next few years as he made his visits around the Force.

Before our new leader, John Over, had reached the dizzy heights of chief officer and undertaken his period in the Far East, he had served as a traffic officer, so I should have had a little affinity with him, but initially, some of us thought he had too much 'bull' and too little substance. His deputy at the time was John Woodcock, a much more astute man who in time became Chief HMIC (Her Majesty's Inspector of Constabularies) and had, in practice, been running the Force since our previous Chief had announced his retirement. Irrespective of any failings I had at the time, I must have been a personable individual because, apart from my annual present from the Chief's wife, Mr Woodcock chose to play quite an athletic game of badminton with me each day in the gymnasium which was provided in the new building. I had been playing each day when work permitted ever since our move to the new HQ, and on Mr Woodcock's arrival he asked if he could join our group when there was an opportunity. I always had admiration for the man because he reminded me of that famous Kipling poem hanging on Bill Collier's kitchen wall: "If you can walk with kings nor lose the common touch". I can fully understand how he got where he did.

That first promotion board was a bit of a tester and after 30 minutes of gruelling questions I didn't know whether my rear end was punched or bored, so to speak. The Chief Constable didn't say a lot; he stuck to the usual mundane issues, asking why I wanted promotion, what I could offer the Force and so on, and left the contentious matters to his two colleagues. The awkward one was the 'C' Divisional Commander, who really tried to wind me up by suggesting I'd had little operational police experience, and that I'd only been in charge of civilians for the past four years. I knew only too well that all workshop staff collectively had identified the officers of the two large police stations under his command as probably the worst abusers of police transport in the Force, so I attempted to give him as good as I got. The third member of the panel was, to my utter delight, Mr Woodcock. He posed several questions which allowed me to suggest that my management skills, interaction with other agencies and level of decision making were way above those of someone with twice my service. There was no official feedback from these boards, but Mr Woodcock did mention in passing some days later in the gym that I hadn't let myself down.

It was about three weeks later when Harry, one of my drivers/handymen, popped his head round the office door to advise me that two uniformed sergeants were due to see the Chief that afternoon. I never questioned Harry too deeply about how or where he got his information; his role enabled him to make personal contact with grass roots members of the Force all day and every day. I just soaked up all his news. It was, however, very interesting to me that the sergeants concerned had appeared two days before me on the board.

By command, I stepped onto that white carpet on the Monday morning of the following week and was invited by the Chief to take a seat. In those milliseconds while you adjust your senses as you walk into a strange environment, I can remember thinking what an odd and extravagant choice of carpet it was for such a busy office, but on all the occasions I entered that room, and there must have been many in my subsequent career, I never saw the slightest dirty mark. Mr Over told me, without any exciting preamble, that he was going to promote me to the rank of inspector, but for the time being he was going to retain me within the Traffic Department. He congratulated me and shook my hand, as he did with everyone, before I was politely dismissed. My transfer would take place within a fortnight, which meant a move of office to the other side of the traffic yard where the operational officers were based. I was to head 'D' relief, consisting of two sergeants and an establishment of 22 officers. I say 'establishment' because the Traffic Department always shouldered any shortfall of patrol constables within the Force due to lack of recruitment or finance. Each of the four traffic reliefs were always carrying at least one vacancy. We worked a continental three-shift pattern, so one of my first jobs at home was to make sure we still had that reliable, loud alarm clock.

My other role on promotion, which I was unaware of at

the time, was to carry out the duties of Vice-President of the Officers Mess. Many forces throughout the country had this social association, which encompassed officers of inspector rank and above; they were probably brought about by the large number of senior military officers appointed to command police forces after World War Two. Personally speaking, I saw nothing wrong with them; they allowed senior officers throughout the Force to get together for a meal, a drink and an informal chat in a social environment, usually every three months or so. During my service in Gwent, I attended two occasions where the wives were invited with a dinner-dance organised and I know Shel really enjoyed them. Officers wore mess-dress and the ladies took the opportunity to show off that ballgown. There was some hostility to this fraternisation shown by some Federation members and local left-wing politicians, who thought it suggested a 'them and us' culture. However, the majority of chief constables back then were men of conviction who made it clear that it was they who 'ran the force' and they would do as they pleased. As these men retired and were replaced by the cloned individuals who were bred at the National Police College, which of course was strictly directed by the Home Office, the Officers' Mess as such was doomed by the early 1990s. However, while the one in Gwent was flourishing in 1973, I was its Vice-President and had to propose the 'Loyal Toast'. The Force held a Mess dinner only three weeks after my promotion and I was required to ask my fellow guests to raise their glasses to 'The Queen' on that one occasion. I was replaced well in time for the next function as it was the youngest or most recently promoted inspector who was given the task.

I've mentioned the animosity I felt among some officers when I moved to Abergavenny with three stripes. Well, that was nothing to the reception I had from a couple of traffic sergeants, who were both, incidentally, ex-Newport Borough, when I took on patrol supervision with two pips. The Traffic Department, shortly after amalgamation, had a high percentage of officers from the Borough force because, on amalgamation, officers who had originally joined in Newport could not be moved outside the Borough's boundary against their will, because of their conditions of service. However, quite a lot of their die-hard traffic officers wanted to remain in their preferred department (they had no intention of returning to foot patrol wearing a tall, pointed helmet) and this new state-of-the-art headquarters was only a mile or so outside their old northern boundary. Most of the officers would have less travelling than if they were to remain within their own force area, so when they were given the opportunity to move to Croesyceiliog, they jumped at it. Furthermore, the Chief was happy to approve the transfer of quite a few, because the integration figures would go down well with the Home Office, who were monitoring these police amalgamations with great interest.

One such officer who accepted such a move was Vic (Victor) Tuck, one of the supervisors reporting to me on 'D' relief. It was quite obvious on my first shift that he considered me to be a country bumpkin who was still wet behind the ears and too young to have any experience. Well, there certainly was an age gap; I had just turned 29 and Vic was probably in his late 50s, with retirement looming. I decided to plough on and demonstrate my ability. After a month or so I could see that his attitude was not tempering and I became even more concerned that he had a small group of ex-Borough constables who were supporting his stance.

I dealt with the situation during one night shift, when I arranged to confer with him in a large lay-by on the A48 just west of Newport. These conferences were a regular feature on traffic patrol; they allowed a briefing session between patrol officers and supervisors. As soon as I sat beside him, Vic found out that this was no usual meeting between two officers. After a frank discussion, I informed him that if he did not alter what I considered to be his childish attitude, I would ensure he was moved to another relief, or if the Divisional Commander was of the view, another station. My ultimatum was not given until after I'd explained to Vic that I valued his experience, which at that stage was far wider than mine, and said that with his support we could mould 'D' relief to be the envy of all our peers.

Our relationship improved almost from that moment; 'D' relief did become top dog, certainly in our eyes, and I started to really enjoy my role once more. I'd spent a very happy 12 months on traffic patrol, despite the occasional disruption to domestic life caused by the continental shifts. Many people say they give you far more free time at home, or to pursue hobbies or leisure pursuits, and I agree, to a certain extent. The downside is that when you're at home, your wife is often at work and your children are at school.

At this point I must mention that my wife was now back in work. Our new house had kept us pretty busy for some months with Shel sorting out her bits and bobs and me in the garden, so we'd had no real time for socialising; in any event the two lads were still at primary school and needed babysitting. We were able however, to visit the Country Club, which was only a couple of hundred yards away through the estate, on the occasional weekend evening, and within a few months we became quite friendly with the licensee and his wife, who to my satisfaction, kept a very clean and orderly establishment. Our idle conversation one evening led to Shel being asked if she'd like to take on a couple of hours cleaning work each day. That was the start of another brief career for my shorthand typist. Shel fitted in well and before long she was helping out at various functions and had become quite proficient at 'silver service'. The added bonus was that during school holidays she could take our two boys with her, and they would play with the licensee's children.

CHAPTER 10

Everything in our small family seemed to be ticking along nicely. Michael and Brian had settled well into primary school, Shel was actively engaged in something she enjoyed and I was supervising the policing of the county's roads. Then, one afternoon shift, I was called to my Chief Superintendent's office and told I was moving to Ebbw Vale.

I don't believe my Chief Superintendent, Mr Shortridge, who had been promoted from the CID in Newport some three months earlier, had a clue where Ebbw Vale was, but I did. I had no misgivings about the town itself; it was at the Heads of the Valleys, and I was a Valleys boy. I remember quite well that the Chief, when promoting me, told me that he would keep me in Traffic 'for the time being' and it appeared that the 'time being' had elapsed. Furthermore, for most of my service to date, I had been attached to this specialist department and I was only too aware that if I was to progress I needed to become involved in general policing to broaden my experience. The CID had never been of any interest to me; it was a vital part of our police operations but I wanted to be a police officer, inside and out, ready to be visibly present to deal with society's problems. Detectives spend most of their time in the public domain trying to keep their identity hidden, with surreptitious observations and clandestine meetings. No, that wasn't for me.

My only concern about moving to Ebbw Vale was the extra daily travelling that was going to be involved, which obviously meant extra cost and time away from home. Still, that was something you took into account when purchasing your own home. The journey to and from work amounted to about 40 miles and coincidentally, I found I was faced with a similar situation as I was in workshops; helping to prepare the sub-division to occupy a brand-new police station. Ebbw Vale, which has been listed as one of the 10 worst places to live in the UK, had a population of about 30,000 and is situated in the constituency of Blaenau Gwent, with the duffel-coated Michael Foot, the one-time leader of the Labour Party, being its MP during my time there. It certainly was a deprived area, an industrial town born out of the Industrial Revolution. The main employer was the large steel works, part of the British Steel Corporation, which was nationalised by the Labour Government in 1967. I could clearly see soon after I arrived, from the reported crime statistics, the petty theft and fraud that was emanating from the complex, that it was financially doomed. Margaret Thatcher was demonised for her decisions some years later which led to its severe contraction and ultimate closure. As the 21st century dawned, the whole sprawling complex had been razed to the ground and its landscape now encompasses unit factories and an NHS hospital.

Ebbw Vale was then a sub-division of the Force and I was to be its Deputy Commander, working directly under the Chief Inspector in charge, Edwin Jones, who had recently been absorbed, or technically transferred, because he had the choice, when a small section of Dyfed Powys was merged into Gwent in the local government reorganisation of 1972. I basically worked a day shift but had to give supervisory cover between the hours of 6 pm and 2 am for the whole Division, along with four other deputy commanders from other sub-divisions, which meant I worked a couple of late evening shifts every 10 days or so. However, we all knew each other well and would provide cover amongst ourselves to suit any domestic or social activity. Our Divisional Commander was pretty easy-going in that respect; as long as someone was available. My relationship with Chief Inspector Jones, as I always addressed him when in company, was excellent. Like me, he wouldn't tolerate time wasters or shirkers and because of my divisional commitments and our rest days, we would seldom be working together and he seemed perfectly happy to let me run our patch in his absence. The one thing I respected him for, which didn't always occur with other senior officers I have worked with, was that if I made a thoughtful and rational decision, then it stood. He would never countermand it. Once your constables and sergeants are aware of that, then you're half way there.

I've mentioned the planned new police station and the fact that Ebbw Vale was a deprived area. This was reflected in the existing police stations, which stood in the centre of the town's main street. It was an old Victorian building which had seen much use over the years, and two months before my posting there the Police Authority had sanctioned its closure. Because of its prime position within the community, the Chief Constable, who had been clearly swayed by local residents through their elected councillors, decided that the new building would be constructed on the same plot of land after the demolition of the discarded one. The total transformation was to take at least 18 months, so to ensure a constant police presence in the town, two second-hand static caravans were placed on a derelict plot of land directly behind the site of the new building, one to be used as an enquiry office where the public could make contact and the other as a mess room, uniform locker store and generally an Aladdin's cave for any other use that was required. The beating pulse of the police station, including the reception area for prisoners, CID, interview offices and many other functions to which the public are generally excluded, was moved to a sectional police station four miles down the valley in Cwm, a small mining village whose colliery had suffered an explosion on St David's Day, 1927. On that first day of March, 53 miners lost their lives, 39 of whom lived in, and were probably born in, the village. It was a close-knit community and its residents welcomed the influx of police activity.

The officers of Ebbw Vale were just getting used to their temporary abode when I arrived, and I shared it with them until we occupied the new building with all its mod-cons. After tolerating more than one and a half years of what can only be described as atrocious working conditions, for which every member of staff at the time deserves the highest praise, we just didn't know ourselves in our new surroundings. In this second decade of the 21st century, thanks to a combination of establishment-bred Chief Constables, Health and Safety law and a more vociferous Police Federation, it would just not happen, no matter what local residents requested.

My time at Ebbw Vale gave me valuable experience of general policing duties, including monthly cautioning sessions when I would officially interview youngsters at Cwm in the presence of their parent or guardian, and attempt to point out the errors of their ways after they had been reported by an officer for some relatively minor indiscretion. There was also the weekly Magistrates Court, where I would cover for the Chief Inspector and present prosecution cases. My presence in Ebbw Vale allowed me to hone my management techniques and gave me an insight into the various policing methods and systems, which I could not always agree with.

One such laborious and in my view, expensive and time-wasting exercise was in relation to found property. Any property handed into the police as 'found' was documented, locked away and if not claimed by the rightful owner within six months, was returned to the finder. With some exceptions, such as dangerous or perishable goods, that was it; relatively simple, apart from the fact that I saw no need for it to be kept for six months. Bus companies and other organisations dispose after 28 days, but I was in no position then to have National Police Guidelines altered. Furthermore, a Force instruction that items should be checked each month by a supervisory officer resulted in the supervision of patrol and other policing duties being cut by 50% for hours each month with a sergeant tied up in the property store checking and counting goodness knows what. We lads and lasses in Ebbw Vale had an added problem, because all items received from the public in the town had to be transported safely and securely four miles to the police station in Cwm; there was no security in the caravans.

During my tenure at Ebbw Vale, I had the misfortune to have a Divisional Superintendent who visited his sub-divisions quite routinely and whose forte was to carry out spot checks on property each time he arrived. He was Robert Haines, a rather short man for a police officer, who was promoted into our force from West Mercia. Our Chief Constable, John Over, shortly after his arrival and to the dismay of many of his own officers who were vying for advancement, promoted a large number of officers to the rank of Chief Inspector and Superintendent from other forces, which was a clear indication to his own men that he wanted his suitably qualified officers to apply for posts being advertised nationwide. His two-year secondment to the Royal Hong Kong Police (before the Chinese repatriation of course) may have adversely affected his outlook on the Welsh nation, because his usual comment about his own senior officers in any social gathering was that they were all members of the "flat earth society". That did him a lot of good! Many thought it sarcastic. He was not savvy enough at that stage to understand the patriotism that ran through the veins of many Welsh people, which obviously included some of the men he was struggling to earn respect from.

Meanwhile, back at our temporary police station in Cwm, Superintendent Haines arrived, unannounced, early one afternoon when I was on duty. I was sitting in the Chief Inspector's office upstairs, in which I was provided with quite a nice antique desk in the corner of the room. The first I was aware of this supervisor's presence was when the reserve constable tapped on the door, then put his head around it. He cast a quick warning glance to the ceiling and advised me that my presence was required in the enquiry office.

I will declare at this point that I did not like this man one bit. Some would say that he had an unfortunate arrogant attitude; I was of the view that there was nothing unfortunate about it, he was arrogant and that was that. He came to the Force as a Chief Inspector with a self-declared detailed knowledge of firearms and was allowed to pursue that avenue throughout the remainder of his service in Gwent. Throughout the remainder of my service I was unable to ascertain or find anyone who could advise me where or when he had accumulated his apparent expertise. I can only assume he gathered most of it using his 12-bore shotgun on the sprawling fields of Herefordshire. In any event, it was abundantly clear that this Superintendent did not like me either. I have no idea what prompted his dislike of me and had no inclination to ask him, but our negative view of each other was totally and unsurprisingly mutual.

As I entered the front office, surprise surprise, Mr Haines had the found property book open in front of him. He looked at me and in a tone which suggested we were seeking a thief, he said "This ring is missing". The register entry indicated a gold-coloured ring with red stones, value unknown. It had been found outside the leisure centre three weeks previously and handed in at the caravan to Sergeant Deakin, who had recorded the details. After an in-depth search I could not locate the ring either. The Superintendent caused quite a kerfuffle. He accused almost everyone working at Ebbw Vale of being incompetent and me in particular of being unable to impose discipline and supervision, then put the tin hat on it for me by suggesting that the ring had been misappropriated and that Sergeant Deakin was responsible.

I took stock. Before reacting I recalled that the Sergeant was on leave, and had told me some time previously that he and his family were taking a trip to Brighton. Sergeant Deakin was one of five sergeants under my supervision; I'd worked with him for over six months and although he wasn't the sharpest tool in the box, I'd lay my life on the line that he was not dishonest.

I asked the reserve constable, the only other person in the room, to leave and in as respectful a manner as I could I told the Superintendent that he was completely out of order. I said he was fanatical about property and suggested he left so that I could sort it out. Before leaving he demanded that the ring should be located by six o'clock that evening, whatever action was necessary, even if the Sergeant had to be recalled from leave.

I was sure that Superintendent Haines would have satisfaction in informing the Divisional Commander at the earliest opportunity, so I briefed my Chief Inspector at his home by telephone, advising him that I was sure things would be resolved three days later when Sergeant Deakin returned from Brighton. In the meantime, I would make enquiries with the Sergeant's shift members to see if they could shed any light on the situation, but that proved fruitless. There was nothing that could realistically be done at that time so nothing was. I had a feeling that I wouldn't hear anything more from Mr Haines that evening and I didn't. He was more than arrogant – he was all wind.

I spoke with Sergeant Deakin by telephone at his home the following Saturday, shortly after his return from Brighton, and he recalled dealing with the lady who had handed the ring in. As soon as I mentioned the property register, he asked me to hold on. The line went silent for a few moments before Sergeant Deakin sheepishly advised me that he had just retrieved the ring from the breast pocket of his tunic, which had been hanging in his wardrobe for the past two weeks. No, he wasn't the sharpest tool in the box, but nor was he a thief. I left my Chief Inspector to advise Mr Haines the following Monday morning that Sergeant Deakin had simply placed it in his pocket to transport it to Cwm and then just forgot.

Figures and statistics have always played an important role in the Police Service, and are still being sought by the Home Office, almost on a daily basis, so that they can be fed into the Government's machine to prove or disprove any theory which is currently top of the agenda. With our new all-encompassing Freedom of Information Act, all kinds of pressure groups are clamouring for statistics so that they can actively channel their efforts in the direction of whatever campaign they happen to be pursuing. But most people with an iota of common sense realise that figures can be juggled to show anything, and from one who has been at the initial collection point for all this misinformation I can say that very often, they are purposely recorded incorrectly at the start.

Nothing springs to mind more readily than crime figures, the basic source on which the state of our society is constantly judged and monitored. Back as far as 1974, I observed them being freely manipulated to reflect a favourable picture of the performance of a force, and each division within a force would vie for the best result. A common occurrence in all valley towns was the theft of milk each morning, shortly after the roundsman had deposited the bottles at each front door. It was usually taken by young lads who had either been specifically directed to do so by their parents, were genuinely in need of sustenance or were just playing a childish prank. There would usually be around half a dozen law-abiding citizens deprived of their breakfast menu and when reported to the local station, the CID office would not officially record the matter forthwith but would wait to see if there was any likelihood of apprehending the offender(s). If the crimes were solved, they would be listed as six detected offences of theft from six different addresses, but if no miscreant was forthcoming, a single undetected offence of 'theft of milk in High Street' would be added to the figures. Most officers in the Force knew this happened, certainly all those in the CID, which included the Detective Chief Superintendent. Of course, any Chief Constable would deny such knowledge, but if he wasn't aware of the practice his lack of experience and naivety should have barred him from high office. This is a simple example, but such misrepresentation took place across the whole spectrum of offences.

Earlier in my tale, when describing the social conditions in the South Wales valleys, I explained how the miners' welfare institute was an integral part of most communities and how the registered clubs differed from public houses in the way they were permitted to dispense alcohol. I held the belief that it was a farce then, and I still had the same view when I was attempting to police the community in Ebbw Vale. One of the problems I had whilst trying to foster a community spirit in this deprived valley town was my Chief Superintendent, sitting in his Divisional HQ some 15 miles away, who had an inherent dislike of these registered clubs, coupled with a desire to improve his prosecution figures month upon month. Whether he thought there was wide-scale debauchery taking place in these establishments on a nightly basis I know not, because he never took the trouble to discuss the issue with me. Up until this present posting I had been part of the Traffic Department when I had often taken part in a raid on such a club in other areas of the Force, because when such a raid was undertaken, manpower became an issue and the best place for divisional officers to seek assistance was Traffic.

My Chief Superintendent, Mr William Holder, had spent most of his service sitting behind a desk in the Training Department and I doubt if he had any practical knowledge of what actually happened behind the clubs' entrance doors. If he had asked, I could have explained that members enjoyed themselves with social chit-chat over their favourite tipple, usually best bitter. On two or three nights a week there would be a bingo session, to which most wives would be welcome, and the *pièce de resistance* would be a visiting musical act performing on a Friday and Saturday night, when wives and girlfriends took the opportunity to don their glad rags. I ask the question – as long as exuberance didn't turn into quarrelsome behaviour, as it seldom did, what was the problem? Incidentally, on many an evening in the late 1960s, such a club near Pontypridd secured the attendance of a musical group who called themselves Thomas Woodward and the Senators. The singer went on to entertain the world for decades with the name Tom Jones.

Of course, Mr Holder's annoyance was triggered by those persons allowed to purchase alcohol who were not bona fide members, and that was technically unlawful. When a raid was carried out somewhere in the Force area, which was quite often, officers would discover perhaps upwards of 20 local persons who were there drinking 'illegally', and they would eventually appear before magistrates and be fined. The club would also be prosecuted, but in my experience, I knew of no Registration Certificate that was ever revoked; the Magistrates knew it would cause uproar in their town. The whole procedure was totally counterproductive, because it only promulgated bad feeling between the local residents involved and us, the police. The strength of the British Police Service relies on the fact that it carries out its duty with the consent of the community from which it is drawn, and no individual's whims or wishes should contradict that.

If Chief Superintendent Holder had spoken to me direct and ordered me to carry out a raid on any particular club I would have been duty bound under the Discipline Code to do so, but he never did, although my immediate supervisor, Chief Inspector Jones, had told me he had been asked to advise me. We spoke about this subject quite often and Chief Inspector Jones shared my view, so our supervisor's suggestion never got anywhere. It was obvious that my inspector colleagues in neighbouring sub-divisions had been leaned on, because raids were carried out in each of their respective areas, at the rate of two or three every year.

Chief Superintendent Holder and I never did have any type of confrontation, unlike that with his deputy concerning the missing ring, but we just didn't see eye to eye and there was only going to be one winner. I continued working at Ebbw Vale throughout the summer of 1974, thoroughly enjoying it, but expecting to be summoned at a minute's notice to see my Divisional Commander, who I envisaged would give me the usual spiel about how good it had been to have me on his team but say it was time for me to move on. Well, that invitation didn't arrive, but towards the end of August, just after Shel, the boys and I had returned from a holiday in Brittany, I received one of those personal memos from HQ, which, as always, had been scrutinised and noted by every supervisory officer who had spied it on its journey through the internal mail. It advised me that I was to attend an Inspectors' Course at the Police Staff College. It was to last for 13 weeks from September right through to the week before Christmas. Shel was really going to be pleased!

The National Police College, as it was initially called, was established in 1948 at Ryton-on-Dunsmore in Warwickshire, within the confines of one of the national recruit training centres, with the aim of giving a common standard of training to senior officers drawn from all forces of England, Wales and Northern Ireland. In 1960 it was moved to a permanent base, in a 402-year-old Grade One listed Jacobean building named Bramshill House, set in acres of woodland near the village of Hartley Witney in Hampshire. In 1979 it was renamed the Police Staff College.

To be honest, I was full of apprehension that Sunday afternoon as I set off from home for my initial registration. Shel had prepared a sandwich pack because I'd no idea how long it would take to get there or what I'd find on arrival. I'd been away on my recruit training for three months, but that was just a hop and a skip down the road. This time it was to a foreign country, and I was leaving a wife and family at home. Although we didn't speak too much about Shel's health issues, I knew she quietly thought about it and I tried not to show too often that I was concerned, but at times like this it was foremost in my mind. The Severn Bridge slowly disappeared in my rear-view mirror as I made my way up the M4 and my eyes welled up on more than one occasion.

The setting of Bramshill Estate was impressive. The country house appeared as a dot in the distance as you began the long drive from the road junction down the never-ending straight drive, but as you drew nearer it was awe-inspiring to view it in all its autumn splendour. The house itself contained a large ornate dining room with the teaching staff and visitors occupying the top table and we mere mortals regimentally sitting at long trestle-type tables running the whole length of the room. It often made me think I was young Oliver Twist sitting with his doomed friends awaiting Mr Bumble's booming voice telling us to be quiet. The rest of the grand mansion housed a very comfortable bar area, a billiard room with two tables for our recreation, a library so vast I could never have imagined it before I saw it, and all the administrative offices. The students' accommodation and lecture rooms were housed in adequate buildings in acres of ground surrounding the house itself, which was the focal point. Most of the Metropolitan officers were quite blasé about the whole experience; after all, this was what life was all about to them, but we lads from the shires and backwaters were somewhat overwhelmed.

All in all, I settled better than I had expected and got on reasonably well with the 19 other officers in my syndicate, one of whom had travelled from Belize in Central America. The only woman was Inspector Peters from Derbyshire, who must have felt a little isolated. Our studies were a little more involved than learning definitions; we were given individual subjects to research and after a couple of weeks studying, we were expected to present a 10,000-word thesis for evaluation. My first such exercise was 'Discuss the Life and Politics of Joseph Stalin'. Yes, I found it hard; enjoyable but hard. It was good to unwind on a Wednesday afternoon, which was set aside for recreation, and having got to know a few chaps from the South Wales Constabulary in another syndicate, I played several times for the college rugby team, visiting other establishments such as Sandhurst, where I must admit our experiences were widened, both on the field and during the after-match refreshments.

It didn't take me long to pine for home; by the first Monday morning after breakfast, while patiently waiting for the first session, I was longing to see Shel and the boys, and to be perfectly honest, it didn't get any easier during the rest of the three months. The only thing that kept my mind in some form of equilibrium was the telephone call I made home to Shel every evening, between 6.30 and 7 pm. The half-hour slot was introduced because although I was fortunate that one of the few red telephone boxes on site was positioned right outside the main door of our accommodation, there were invariably three or four others who had managed to get there before me, equally anxious to communicate with loved ones far and near.

To our dismay, the syllabus included two or three weekend visits to public body establishments, but generally speaking we students were set free at 3.30 on a Friday afternoon, or a little earlier if we could bribe the instructor with us at the time, and expected to be back on campus by 9 pm on the Sunday. The road from the college entrance to junction 11 of the motorway was like Silverstone circuit each Friday afternoon and after a month or so I knew every individual characteristic of both carriageways of the M4 between Reading and Newport.

For the whole of the last month every student was looking forward to Thursday 19 December, when a formal mess dinner was to be held, followed by a dance. More importantly, you were allowed to invite a guest. Shel had been planning the visit from the moment I told her; the family was toddler-sitting and Shel's Uncle Frank was to drive her up on the Thursday afternoon. The guests' accommodation was the responsibility of the students, and although there was no public announcement, the staff surreptitiously advised us that there would be no objection to the student's rooms being utilised. Shel and I and I'm sure most others thoroughly enjoyed the evening, although the night's sleep in my single bed was a little cramped – but who was complaining?

I believe the course did its job as far as I was concerned; my outlook on life was certainly broadened, the interaction with other students and delivering presentations gave me more confidence and I certainly knew a lot more about Joseph Stalin. However, one aspect did surprise me and gave me some concern, about the direction in which the Police Service was heading. Although each syndicate director was a senior police officer seconded from various forces throughout the country, we seemed to have a vast number of lectures and presentations from the academic staff, most of whom had studied psychology and social sciences, together with visiting chief executives from county social services departments, all trying to convince us that there were other ways of dealing with crime than prosecution and punishment. When I joined the Police Service I was told the primary role of a police officer was the protection of life and property, the maintenance of order and the prosecution of offenders against the peace. In my mind, that didn't exactly accord with what these people would have me believe.

Meanwhile, back in Ebbw Vale things were ticking along just fine as far as I knew. Before I had left for the bright lights of Hampshire my Chief Inspector had told me to switch off, go and enjoy the course and forget about Ebbw Vale, and that's what I did. Within a week of my return I did get the summons I had been expecting three months earlier, but it was my Divisional Commander who came to me. Yes, he had been pleased to have me on his team, but for the good of my future I was to move stations so that I could broaden my horizons.

Where had I heard that before? I knew full well that it was the Chief Constable who sanctioned any type of transfer for inspector rank and above and it was he who had decided that I should go to Maindee, back as a relief inspector working similar shifts to those on Traffic. Shel always had the habit of telling me, whenever any problem arose, to look at the positives, and the only positive I could see was that my travelling costs would be slashed. My new place of work would be only six miles down the valley from our home. The other thing to be thankful for was that nine years had gone by since amalgamation, and there had been so many retirements and transfers in the intervening years that there was no longer any antagonism or bitterness between warring factions of the two individual forces. The one policing issue however that dominated life in the Gwent Constabulary was that to all its officers, Newport was busy.

On the domestic scene, I'm pretty sure Shel was glad to have me home; I was certainly glad to be back. I could now continue to shape my garden in the coming spring and was looking forward to growing my first vegetables in uncultivated virgin soil after clearance of all the bricks and lumps of concrete left partially buried by the builders.

CHAPTER 11

At this point in my tale I will introduce you to a man I came into contact with just a little too often in my police career, although he was only a passing acquaintance. To save any embarrassment to his family, I will refer to him by the name of John Green. He was a married man of roughly my own age who had moved into a dormer bungalow on the second phase of our estate. Because of the topography it was next to our house and he would have been a next-door neighbour if we had not been separated by an access road. He had moved to Gwent from the Home Counties to take up a position with the Magistrate's Courts Committee in Newport, working out of the same building that housed our Divisional HQ. The few enquiries I made revealed that he had originally joined the Metropolitan Police, but during his first two years' probationary period he had either decided the job was not for him, or the Met had decided he was not for the job. In fairness to him I know not which, but if my instincts were correct, from the assessment I made over the first few months, he just didn't have the temperament to become a police officer. He and his wife had a son the same age as my lads and a slightly younger and very pretty daughter.

In addition to my assessment of this new arrival, I noted that my two boys, over the spring and summer months made no contact with the two children or spent any of their playful leisure time in their company. Perhaps my boys had similar thoughts to me. Mr Green was, as I said, just a passing acquaintance at that time, but because he was a neighbour I was forced to acknowledge him on the odd occasion I would see him within the confines of the Court precinct.

Newport, the town to which I had been posted, was at the mouth of the River Usk and was Wales' third largest conurbation, with a population of 137,000. When I arrived, it was, to the dismay of most local councillors, still only a 'town', and although it has had a small cathedral since the 17th century, it was granted city status only in 2002. The city itself dates back to medieval times and its castle was built when the Normans conquered Wales. It has progressed somewhat in recent years, playing host to the Ryder Cup in 2010 and a NATO summit in 2014, but to me, and a favourite aunt who lived there for 62 years, Newport always has been, is, and always will be a sad and depressing place, unless some future group of local councillors gets a total grip on their delegated role.

From a policing aspect, when I arrived in 1975, there had been no improvements to police buildings and facilities since its days as a relatively small borough force and the immigrant population, like several other towns and cities in the UK, had been allowed to expand out of all proportion to the indigenous section. Without being in any way racist, this put added pressure on the police and other agencies because of the different cultures and religions.

Apart from three or four outstations which had been converted from semi-detached houses on large estates and opened in an attempt to appease the public, to no avail whatsoever, there was the Divisional HQ, which also housed a sub-divisional unit. They were located in the town's Civic Centre building, accommodating the administrative offices of all the Local Authority's facilities and with all councillors intent on looking after themselves, I can assure you that the police were the poor relations.

The other police station was the sub-divisional HQ which policed the Maindee conurbation and its surrounds. I was to take control of its 'A' relief, a motley crew if ever I saw one, but I soon learned that you had to be to police Maindee. I worked with three other relief inspectors and was guided from above; well, from a very small office at the top of one flight of stairs, by Woman Chief Inspector Barbara Jones, a proper tyrant, who made it clear that she was as good as, if not better than, any man in the establishment. I got on with Barbara, probably because of my charm, so I'll criticise not. At the head of this thriving hive of workers was Superintendent Bees (no pun intended). If he had anything to say to you, he would, but seldom did. He was quite busily occupied most of the week arranging his golf outing, which took place each Wednesday.

I have mentioned that Newport was busy; all aspects of human misbehaviour contributed to this, including the theft of anything if it wasn't firmly secured, with shoplifting almost a social pastime. Juvenile crime was most prevalent, with burglaries commonplace. It was quite normal for one of my lads to go out at the start of a shift to pursue enquiries regarding some reported house-breaking and arrive back at the station some hours later with a panda car filled to the gunnels with juveniles all admitting their involvement. It seemed that every small estate, or even one average street, would have formed their own 'gang' which was vying to be top of the pops. In Maindee at that time, there was no such term as 'pro-active' in police terminology, it was just a case of response policing. We were trying to keep the lid on an explosion of social depravation. This, of course, was added to by the nightly circus which was promulgated by the large number of unruly and drunken revellers as they spilled out of the discos and nightclubs on Friday and Saturday evenings, and it was not unknown for our central control room to advise all patrols by UHF radio that "no more prisoners were expected". Everyone knew that meant the cells were occupied to their maximum capacity. Our Divisional Chief Superintendent at the time, Mr Castree, had recently been seconded to the Home Office for two years, so he knew his figures and I believed him when he often said that Newport Division had more arrests per year than West End Central in London.

One thing that John Over did within days of taking up his post in Gwent, apart from irritating most of his senior officers with his comments about Welsh blood, was to make his views known, not only to his men, but to Local Authority members and particularly those who served on his Police Authority, about his absolute disgust at the state of Maindee Police Station. He was appalled that his officers were forced to work in such conditions and there were many press reports in which he described the building as 'Dickensian'. It certainly was of 19th Century construction, but to exacerbate the situation, there was no evidence of any improvements being undertaken since the day it was opened. It had a listed façade abutting the main A48, which one or two locals who were, no doubt, members of a historical society, thought enhanced the area, but inside, the building's space was shared with the local library and one or two other offices attributed to other agencies. I have mentioned that Newport was suffering from social deprivation; well, the police station certainly matched that criterion.

I will freely admit that throughout my police career I was proud of being an officer, and as I progressed through the ranks it became clear to me that my wife and two boys were too. That gave me added pride. Advancement in any chosen employment is pleasing and acceptable, even if only for the financial implications, but unlike some of my contemporaries, whatever rank I held, I considered myself first and foremost, a police officer. Many of my colleagues who had been recognised by having two pips placed on their shoulders were happy to keep the seats of their office chairs at a confortable temperature and issue instructions from behind the line. To the annoyance of my patrol officers and sergeants on occasions, I was always happy being alongside them, whenever possible, experiencing the things that I otherwise would have thought I was missing.

We had three cells at Maindee, so old, crude and basic that they were not approved by the Home Office for any lengthy detention of prisoners. It was divisional procedure that anyone detained overnight had to be transferred to the divisional police station before 6am, which was the time of shift change, if their detention was to be extended. Central police station had a large suite of cells which also served the Crown Court, and the unwritten rule at Maindee for all four shifts was 'whatever you create at night, you clear up before going home'.

It was late one Thursday evening; we had not long started the night shift and it had the makings of being an exceptionally busy one. It would have been around 11.30 pm and I was sitting at my desk vetting reports, only about three yards down the corridor from the public enquiry counter, which was just inside the front entrance door. Both my sergeants were in the charge office documenting two or three prisoners, with four juveniles who had been arrested for house-breaking handcuffed to the large central heating radiator to prevent their escape (this practice was obviously not condoned, but it was the only thing the custody sergeant could do when the juvenile detention room was occupied). Suddenly, I heard an almighty thud; I raced down the corridor and as I passed the enquiry office to investigate what I thought was charge room activity, I saw to my right that the front entrance door had been forced open so hard that it had broken the self-closing mechanism. On the floor, half in and half out of the building, was a man in a dishevelled state who I recognised as Tommy (I shall call him Tommy to protect his true identity) and lying on top of him was Police Constable Patrick (Pat) Lannigan in full uniform apart from his helmet, which I could see sitting sedately in the road, inches away from passing traffic.

Tommy was a regular visitor to both police stations in Newport. He was an unemployed alcoholic who slept under the stars most nights and made his only income, apart from benefits, by odd-jobbing and selling any bits and pieces he could purloin. Tommy was always intoxicated but never gave any intentional trouble. He was regularly arrested for being drunk and incapable, which was nearly always for his own safety. This type of individual really needed long-term help from other agencies within the Local Authority, but during their hard-working day shifts they were far too busy attending meetings (I admit to sarcasm).

Constable Pat Lannigan had been part of my shift when I assumed command several months previously. He was in his last few months of probation and was a first-rate officer. He was in his early 20s with an appetite for all kinds of police work and I could honestly say that if I was faced with any situation with just one officer to stand beside me, I would choose Pat. Coincidentally, his twin brother also served in the Force and his father, a pharmacist who owned a chemist's shop, occasionally took a pint of beer in the country club I frequented.

I immediately went to Pat's assistance at the front door and helped him to his feet before we manhandled Tommy into the main body of the police station. Pat could see how busy the place was and apologised to me for bringing Tommy in. The prisoner was so drunk that I fully accepted the officer's word when he explained that Tommy was in danger of staggering into what was quite a busy flow of traffic on an arterial road. Tommy was incapable of supporting his own weight and certainly not fit to be taken into the charge room amongst the other prisoners, so we carried him into the passageway outside the cells. That was the easy bit, because we now had to search the prisoner to take possession of any items he had with which he could cause harm to himself or others. We removed his short outer jacket and hung it on the hook provided outside the cell door before we made an inventory of all other items found on his person. These were listed on the charge sheet and secured. To be honest, everything recovered should have gone straight in the bin, and back then in 1976, we weren't even issued with vinyl gloves to undertake such tasks.

The last I saw of Tommy that night was as we lay him down on the two-inch-thick mattress to allow his body to recover its senses. He wouldn't have got a great deal of rest because Force Orders stipulated that all detained prisoners should be checked and roused every 30 minutes. I would, generally speaking, have nothing to do with prisoners in detention unless there were unusual circumstances, so I saw no more of Tommy and terminated my night shift along with all my officers at 6 am looking forward to a good day's sleep.

At approximately 10.30 that Friday morning I was awakened by Shel, telling me there was someone on the phone from Maindee police station. It was my relieving colleague on the morning shift, who had decided to inform me that Tommy had apparently attempted to commit suicide whilst in custody and Superintendent Smallcombe from our force had been appointed to investigate the matter. I had no more information than that, but even that scant knowledge ensured that no more sleep was to come my way. Obviously, the words 'attempted suicide' gave it a ring of real concern, but I knew that if any real harm had befallen Tommy there would have been someone from another force to investigate, or indeed the Police Complaints Board would have been notified. In any event, that did not stop me from worrying.

Around midday, I had a further call from my boss, Superintendent Bees, who placed the whole episode into perspective. Before we terminated duty that morning, two of my officers had transported three prisoners over to Central Police Station, as was the procedure. One of these was Tommy and as they left they collected his jacket from the hook outside the cell, as they should have.

On arrival at Central, Tommy was placed into the care of the custody sergeant and was allocated a cell by the 'gaoler', an individual who was a police constable, dedicated full-time to supervising a suite of 12 cells. Before the door was slammed shut on Tommy, the gaoler, apparently, threw the jacket in after him. This was the jacket we had withheld from the prisoner during his earlier detention. Sometime during the morning, our Tommy had recovered enough to rifle through his jacket pockets, where he found a Gillette safety razor and, for whatever reason, he managed to scratch his left wrist. This was obviously noticed on the next cell visit and as they say, 'the balloon went up'. The duty inspector at the time interviewed Tommy, who refused to make any kind of complaint and no medical action was necessary. Tommy was taken before the Court at 10.30 am when he pleaded guilty to the charge of being drunk and incapable and made no mention to the magistrates of his escapade. Superintendent Bees surmised that Pat and I should perhaps have searched the jacket, but Tommy had not been allowed it whilst in our custody and maybe the gaoler at Central should not have thrown the jacket into the cell. My Superintendent advised me not to dwell on it too much and to be open and frank with the investigating officer. He ended the conversation by simply saying he thought that the whole investigative procedure was political and before putting the phone down he acknowledged my request that he would put Constable Lannigan in the picture.

There was no reason to ignore Superintendent Bees' advice, and when I was interviewed in my office at 10 pm that night by Superintendent Smallcombe, I spoke the truth, the whole truth and nothing but the truth. That did not stop him informing me at the conclusion of our meeting that he was going to report the issue to the Chief as an act of 'Neglect of Duty' under the Discipline Code.

A dark cloud hung over Maindee police station for several weeks and both Constable Lannigan and I were grateful for the support shown to us by all officers up to and including the Sub-Divisional Commander. We were both subsequently charged with 'Neglect of Duty' and I was quite forthright with my "no" when a member of the Complaints Department, who in addition to investigating complaints from the public, also coordinated disciplinary hearings to be held in front of the Chief, asked me if I had any objection to the cases against Constable Lannigan and myself being heard together. The regulations allowed us to be represented by what was legally termed 'a friend', and whilst Constable Lannigan chose Sergeant Simmonds, secretary of the Gwent branch of the Police Federation, I chose Chief Inspector Jones from Ebbw Vale.

During the intervening weeks, we were given lots of advice from both genuinely concerned colleagues and many barrack room lawyers, but Constable Lannigan fully accepted my suggestion that we should plead guilty and throw ourselves on the mercy of the Chief Constable. I was perfectly happy in my own mind that we hadn't been purposely neglectful and there were such extenuating circumstances that a competent 'friend' or even if we conducted our own case the Chief would deal with us leniently. In addition, I had been discussing the issue in depth with Superintendent Bees and he was still convinced that the whole episode was a political façade.

The fateful day arrived and we stood to attention in the conference room, next to the white-carpeted office as the charge was read out. Chief Inspector Jones spoke as eloquently as I knew he would, and Sergeant Simmonds did his best. Like my Sergeant Deakin at Ebbw Vale, Sergeant Simmonds wasn't the sharpest tool in the box, in fact, after a disciplinary hearing some years later in which he spoke for a traffic officer and I was successful in presenting the case, the Chief Constable said to me, "The trouble is Alan, Sergeant Simmonds is as good as gold, but as dull as hell".

The Chief Constable responded the moment Chief Inspector Jones stopped speaking and in acknowledging the fact that we had saved a great deal of time and effort by pleading guilty, he described how he was somewhat ashamed that his officers were forced to work in the conditions that existed at Maindee. He issued us both with a 'formal caution', which was the most lenient penalty at the time, and told us to leave with our heads high and carry on the good work.

In the following weeks, I was informed on good authority, and by that I mean the Chairman of the Police

Committee, that Mr Over was using our disciplinary misfortune as ammunition to strengthen his case for building improvements at Maindee. He apparently made it quite clear that he would no longer have his officers placing themselves in jeopardy by having to work in such Dickensian conditions. It took a little time to alter Maindee because the large amount of capital expenditure needed required budgeting, but apart from pleasing the group of architectural buffs by retaining the façade that faced the main road, the whole building was gutted and brought into the 20th Century. Neither Constable Lannigan or I suffered any serious fallout, because within 18 months he was appointed a Detective Constable, a post he had longed for, and I was promoted to the rank of Chief Inspector.

Within six months of my escapade with the Discipline Code, I was transferred across town to Central Police Station where Mr Castree, my Divisional Chief Superintendent, told me I was to undertake a role in the Prosecutions Department. At that brief meeting with him, he could obviously see the concern and disappointment on my face, because he did his best to paint a rosy picture, pointing out what he saw as all the advantages and saying that most importantly, it would be wonderful experience. Where had I heard that phrase before? Yes, it would be a nine-to-five role with every weekend off, no hassle, no unruly prisoners and no supervisory officers looking over your shoulder suggesting what you should have done – but no, I still didn't want it.

I've pointed out how busy policing in Newport was in the latter years of the 1970s, with more prisoners than one of London's busiest police stations. Well, it followed that its

Magistrate's Courts shared the same level of activity. I had experienced prosecution duties in Ebbw Vale, an average sized sub-division where there was one court sitting each week, which invariably terminated before lunch, together with one juvenile court held once a month. To service the workload in Newport it necessitated three courts sitting each day – very often four – with a juvenile court sitting twice a week. In addition, there were two Crown Court sittings each day and although we obviously had no prosecution staff involved there, each court had a dedicated plain clothes liaison officer. It all helped to create a very busy working environment.

I was one of two inspectors presenting the prosecution cases each day between 10 am and usually 4 pm to 4.30 pm, with a sergeant dealing with the more minor motoring matters. We were assisted, yes, assisted by a solicitor from the Criminal Prosecution Service (CPS) whenever they could spare someone, but because Newport had a dedicated full-time Courts Department, the CPS assumed that we could manage, so they allocated their staff most days to other courts throughout the county. It took me a good three months to settle into that role; it was busy, very busy, although once I'd nailed the basics and procedural details I started to very slightly enjoy it. It gave me some satisfaction pitting myself against the array of private practice solicitors who were invariably representing most cases, the vast majority being paid for by Legal Aid. Having to think on your feet when a surprise course of action was suddenly adopted by a defending solicitor gave you inward satisfaction when you successfully counteracted it, but there were days when you didn't.

I was, however, mentally exhausted by the time I got back to my office chair every afternoon, with only enough time to quickly scan the file of cases that had just been placed on my desk for tomorrow's court. I never got into the habit of staying late to prepare in more depth; I relied on the one hour in the mornings before court to do the best I could, and on those odd adjournments throughout the day when the magistrates had to privately discuss a case or more truthfully, have a cup of tea. However, I got through my stint in prosecutions without too many bruises. I got to know most of the solicitors practising in Newport, some of them quite well, and by the time I left them all to further my travels, I believe most of them had some respect for me in the courtroom.

I had been there well over 12 months when one morning as I carried my file of cases through the corridor towards Court Number One, I passed Inspector John Davies, my prosecuting colleague, who was standing talking to one of that day's solicitors. He had asked John if he was the prosecutor in his court, to which he replied "No, it's Inspector Thorne". As I walked behind the solicitor I clearly heard him say "Oh no, not him". I took that as a compliment. Mr Castree was right with his comments; the role had given me good experience. I had become a much more confident individual, happy to face any issue with a more authoritative air.

During this period, within the Prosecutions Department at Newport, I had seen a lot more of my new neighbour, Mr Green, although my view of him had not changed one iota. He had been transferred to the Clerk's office and was quite often carrying out his duties in the court I was assigned to.

The surreptitious enquiries I made with his staff revealed that they were not too enamoured with him either.

During my six and a half years in the rank of Inspector, I took note of the Chief Constable's comments concerning the 'flat earth society' on three occasions and applied for posts which were being advertised nationally. The only way to become aware of such national vacancies in the 1970s was to regularly read a copy of *Police Review*, a weekly magazine designed for the serving police officer, founded in 1893 (it ceased publication in October 2008). Every force in England and Wales would publish those posts that each Chief Constable wished to advertise, but Home Office guidance set out the annual percentage to which they should adhere. Whether the Chief Constable concerned actually appointed such candidates would be his prerogative. Mr Over brought his fair share into Gwent during his tenancy and he certainly encouraged his officers to spread their wings with a view to joining other forces. I must be honest, the two that I applied for were simply to demonstrate to my Chief that I had ambition, for I had no real personal drive to uproot my family and move to another area, not even for promotion.

The first post was in the Norfolk Constabulary and I attended their interview in Norwich. I was interviewed by just two people, the Chief Constable and his Deputy, who both looked to be on borrowed time in the police service. That perennial question was thrown at me, inviting me to outline the qualities I had to offer their Force. I had not long completed my Inspector's Course at the police college and during one of the many lectures we had on man-management, I clearly remember being advised that as a supervisor I should always remember that everyone is human. We are not automated machines, capable of performing at 100% all day long, and that circulated through my mind as I directed my answer to them as clearly as I could. I rounded my answer off by politely telling them that they could be assured that I would strive for 95% effort at all times. It became immediately clear to me that these two elderly senior officers had never attended a similar man-management lecture and I realised I'd said the wrong thing. They thanked me for attending and their rejection letter almost got back to Gwent before I did.

The second post I applied for was in the Surrey Constabulary, but I have no significant recollection of that interview, which was conducted at their HQ in Guildford. I can only recall that, probably to save on the expense of accommodation, which in those circumstances was usually at a local hotel, they seemed to have opened up a dormitory in their cadet training unit, and I spent the night occupying a lonely single mattress in a 12-bedded room. Really cosy! I was unsuccessful, thankfully. I would have had no impetus whatsoever to move to that force, which during my brief visit seemed like an enclave of the Metropolitan Police. I will mention my third application later.

My very special maternal grandmother, Amelia (Millie) Prosser, who effectively raised me until I was 11 years of age.

Me, aged about seven, outside the newly constructed 'prefab' we had occupied.

My first pair of long trousers as part of my uniform just before entry to Pontllanfraith Technical School.

Shel and me holidaying in Clacton about three months before I joined the Police Service in 1965.

On completion of my initial training at Bridgend in December 1965 – yours truly is second from right, back row. Poor Constable Wall (far left, second row) from the Merthyr Tydfil Constabulary was still awaiting his uniform having completed three months training in civilian clothes – things were tight back then!

Shel and me on our big day, June 1966

Tour of workshops with HRH Princess Anne and the Chairman of the
Police Committee during the official opening of Police HQ, 1972. On the
right is Tom, my foreman.

Shel, the proud mum, with our two boys Michael and Brian,
on holiday in Newquay, Cornwall, 1976

The Holly Tree shrouded in mist on the day we viewed it in April 1991.

The Holly Tree three months later after renovation, with Ben, our retriever, making sure he's in on the act.

Shel and me with the Mayor of Bromyard, who sampled the first pint after officially opening the Holly Tree.

Gill and me relaxing in the South of France on holiday, July 2004

CHAPTER 12

The 1980s were slowly dawning when the Chief Constable, during a one-to-one chat in his office, told me he was bringing me back to HQ. I was to have one more pip on each shoulder as a Chief Inspector back in the Traffic Department. He reminisced somewhat and explained that his early career had been spent patrolling the roads of Dorset and therefore, quite naturally, he would probably exercise that little bit of extra scrutiny over its activities in this, his new force. I knew his forte had been traffic – I had gleaned this during my earlier service – and I was also fully aware of the fact that he insisted on traffic officers wearing their uniform caps whilst in their vehicles and that sunglasses were totally banned. Any early complaints from the Police Federation had been met with the statement "If the officers cannot comply with my directive they can return to walking the beat". The complaints soon dried up. I happened to agree with his sentiments and not just because he was the Chief, although I wouldn't have dared contradict him anyway. But even now, I feel that it's rude, whether a police officer or not, to talk to someone when you're wearing sunglasses obscuring your eyes. Back in the 1980s the cap and helmet were the only articles of uniform that clearly signalled to the public that you were a police officer. The peaked cap had a chequered band, and without that or the traditional helmet, the officer, in public, looked no different from a bus driver or a domestic meter reader. Not that there's anything wrong with those occupations, but they didn't have the wide-ranging powers of a policeman, and a patrolling constable should always be identifiable to the public. It was something I kept lecturing my probationers about back in Ebbw Vale.

The nucleus of the staff in Traffic was the same as when I'd left them some six years earlier. There'd been a few transfers, but by and large I knew them and they knew me. The Chief Inspector role within the Police Service is, however, something of a hybrid, because whilst you are looked upon by your officers from below as the head of operational matters, or where the buck stops so to speak, to supervisors above you are really the first rung of administration with man-management and personal development at the forefront, together with being the lynchpin for cooperation with other agencies. There's nothing could have been as busy as Newport, but my new role in traffic was time-consuming. I would be in my office by 8 am and rarely got home before 7 pm, which left Shel coping with Michael and Brian far more than she should have.

As I look back now and reflect, it was really inconsiderate of me. I was out from home each morning before the boys got up, and would have little time to spend with them after we'd finished our evening meal. Sunday was the only full day I could put aside to actually accomplish domestic chores, as I would catch up on office work most Saturday mornings, or visit some part of the county for a variety of reasons. I did manage, somehow, to keep the garden in hand and continue to produce a little sustenance from the fruit and vegetables.

The hobby I did enjoy, back in the days when I worked continental shifts, had long diminished. I was in the habit of visiting the British Car Auction sales in Cardiff, and sometimes Tewkesbury, where I would buy some saloon or other which appeared to have potential for being a bargain. I bought several over those few years and enjoyed bringing them back to the state that the manufacturers had intended. We would use each as transport for the family for a few months before making a few bob to cover our expenses. Well, that's what I intended to tell the tax man if he ever asked!

I had completed 15 years' service by the time I returned to traffic, fairly rapid advancement in those days, and my rose-tinted view of the police service had somewhat mellowed during that time. The strength of the British police service is that its membership comes from the community it serves, with all the weaknesses of human nature, but although a rigorous selection process should have sorted the wheat from the chaff, it didn't always work, especially with those few individuals who were hell-bent on defeating the system. There are some characters who have the inbred desire to impose 'authority', no matter what it takes or whoever tries to alleviate their efforts, and the police service is the ideal place for this type of individual to thrive. Thank God there are so few who get through. However, they do get through in all forces and Gwent had its share.

As I have mentioned, the Home Office at that time was using every effort to persuade Chief Constables to appoint senior officers from other forces, so that the service as a whole would benefit from the exchange of ideas and working practices. The rank that seemed to attract the most applicants was that of Assistant Chief Constable. One such officer was appointed in Gwent shortly after my return to traffic. I had very little to do with him in his early days due to his exalted position, but his reputation spread through the force like wildfire within weeks. In not too long a time, I was to work directly under him on a daily basis and found him as an over-officious and pompous individual. It seemed to me that his daily objective at work was to criticise everyone's efforts, and during the whole period I worked with him, I was never at ease in his company.

My first brush with this person was at 8.30 am on Thursday 29 October 1981. I remember it well. Prince Charles, Prince of Wales, had married Lady Diana Spencer at St Paul's Cathedral in July of that year and after their honeymoon, they undertook a whistle-stop tour of Wales in order to give the residents of the Principality the opportunity of seeing the newly-married couple. They were to travel by limousine through our county on 28th October and a fair amount of planning took place in the preceding weeks. I attended several meetings with the Lord

Lieutenant of the County, our Chief and the Assistant Chief Constable, who was to be the senior officer in charge of operational matters on the day, supported by other officers whose departments had a role to play. The route had been earmarked, the stopping points and walkabouts noted, with protocol and security being arranged accordingly. My area of interest was the cavalcade and its security, bearing in mind that we were experiencing problems from the Free Wales Army with their constant threats of disruption, and the IRA were still active, giving publicity to their potential for mainland bombing.

Our final briefing session, with only two days to go, determined that the cavalcade would be led by the Chief Constable, who would convey the Lord Lieutenant, followed by the limousine carrying HRH. Their vehicle would be closely followed by members of the Diplomatic Protection Squad from the Met, and the tail vehicle would contain the Assistant Chief Constable, who, it was made quite clear, would be in overall command of the cavalcade during its presence in the county. There would of course, be motorcycle outriders; two in front of the cavalcade, two just behind the limousine and two at the rear, with Special Branch, CID and firearms officers in their own vehicles monitoring progress, but keeping at a discreet distance. My specific role (well, not so specific) was to trail the cavalcade, maintain overall supervision of the remainder of the traffic fleet in the county and be in a position to provide back up if the need arose.

The day's itinerary went fine until approximately 4.30 pm. The cavalcade was travelling west along the M4 in the south of the county. The last scheduled stop had been completed and our royal couple were speeding along towards our border with the South Wales Constabulary, which was only two miles away, with everyone involved probably starting to breathe a sigh of relief that everything had gone according to plan. The cavalcade was approaching junction 28 of the M4 at Tredegar Park, which consists of a very large roundabout controlling traffic entering Newport from all points West. The M4 carriageway at this point involves a long flyover, about 300 yards in length, so you will therefore appreciate that there were no sightseers and no flags waving; in fact, I doubt whether anyone not involved with the escort knew of the auspicious company.

I was told later that the Chief Constable in the lead car was about a quarter of a mile from the junction when Control Room at Police HQ passed a radio message to 'Quebec 3', the call sign of the Assistant Chief Constable, who was in overall command. The radio system was on 'talk through' so I could hear quite clearly that he was being told that a bomb had been placed under the flyover and the message which they had received had been preceded by a code, which indicated its authenticity. There was no reply.

I waited for the response and there was none. Prince Charles and his new wife were hurtling towards this apparent problem at 60 miles per hour; someone had to say something – and quick.

I immediately instructed the two advanced motorcyclists to lead the cavalcade down the exit slip road, around the roundabout and back up onto the M4, thus negating the need to travel across the flyover. This they successfully did, without fuss, and our exalted cargo went safely on its way. A few minutes later, Control Room transmitted a message to all units advising that 'the cargo' had been successfully transferred to our neighbouring police force and instructed everyone to stand down. I made my leisurely way back to HQ and that evening I finished work at a respectable time, as I remember calling at the country club for an early evening pint, where those present were interested in the day's events. I was back at home with Shel for an early meal well before six o'clock.

I reported for duty as usual the following morning and whilst reading the night report with that first cup of coffee, my internal desk telephone rang and the small light indicated that it was the Assistant Chief Constable. I'd hardly had time to raise the handset to my ear before he started to rant and rave in a manner which could only have come from him. The obscene language being blasted in my ear was to some extent, quite comical. He had really lost it. There were bits of his dialogue I just could not decipher, but his last sentence before I replaced the receiver without acknowledging him was "Don't you ever f***ing usurp my authority again!" I'd heard before, from several colleagues, that he was prone to this behaviour; now I was part of that small group with first-hand experience. I thought my act of slamming the receiver back on its cradle would have induced a summons to his office, but I heard nothing. As I've mentioned, I was to work much more closely with him in future years and he never mentioned the subject again. I was perfectly happy in my own mind with my actions. I had no idea at the time that the call received at Operations Room would turn out to be a hoax; nor did he, but somebody had to make that split-second decision. He had proved to me that he was fallible, which I remembered for the rest of my service.

That summons never did come from the Assistant Chief Constable, but it was not long after the royal visit that I received a message from the Chief Constable's secretary directing me to see the Chief the following day. She couldn't or wouldn't help me with the reason and that left me pondering all evening. It was unusual to be summoned to the 'inner sanctum', as such visits were only for promotion or unusual transfers. I knew it wasn't the former and if the latter, I was pretty certain my Divisional Commander would have warned me.

However, I duly arrived and was invited to sit down, which threw me even further. We had quite a sociable chat for several minutes, about the Force in general, what he had in mind for Maindee after my ordeal, and how he was pleased that the royal visit had been a success, without any reference to the unofficial detour. He eventually came to the crux of my visit and explained that on arrival in Gwent he had purchased a house in Llantarnam. I knew that; it was quite a nice looking detached property set near the Three Blackbirds public house in Ty Coch Lane. I thought for one second that he was experiencing problems with what I knew to be quite a pleasant hostelry. If this was the issue, then I was the wrong man to be speaking to, as this was a sub-divisional problem for Cwmbran. He obviously knew that.

No, it wasn't the public house, it was Ty Coch Lane itself. He explained that it was in a terrible state, especially the section near his home. He added that the surface had deteriorated so badly that there were more potholes than tarmacadam, and surface water could not drain away. He ended the conversation by suggesting that the lane was a road safety issue and he wanted me to do something about it!

Road safety my backside. I knew Ty Coch Lane well; some 200 years ago it would have been the main highway leading down the valley to Newport, on which the Chartist marchers may have trod, but over time, with all the road improvements to cater for traffic increase, it was, and still is, what its name suggests, a lane, and an access lane at that. It is no more than 12 feet wide and led to the Chief's house and a few other properties before terminating after several hundred yards in a dead-end.

There was no way I was going to disagree with my Chief Constable at that point, so I said "Right sir" and made a swift and grateful retreat. I visited the site during the next few days, which totally confirmed my suspicion. With budget constraints and priorities to consider, there was no way the local authority could justify any remedial work from a road safety point of view. I thought about the issue for a few more days and considered the best way to approach my problem, and it was a bit of a problem. I discounted the political approach because there was absolutely no one in the force with more political clout than the Chief, so it was clear he didn't want anyone of that persuasion involved.

I finally decided to seek a meeting with the engineer in charge of the Highways Department, which was arranged to take place in his Town Hall office, where I tackled the issue. Our paths had never crossed before, but in the first 30 seconds I trusted my judgement that he was a straightforward, genuine chap. Like me, he had lived locally for quite a few years and we seemed to hit it off. I wasn't going to look ignorant and push the road safety angle as I knew he wouldn't wear it, so I explained that the Chief was relatively new to the Force; he was going to act like the 'new broom' and in relation to the Traffic Department, he wanted to give traffic management far more prominence. I added that he had asked me to develop our one-man band section into something more in keeping with modern developments and I was to concentrate on closer liaison with local authorities. I could see at this point that he was on my wavelength.

Then, as an aside, I mentioned Ty Coch Lane, explaining that the Chief was inviting relatively high-ranking acquaintances and official guests to the Force, many of whom would visit his home to meet his wife, and several close friends that he had made during his travels throughout the UK would actually stay the night there. I added that one or two had already made a few comments about the state of the lane, and pointed out that it could well be a reflection on his department. I simply asked if he could do his best to improve the area. He posed a few more questions about our proposed traffic management changes and suggested a few areas in which we could make our way forward, before asking me to 'leave it with him'.

Within six weeks, the whole length of Ty Coch Lane had been resurfaced by machine with what appeared to be the finest tarmacadam available. The Chief Constable never mentioned Ty Coch Lane to me again throughout the remainder of my service, but approximately four months after the lane was resurfaced, his house was put on the market and I recall that it sold rather quickly. For Mr Average, who might have been relocating for work or domestic reasons, to have the 'kerb appeal' of his property enhanced in such a manner would have been entirely fortuitous, but this was a Chief Constable, and he had manufactured the situation. Now that was quite naughty, and I had unwittingly been a party to it.

John Over and his wife moved to a rented cottage set in the sprawling Llanover Estate just outside Abergavenny, which was owned by Robin Herbert, who at that time was a wealthy individual and President of the Royal Horticultural Society. The Chief had, in the eyes of many of his senior officers, become one of the 'county set'.

Meanwhile, back at my humble abode in Cwmbran, things were running pretty smoothly. Shel was still enjoying her role at the country club, carrying out far more work on the catering side of things and less on general cleaning. She was assisting the proprietor's wife, Judy, in food preparation for functions. I'll mention my neighbour Mr Green again at this point, because although I'd had no contact with him outside work since my move from Newport, I had to acknowledge him whenever we saw each other around and about, to be polite if nothing else. Then, one Sunday afternoon, I was sitting digesting the weekend newspaper when he came a-calling at the front door. Now I was aware that he had acquired a second-hand MGB sports car for his son, who was not quite old enough to have a driving licence, but what else would you get for a rather spoilt young lad, I ask? Mr Green explained that his son was slowly reconditioning the vehicle and was experiencing some problems with the front suspension. He, or in fact both of them, would be grateful if I would pop across and offer some advice. The young lad explained that he was attempting to renew the front offside suspension, and from the state of the vehicle and the parts scattered far and wide, he had taken on something way beyond his capabilities. This particular job is not for those with very limited knowledge, and in my view, should not be undertaken in a domestic garage with few facilities. Well, by utilising my array of tools I somehow completed the task, but I was away far longer than Shel was expecting. That was another of my precious Sundays ruined.

On another occasion, I was accosted by Mr Green as I drove from the house one day. He flagged me down and gave me a detailed account of how he'd bought a Golden Retriever puppy for the family, and because he was having trouble instilling it with a little obedience, he was under threat from his rather houseproud wife that in the not too distant future it would be a case of the dog or her. He asked if I could arrange for a dog-handler to call and give him some advice, or even take the dog for a few sessions of behavioural training. I quietly thought to myself "What is this man like?"

Shel and I had decided to get a dog when the boys became teenagers and we'd bought a pedigree Golden Retriever, after vetting many adverts from right across South East Wales. We finally bought 'the one' from the seaside town of Porthcawl at a cost of £100 – I still cannot believe that I paid that amount; it certainly was the heart ruling the head. However, we named him Ben and as I picture him now, he brings back 16 years of lovable memories. We trained him to an acceptable standard, which he displayed when he thought fit. In his early months he would enjoy lying quietly on the front drive watching the world go by and waiting for a bit of mischief to grab his attention, which is probably where Green saw him and made the decision to follow suit.

In answer to Mr Green's request, I told him clearly that

it would be out of the question to involve a force dog-handler to give obedience training to his pet, but that I would ask Sergeant Phillips, the supervising officer of the Dog Section to call at his office the next time he was at Newport Court and perhaps he could offer some general advice. This seemed to satisfy his request, but whatever the Sergeant eventually said proved to be fruitless as before six months had elapsed, Mr Green's wife won the contest and the young retriever disappeared from our community. My only hope is that it went to a good home, because Shel and I had said from the start that Mrs Green just would not tolerate those muddy paws and hairs everywhere.

During the 1970s and early 1980s, the Irish Republican Army had been active, both in the Province and throughout the British mainland, with notable atrocities such as the Balcombe Street siege in 1975, the killing of Airey Neave in the Palace of Westminster in 1980 and the bombing of Chelsea Barracks in 1981. However it was the Iranian Embassy siege of 1980, when a group of six armed men of Middle Eastern extraction held 26 people hostage, before the British Police, probably under governmental pressure, took the issue of hostage-taking seriously. The Met had done so for several years, but the leaders of provincial forces began to realise that such outrageous behaviour had no boundaries. It was decided that forces throughout England and Wales should train up a number of hostage negotiators. In the leafy backwaters and industrial scarred valleys of Gwent, it was decided to have two, both of chief inspector rank, Detective Chief Inspector Martin and yours truly. We had no choice in the matter, at least I didn't. When my

Divisional Commander told me I was being nominated for training I honestly didn't know what the role entailed. It was a sign to me that the decision to train such personnel had been a political one and made fairly high up, if not at the top, and that it was to be high priority because our training commenced only days after being nominated.

The first few sessions were classroom based with visiting military staff from the Welsh Army HQ in Brecon, when we discussed strategies, the need and use of firearms and the liaison and specific areas of responsibility between the armed forces and civilian police. This was followed up by practical exercises involving force firearms officers, where the scenario was set around some disused farm buildings on a windswept mountainside, with the full knowledge and permission of the farmer, I will add. An interesting two days were spent at the SAS HQ, just outside Hereford, where they gave us a lot of information regarding their involvement, but only the bits that had been authorised, no doubt. We were fortunate in Gwent at the time because we had a large coal-fired power station on the outskirts of Newport which had just been decommissioned, with demolition planned so that residential housing could be erected. Our force, in conjunction with the military, and other agencies, who could well be involved in such an incident, organised a day-long exercise when the SAS attended to act their part in the scenario. My colleague, Mr Martin, and I worked as a team throughout the whole 15 hours to absorb as much knowledge as possible, but our negotiating efforts were deliberately planned to fail because the SAS wanted to take advantage of this opportunity to carry out a final assault on this empty building for their own training purposes. The final action took place in total darkness at around 10.15 pm, and the local police station and HQ were inundated with telephone calls for an hour or so afterwards from concerned local residents. That was it; we were both fully trained negotiators and wondering with concern when we'd be called upon for real.

Everyone makes acquaintances as they pass along life's highway; some you wish you hadn't, some you tolerate and some you are only too pleased to retain, and I am no exception. I never did socialise a great deal, but Shel and I would attend official functions, which included those we wanted to and those I was expected to, and we would visit the country club on the odd Friday or Saturday night. That was really because we were friendly with the proprietor, which stemmed from Shel's work, although I would pop in on the odd occasion for a swift glass and take part in some social intercourse with regulars. The Cwmbran Rotary Club used the premises as their HQ and held their weekly lunch there every Wednesday, and the proprietor, Mr Booth, had invited me as a guest once or twice. He had in fact told me that he would have invited me to become part of the branch, but they had a Chief Inspector Williams as a member and the Club's rules allowed only one person from each profession.

I knew Chief Inspector Williams very well. He was 'little John' who had lived down the avenue near our first police home, as opposed to 'big John' who had lived up the avenue. Remember? However, I was not perturbed one little bit about not being allowed to join. Then, one Wednesday, at the bar after one of my free lunches, I was introduced to Mr Don Robinson, a Lancastrian who had moved to Cwmbran to take up the post of manager at the crematorium when it was built in the 1970s. His official title was 'Superintendent', which he used as often as possible. I was introduced as a member of the force Traffic Department and that was that, until three days later at work I was asked to take a call from the crematorium superintendent. Mr Robinson told me that he had been stopped the previous day by one of my patrols, and he was afraid that the officer might decide to submit a report. After giving all the usual circumstantial excuses and bringing the Rotary Club into the conversation, he asked if I would look upon the matter favourably. I told Mr Robinson that I was not in the habit of interfering with the due process of the law and I wasn't going to start. I did however later check the records, and found that my officer had reported him. He was summonsed for speeding, and I made my mind up there and then that membership of the Rotary Club was not for me.

Another acquaintance I made at the country club was one John Baillie, Lieutenant Commander RNR OBE. He was a broad Scotsman who, along with his wife, like our Lancastrian, had moved south to take up employment in public service and was employed within the county as a senior probation officer. John's wife met Shel once or twice and they became quite friendly, which culminated in the four of us attending the odd function together. I would invite my naval reserve friend to a mess dinner occasionally and he would respond by taking me to his annual naval function held at their South Wales HQ on the coast at Sully, which is just outside Barry Island, of Gavin and Stacey fame. With his full-time role in the probation service and his part-time role in the Royal Naval Reserve, John did his best for the youngsters under his care by organising extra-curricular activities for them, which, along with the time he devoted to the Sea Cadets, was why he was awarded his OBE in later life.

John had been active in the Royal Naval Reserve for most of his adult life, hence his rank. He had many strings to his bow and he knew when to pull them. He would arrange to take a minibus of young lads who were serving some type of Community Order down to HMS Raleigh in Cornwall, the national training centre for all new recruits taken on by the Royal Navy. One can imagine that the facilities there were first class. The boys would be billeted in their own dormitory and take part in daily activities, with a view to broadening their horizons and showing them that there are alternative ways through life. The activities would have the full support of the naval staff and ranged from daily participation over the assault course, swimming instruction in the indoor pool and day-long treks over Dartmoor to experience map reading. The really enjoyable one for them would be the trip to Devonport dockyard in one of the Navy's inflatable assault craft to view the section of the fleet in port at the time. These lads would obviously require supervision and on his first venture, John was able to take a few of his probation officers, although he did tell me that his Chief Officer was somewhat concerned about the amount of probation service resources being used.

That's where I came into the equation because on his second trip, John suggested that I should go along to share the experience. This obviously appealed to me; five days away in Cornwall would suit me down to the ground. When we discussed the arrangements in a little more depth, I suggested that I should invite a group of police probationers, which I knew would be no problem as long as I could secure the Chief Constable's approval. The young men I would take could easily cope with the duties of supervision; it would give them an experience not available elsewhere and it would help to break down any barriers these youngsters might have towards the police service in general. My official request only had to get as far as the Deputy Chief Constable, who thought it was a wonderful idea. He endorsed my report with his 'APPROVED' stamp and added that although no overtime, subsistence or expenses would be paid, I and three probationer constables could attend in duty time. I had no trouble selecting three volunteers, and because the wayward youngsters were all being dealt with by the probation office covering the Ebbw Vale valley, I chose my three officers from that area. There were six young lads, so we all travelled down in a 12-seater minibus and had a thoroughly enjoyable and, I believe, beneficial week.

It was so successful that John's group badgered him and my officers badgered me to repeat the exercise, so we agreed to give it serious thought for the following year. However, only 10 months elapsed before we went again because we had to slot in with the available room at the naval base and I took different participants to share the experience around. The last time I saw one of the young officers I took on the first trip was about six months ago, and he was a Detective Superintendent. It hadn't done him any harm.

During our time at HMS Raleigh, John and I stayed in the Ward Room (naval term for officers' accommodation), and on the first evening of our second visit, the base Commander joined us at the bar for a drink. His opening remarks to John were "I hope you and Mr Thorne enjoy your stay, but I must ask you to be on your best behaviour". His remark was light-hearted because he continued by informing us that Prince Andrew would be arriving the following morning for a three-day visit. The Prince was, at that time, on a short service commission as a seaman officer, sub-specialising as a pilot, and although the Commander would reveal no more, I would have thought that his stay was in some way related to his training.

I saw nothing of the Prince until about 7.45 on the Wednesday morning when I visited the 'heads' (naval term for the gents' toilet) shortly after arising from my slumber. I was standing at the urinal contemplating whatever one contemplates in those circumstances, when the door opened and in walked the Prince, encased in a dark burgundy dressing-gown. He stood about three paces to my left, and without actually turning his head, quietly said "Morning". I replied in a similar vein "Morning sir". The room was silent for a few seconds until I turned to leave, and as I started to pull the door open, a voice said, "Excuse me, my good man, at Gordonstoun they taught us to wash our hands after visiting the toilet".

I turned towards the Prince and said, quite respectfully, "Well sir, at the school I went to they taught us not to pee on our hands…" No I didn't! That was a joke that's been in my repertoire for years. But it's true that Prince Andrew came in. We acknowledged each other and I quietly left. I had great pleasure in advising the whole group of my casual encounter, but unfortunately, they didn't get to see the Prince at any stage.

CHAPTER 13

It was early summer 1982; Shel had kept an appointment to monitor her progress following the operation. She felt well and after various tests and X-rays, we were told that things looked 'pretty good' and they would reappraise the situation in another five years, if the intervening period proved trouble free. We both breathed a sigh of relief and enjoyed a holiday with the boys at a country cottage in Cornwall, not far from Newquay. We all returned refreshed, Shel and I to face work and the boys a new term at school.

Shel, however, was to face some upheaval in the coming weeks. First the proprietors of the country club announced that they had booked a cruise to celebrate a wedding anniversary. They would be leaving the children at home and the proprietor's mother, Mrs Booth Snr, would be coming to look after them during their parents' absence. This caused no problem for Shel. She knew Mrs Booth well and they got on like the proverbial house on fire. The proprietor's sister, who worked at the premises, would supervise the business activities.

Everything seemed fine, but on the first Monday of this holiday, Shel received a telephone call from the administrator of the No 8 District Police Training Centre, which had been built in Cwmbran in the early 1970s. They had advertised a secretarial position which Shel had noticed in the local paper before we went on holiday; she had submitted an application form together with her CV. The telephone call was to ask if she could attend an interview the following day. She agreed and explained the situation to Mrs Booth Senior.

Yes, you guessed it, things were now really awkward. Shel was offered the job and to make matters worse, they wanted the successful applicant to start on the following Monday; that would be the day after Mr and Mrs Booth returned from their cruise. Shel agonised all that evening and well into the small hours. What would the Booths think? How could she let them down like this when they'd been so good? The police training college was the only purpose built one in the country and the role was to be personal secretary to the Commandant. The pay would be according to the current Civil Service scale and was pensionable. It was a 'no brainer' to me and I told Shel so clearly. That didn't stop her worrying.

The following morning at work, Shel had a long and detailed discussion with Mrs Booth Snr, who fully and unequivocally accepted the situation and told Shel that she would be silly to turn it down. But the proprietors returned from their cruise the day before Shel was to start her new job and refused to see her when she rang to ask if she could pop in to explain. Neither of them ever spoke to us again from that moment on.

I'd been head of operational traffic for just over two years and was expecting a move at any time. I hadn't picked up any substantial vibes or gossip, but the Police Service, like many other fluid occupations, always seems to uproot and move you at the most unexpected time, when work is enjoyable, and so it was. I wasn't ready to move on, but the internal mail arrived one morning with that memo headed 'personal' which seemed to contain everyone's 'noted' signature bar the evening cleaners, directing that I was to attend the Junior Command Course at the police college. This session of training was designed for officers of Chief Inspector rank who showed promise for advancement.

It was eight years since I'd spent those three months at the college previously and although, on balance, I had enjoyed my time on that first occasion, this course was to last six months, keeping me away from home from Sunday afternoon through to Friday evening from now until Christmas. I did not relish the thought one little bit and nor did Shel. Reflecting on it in the years after, it became quite clear that from everyone's perspective, it was too long. There was the basic issue of my time and effort being lost to the Force and to the community, not to mention the vast training costs, but more importantly, it was detrimental to the boys, Shel and me. I would have no real input into my family life for far too long. Yes, we were allowed home most weekends, but I had found from my previous course that you can't head a family sitting at a desk in Hampshire. There are decisions to be made every day bringing up a family, only minor perhaps, but still decisions, and everything was to fall on Shel. A new job, running the home, and looking after two young lads who were developing through their early teens, all on her own, was not going to be an easy task. Even when I arrived home at weekends, Shel would be cooking the meals I'd been looking forward to all week, and I would arrive with a pile of clothes to be washed, dried and ironed before Sunday. It seemed perfectly clear that I had the easy bit, but we marched on relentlessly.

My first course in Hampshire had been something of a novelty really, an academic existence that I had never experienced. This second course, which extended over half a year, was more involved, but I did have the benefit of now being an 'old hand', knowing all the procedures and shortcuts backwards, and feeling a little bit superior when students on their first visit sought out some unofficial advice. The theoretical work was far more intense, with much harsher criticism from the tutors, and we were thrust into practical problem-solving scenarios far more often. We would be taken in small groups to locations throughout southern England to investigate and analyse real life issues before compiling our written findings back at the college prior to them being sent off to the individual organisations concerned for scrutiny. There were only 13 of us in syndicate K, who lived and worked together for the whole six months, so as you'd imagine I got to know them pretty well, in varying degrees. Before the course ended, we decided to hold a reunion each year to be organised in turn, in each member's own county, and that continued uninterrupted through until 2015, when, because numbers were dwindling, it was decided to call it a day. Christmas wishes will, no doubt, continue to be passed between the stragglers.

That prolonged absence on my second course really gave me time during those small hours to think of my family; where we'd been, where we were and more importantly, where we were going. I was concerned that there was going to be a big chunk missing from the bond between me and my young lads. I often thought whilst writing in that tiny little room that was my home for six months that they were of the age when I should have been at home with them. The fact that I saw little of them at weekends because their mates were, apparently, far more important, didn't help one little bit. There were a few things however, that those six months did. It reminded me how to write a love letter, it made me an expert at soppy telephone calls and it made me realise how much I loved my wife.

Whoever drew up the curriculum for the Junior Command Course must have had a little compassion for its participants, because they slotted in a week's leave halfway through, with two long weekends, one after 12 weeks and the other towards the end, and it was on this short mid-term break that I was asked to go into HQ to see the Chief Constable. He told me that on my return from Hampshire, I was to transfer to the Complaints Department, and because that role necessitated, on occasions, carrying out investigations into complaints against senior officers, he was going to promote me to the rank of Temporary Superintendent. I was obviously elated. The first thing that triggered in my mind was the pay rise – it would be considerable.

In 1977, Lord Edmund Davies was appointed to chair a

commission into the levels of pay and conditions of police officers, because of the severe problems being experienced with recruitment and retention, and his recommendations were implemented in full by the incoming Conservative government in 1979. Police pay increased substantially and I shared in that little bonanza. A significant issue was that officers up to the rank of chief inspector were incurring considerable amounts of overtime because of their operational duties, whereas those of superintendent and above, who had to make more far-reaching decisions, worked long hours and were not paid overtime. He therefore gave superintendents a pay rate to reflect this anomaly, which I would be entitled to in my new role. We were talking about an extra £6,000 per year, and that was a great deal back then.

Having thanked the Chief, I made my way back to the car park pondering the one thing that could very well be a problem; I would be working directly under the supervision of that man who had the view that I'd usurped his authority. Since our altercation over the Royal visit he had been promoted to Deputy Chief Constable, the person who in most forces takes direct control over administration, personnel and discipline, which encompassed complaints. Oh dear!

I started my new role in late December, after Shel had again visited the college for the final night Mess dinner and dance. This time, she made some acquaintances with other wives, which would turn into friendships that lasted several years. Complaints Department staff operated in civilian clothes and I, as one of the investigators, was paid an essential mileage allowance for the use of my private car, but at the outset I just didn't realise how much travelling was involved. I had to visit several locations both within and outside the county most days.

My move into the Department was not to replace anyone, for I was an additional member of staff, the post introduced because of the general disquiet about the manner in which complaints from members of the public were apparently being handled. Until the creation of the Police Complaints Board (PCB) in June 1977, complaints against police officers were all handled directly by the forces concerned, although the Home Secretary could refer a serious matter to another force for investigation. This newly-created Board now had the power to scrutinise a report produced by any force, to satisfy itself that justice had been done, or they could actually instruct Chief Constables to take disciplinary proceedings against his officer(s). This was the system in operation upon my appointment. However, the Brixton riots of 1981 and the Scarman Report which they initiated brought widespread criticism of the Metropolitan Police, which included allegations of racism, and the pressure that was brought upon the Home Secretary by left-wing liberal groups and quangos resulted in the Police and Criminal Evidence Act 1984 abolishing the Board, which was replaced by the Police Complaints Authority in 1985. This authority not only scrutinised a far greater number of investigations but could actually supervise many of them. Chief Constables, if they could not see what was being written between the lines themselves, were surely advised of what was to come by the Home Office and in many areas, the complaints departments of forces were 'beefed up'. Hence my move from Traffic.

My opposite number in the Department was Superintendent Derek Helps, who I had known for several years but had never worked with. He was a wily old fox, and I mean that in the nicest way. He was an experienced officer with about 27 years' service, and we hit it off from the start. I'd always considered myself a worker; I don't believe anyone is entitled to a free ride in this world, and Derek was of the same opinion. I learned more about the job in six months working with him than I'd managed in the previous five years. Although theoretically we were of equal standing in the Department, because of the respect I had for him, I considered and actually demonstrated to others that Derek was the boss. It was a sign of his character that he never took it on board. We each had an inspector working with us who would take notes of interviews, carry out routine enquiries and generally keep our files and paperwork in order. In jest, we referred to them as our 'gofers', because they would go for this and go for that. In practice, we worked as one team and had a lot of laughs. You really had to, because when all the minor faults, mistakes, stupidity and other serious issues that came to light in an organisation of over 1,000 people, who were very often working under stress, were channelled into one office to be dealt with, there had to be some joviality.

One topic discussed by Derek and me within minutes of starting on my first morning was our boss, the Deputy Chief Constable. Derek had been working under his supervision for several months, and he had the same view of the man as I did. In fact, when travelling around the Force, you rarely heard a good word said about him and everyone tried to avoid him, apart from the handful of officers he purposely nurtured in each division to provide him with the secretive information he needed. I won't labour the point any further, but he was like a large, heavily-laden storm cloud slowly circulating over the Force, making far too many people anxious, nervous and in many cases, downright miserable. I often thought, what a way to run an organisation.

Derek got me through the first few months of what was to me, a totally new aspect of my role as a police officer. My confidence grew as my knowledge increased and I was soon able to sit at my desk and discuss, across the room with Derek, particular issues appertaining to the individual complaints we were dealing with and giving my suggestions on the way forward, rather than just taking advice.

I'd been ensconced within my new department for five or six months when I had to respond to an apparent call for help. The superintendent who was Deputy Commander of the Traffic Department had suddenly become unable to fulfil his role, and to be honest, I cannot recall why. It must have been sickness or domestic issues, but I do remember that it was 8 am on a Monday (we were always in for 8 am) and Dave, my gofer, was making the first brew when a telephone call came from the Deputy Chief Constable's office upstairs. The only message he ever gave to Derek or me was "come up", so I went up. Without a word of explanation, he told me to clear my desk and move to the Traffic Superintendent's office. I was to carry out that role until he told me otherwise.

I had no real problem with that, it was like home from home, although I was somewhat annoyed, as it seemed I was just being used, and poor Derek was left on his own again because no one took over my vacant position. I remained there exactly one month with no real excitement being generated, but I recall that there were some problems in the workshops. The officer who had replaced me had now retired and they had appointed a civilian Fleet Manager who didn't gel with the mechanics or the police officers who visited. He couldn't get his head around the fact that the fleet had been purchased for a 24-hour response. He was no longer working in a prestige dealership where the customers sauntered in and out, and I found it necessary to have him visit my office more than once for advice. My move back to the complaints office was announced by my colleague Derek, who visited me one afternoon and over a cup of coffee explained that he'd been asked to advise me that my temporary stint back in traffic was at an end

The following week I was alone in the office, quietly writing at my desk, when the Chief Constable appeared at the door and literally without entering the room, informed me that as and from the following Monday, he was going to make my promotion substantive. I had no one to share my news with, so I telephoned Shel at work, and she was able to pass on good wishes and congratulations from the police college Commandant, who happened to be in her office at the time.

The most unusual experience I had whilst serving in the Complaints Department affected not just me but thousands, perhaps millions, of other people throughout the United Kingdom, and will go down as a watershed in British industrial relations history. It was the miners' strike of 1984, which started on 6th March with a walkout at Cortonwood Colliery in Yorkshire and at its height, involved 142,000 mine workers with over 26 million days of work being lost to the nation.

It was led by Arthur Scargill, the ultra-left-wing trade union official, who, whilst publicly announcing his aim for better working conditions for his members and a stop to pit closures, no doubt had the real goal of bringing down our democratic government. His problem was that to achieve it, he also had to bring down a Prime Minister, in the form of Margaret Thatcher. Written into the Discipline Code when I swore an oath to become a police officer was a stipulation that I would take no active part in politics, so I will adhere to that principle here for fear of annoying anyone who has chosen to read this tale. I will restrict my comments to the facts and my personal experiences.

More than half of the county of Gwent was dedicated to coal mining, so we had our fair share of picket lines and unfortunately, violence. Our area suffered the only death of the conflict, when a taxi driver was killed by a concrete block that had been dropped by striking miners from a bridge over the A465 trunk road, just outside the town of Rhymney, as he was driving a non-striking miner to work. I have no direct evidence of this, but several miners indicated to us in the course of our investigations that they had been told to make an official complaint if any police officer in any way manhandled them, or if they were reported for any offence whatsoever. I am certainly not trying to portray the views of all miners we came into contact with during our investigations, but I can say quite honestly that there was a sizeable percentage who didn't agree with the course of action being directed by their leaders, because there had been no national ballot. They were following the direction of their local and regional officials for fear of reprisals against themselves or their families.

The strike finally ended on 3rd March 1985, and I think everyone on both sides gave a big sigh of relief. During that year our office recorded and dealt with about 130 complaints from striking miners or others associated with the dispute, and not one led to the involvement of the Board. The complaints were either subsequently withdrawn or the complainant was completely satisfied with the action taken by the Deputy Chief Constable, which in 99% of all cases would have been that which was suggested by Derek or me.

You may well imagine, after noting my views on the Deputy Chief Constable's personality, that he may well have had a problem having any kind of social life. As far as I and my contemporaries were aware, his social hours were taken up with his family and his membership of the local golf club. Now, I was aware that he had the most charming and personable wife and a number of children, and I fully accept that he was probably the epitome of a good husband and father, but I was a member of the same golf club for over a year and his reputation there was on a par (forgive the pun) with that at work. However, working so closely with him I did see him unwind to some degree. He was most partial to a few pints of local ale and the odd cigar, and he would time his departure from his office to approximately 5.45 each evening, to coincide with the opening time of the nearby Upper Cock. As he left the building he would visit our office (which was adjacent to the front door) on the pretext of some official query before asking if anyone would like a 'swift half'. Derek was a staunch refuser, partly because he could not stand the man and partly because he did not live locally and had a fairly long drive home. I didn't like the man either, but Derek was nearing retirement whereas I knew I might have to suffer his supervision for far longer, and I didn't want to aggravate the situation. Anyway, I was interested in what made this man tick. I would add that this invitation wasn't extended to me until I'd served well over nine months in his department, and I would estimate that because of work commitments in other parts of the County, my inspector and I would accompany him once a week at the most.

These brief expeditions to the Upper Cock revealed our man in a different light. The three of us didn't drink in a round for which I was thankful, because in the 30 or 40 minutes he was there, he would see away at least three pints and the same number of cigars. He would engage us in conversation for a few minutes about our day's workload, elicit any problems we had and discuss the department in general before moving on to genial day-to-day topics, as well as enquiring about our families. He was, in that short period, engaging company. He would however, always leave rather abruptly; we'd see his Vauxhall Cavalier pull out of the car park and that would be it until eight o'clock the following morning, when he would arrive back in his usual frame of mind. He really was a Jekyll and Hyde character. One thing, however, appeared certain to me: that as sure as night follows day, with the volatile temper that he had, I was going to fall out with him again, sooner or later.

It started late one afternoon, about 4.30 pm, when the 'come up' order came over the telephone. The Deputy Chief told me he had information that one of the scenes of crime officers at Pontypool had just left work and was suspected of having unauthorised bulbs and batteries on his person.

He used the term 'stolen' and I knew there and then that the information would have been passed to him by one of his 'narks'. Most senior officers knew he had several individuals in each Division keeping him in touch with the grass roots but I, along with a few others, knew who they were. I was told to get to the officer's house and sort it out, because he didn't want any thieves in his force. I will refer to this officer as Police Constable X in view of the seriousness of this particular accusation, and on the way to his home I thought how stupid and overbearing this course of action was. There were scenes of crime officers in each division. They worked in civilian clothes and came under the general supervision of the CID. Their role, as the name suggests, was to visit the scene of a crime at the earliest opportunity and attempt to elicit evidence. Their role demanded that they had use of a torch (they were issued with a large hand-lamp actually) and they often fitted all types of intruder and detection equipment, so they would regularly have cause to handle and use bulbs and batteries. But with a man like our Deputy Chief, it was a case of 'mine is not to reason why, mine is but to do'. I would however, be doing it my way.

I arrived at the home of Constable X to find that he and his family were in the final stages of packing their possessions; the removal van was due the following morning to transport them to a new abode. I was invited in and immediately saw a police issue hand-lamp on top of a cardboard box. On questioning the officer, he explained that he had borrowed it from work to help him carry out a final check of the attic that evening. He admitted that the hand-lamp wasn't the one issued to him because that was still in the police vehicle parked outside. The officer was apparently on call until 10 pm that night, which I knew was routine. He denied having any bulbs or other police property in his possession and after searching the police vehicle, I believed him. I wished him and his family a hassle-free move the following day and decided to make a tactful retreat. I had no intention of making an even bigger fool of myself.

Because of the seriousness of the accusation, I spoke with the Deputy at his home by telephone and advised him of the situation. He portrayed his usual disgruntled attitude at the news that I had not recovered any significant damning evidence, and I told him I would visit Pontypool police station the following day to establish what the procedure there was for the issue of ancillary items of equipment. Well, it transpired there was no procedure. All such items, which amounted to various sizes of bulbs and batteries, were kept in an unlocked stationery cabinet to which everyone had access 24 hours a day. There was no check on the issue or use of any of the scenes of crime equipment. Further enquiries revealed that out of the 12 sub-divisional police stations in the force, only two had any type of system to control such issue. Nothing elaborate or time consuming was needed because that would have been counter-productive, but at least the two stations had an administrative assistant to keep the items secure and issue them on request.

The *laissez-faire* system in operation throughout the force prompted me to ascertain what actually occurred at HQ where stock for the force was located. I spoke to the storeman, a Mr Coles (a retired officer, Jack had long finished), who incidentally had been the local bobby in my gran's village for many years and who I knew well. He explained that no form of authorised requisition was required for such items, as was the case for uniform, cleaning materials etc. Anyone from scenes of crime would be issued with whatever they asked for and a single signature would suffice. I believe Mr Coles was quite thankful that my enquiries went no further into his domain.

It only took me a couple of days to put my report together, but whilst I was doing so Derek made mention that there was some history going back a few years, between the Deputy Chief and Constable X, the initial subject of my enquiries. He had no details apart from the fact that our supervisor did not like the officer. He further warned me that I would be treading on thin ice if I intended criticising the requisitioning system, because it was the Deputy Chief himself who was ultimately responsible for administration. I realised that, but I had to list my findings and my report was submitted accordingly, outlining that Constable X had done nothing untoward. I said a force-wide system should be introduced to account for such items of equipment and listed some recommendations.

Nothing stayed in the Deputy's in-tray long, and the following afternoon I was summoned. It was always something of a lottery as to how long he'd keep you waiting after your first knock on his office door, and very often, you were forced to carry out the procedure two or three times before you heard him literally shout "Come!" As I opened the door, I simultaneously heard the whoosh of something being propelled through the air with a fair amount of velocity and saw the familiar dark blue of our standard report cover hurtling towards me from his desk. He had a large office, given his position in the hierarchy, so I had that extra split second to react. I edged backwards an inch or two and my report flashed past my head and landed on the floor at the other side of the room. He roared at the top of his voice "You can take that f***ing rubbish away!" I did exactly as he said and after closing the door behind me I allowed my heart to regain its normal composure as I walked back to my office.

Over a medicinal cup of coffee Derek informed me that although that particular antic wasn't part of his usual repertoire, it was not totally unusual, because he was aware that it had happened to a few divisional colleagues and he himself had experienced it once. I didn't fret too much about it. It was the what followed that upset me.

The following day, the Deputy Chief Constable summoned to his office his protégé, a Detective Superintendent Jones from Newport Division. I have no direct knowledge of the content of their conversation, but I do know that the Detective Superintendent started an enquiry into the past duties and activities of Constable X which went back several years. In fact, he commandeered the officer's completed pocket books, which had been deposited in the archives at HQ for safe keeping; this could only have been an attempt to unearth some inappropriate activity. His fruitless enquiries continued for weeks on end and it was rumoured that Constable X, and probably his family, had taken all they could endure by the time they finished. The saga ended with the officer handing in his resignation. Our Deputy, the high-ranking leader of men, had won. I never liked the man, and now I detested him. I no longer shared his company out of duty hours and the cooperation I gave him was only that dictated by the Discipline Code.

Derek Helps, who I'd had the pleasure of working with for almost three years, was a tough old nut so to speak, but the constant erratic and unacceptable behaviour of our supervisor was even getting to him. One afternoon, he returned to his desk and described how he'd just had the biggest altercation he'd ever experienced with our leader. So much so that although he felt well, he was going home there and then, and if the Deputy Chief Constable were to ring the office, as he thought he would, could I tell him that he (Derek) had suffered chest pains and was going to arrange a visit to his doctor. They must have had one almighty row, which must have concerned the Deputy, because he did ring to speak to Derek and I said exactly what I'd been asked to say. Derek took three day's uncertified sick leave, which must have got something moving in the upper echelons of power, because within two weeks he was transferred to a divisional role at Pontypool.

So I was now the flag-bearing head of the Complaints Department. I was given a newly-promoted Superintendent to work alongside and I did my best to give him the same encouragement and guidance I had received from Derek. He was quite a reserved individual and I could see within weeks that he was going to have problems coping with the Deputy's behaviour. Within three months I noticed he was taking some kind of pill several times a day and when it became obvious that he didn't want to discuss the issue, I let the matter rest. I had no intention of forcing any psychological counselling on anyone.

CHAPTER 14

Apparently it was time for me to move on in the great scheme of things, because within six months of me being joined by a new colleague in the Complaints department, I was transferred to Newport as Deputy Divisional Commander. The officer I left dealing with complaints, Tony Fitzgerald, didn't give the Deputy Chief time to disrupt his career, as he was chosen for interview and subsequently selected for promotion in North Yorkshire, and to my knowledge, completed the remainder of his service there. For me Newport was far closer to home, just four miles away, but still a very busy place for its police officers.

I was working under a dedicated career man, Fred Wyer, who was desperate for promotion to Chief Officer rank and took a great deal of satisfaction from the fact that his office was the one that had previously been occupied by Mr Smeed, the beloved Chief Constable of the Newport

Borough force. I don't believe Fred ever got to know that I used it whenever he was not at work. It really was a grand, palatial room with its own en-suite bathroom. Fred not only aspired to be a Chief but acted the part in his present rank, assuming that the Newport Division was its own little force (as of course, it once was). He devoted all his efforts to general policy, forward planning, resources and personnel, and directed me to take control of all operational matters. My neighbour and so-called friend, Mr Green, now worked two floors below me in the same building, which I don't think did his ego any good at all.

Without detracting from the importance of criminal aspects of police work, which the residents of Newport were showered with in large quantities, one of the main issues I had to face, taking up a great deal of my time, was community relations, which has a direct bearing on the level of crime in any event. Newport had been for a considerable time, and still is, a highly multi-cultural society, dating back to the time when its coal exporting docks were thriving, with a mix of ethnic minorities from all corners of the globe. Communities from the Indian sub-continent, the Middle East and the Caribbean all had separate enclaves in their own area of the Division and were all vying for influence, power and resources through what in the main were self-appointed leaders. They all saw it as a priority to have their local police commanders giving them support in whatever cause they were treating as a crusade. It was for me almost a full-time job and demanded every ounce of tact and diplomacy I could muster. The meetings, discussion groups and workshops (as they were always termed by Social

Services) were constant, but by and large I helped keep the pot from boiling over.

One of my more enjoyable tasks at Newport was to lead a small group of officers to Germany. Newport, like many other towns in the United Kingdom, had embarked on a twinning agreement with a similar-sized town on the continent, and Newport Borough Council had officially forged links with Heidenheim, a town in southern Germany, quite close to the border with Bavaria. There were ongoing cultural links and visits being made by various council departments and charitable groups, and shortly after my posting to the Division, Fred indicated that we should organise a visit to meet our German counterparts and suggested that I might enjoy leading the group. Of course, with that accolade went the job of making all the arrangements. I invited applications from interested officers within the division and our final group numbered six of mixed rank.

We flew from Heathrow to Stuttgart, where we were met by a group of German officers and spent a wonderful four days with them and their families, being entertained and lauded by all and sundry. I'm sure we built bridges somehow and somewhere between our two countries. The best bit of this outing was that we took our wives along and I know that Shel thoroughly enjoyed it. The only cost to the taxpayer was a few force crests and uniform helmets that we purloined as presentation gifts. The following year, the same group of German officers visited our homes when we reciprocated the welcome.

That visit however, took place after some domestic upheaval. Shel and I had been able to achieve quite a good standard of living over the past few years. Her income from the Civil Service, although not handsome, was reasonable for the early 1980s and I had reached the rank of superintendent at the age of 38, which was relatively young in those days. After the Edmund Davies pay award, my salary was to be envied by many in other occupations. Shel and I therefore decided to move up the housing ladder and purchased a detached four-bedroomed house with a double garage, on what the developer described as an executive site. It was only a mile from where we lived and located in Henllys, one of the oldest hamlets that were encompassed when Cwmbran New Town was built. There is evidence that Cistercian monks travelled through this ancient settlement when they founded Llantarnam Abbey in 1179.

The house was set at the end of a cul de sac, and I'm sure it was taming its large rear garden that gave me my lower back problems in later years. It may or may not have been a coincidence (I personally feel it was the latter), but about six months after we occupied our new house, the last one to be sold in our close was bought by the one and only Mr John Green. I was certainly not paranoid, but he'd given me the impression that he could not bear to see my career advancing too much in front of his. I believe he had a problem, and it was envy.

To ease the stress and anxiety involved in selling and buying a house, particularly when you have to coordinate the exchange of contracts with a chain of individuals involved, I spoke with the Chief Superintendent in charge of force administration and he agreed to my occupying an empty police property on the outskirts of Pontypool to ease my sale and purchase. There was a surplus of police accommodation at the time because of the stampede to become property owners. The house in question was a large detached property, usually occupied by a senior officer, which had a long rear garden gently descending down to the banks of the Brecon and Monmouthshire canal. I remember we all had hilarious fun, in the only spring we were there, keeping watch on the hundreds of baby frogs being born in what the local frog population seemed to consider their maternity hospital.

The country club where Shel had toiled for several years was no longer a destination for us, initially because of us being shunned by the proprietors and later because they sold it to a developer for future housing, when it was demolished. So on occasion we visited the Dorallt Inn, which was set in the centre of this once ancient community. Although its owners had, over the years, brought parts of it into the 20th century, the bar area was much the same as it was hundreds of years ago, with the original flagstone floor.

We moved into our new home in late autumn and Shel, quite naturally, wanted to show it off at every opportunity, so her sister and her family came to stay with us for our first Christmas, and on Christmas Eve we all went to the Dorallt Inn, where they'd promised mince pies and carols. It was shortly after eight o'clock and we'd been soaking up the yuletide atmosphere for about 30 minutes when my bleeper activated. In those days, a bleeper was pretty hi-tech, and 'bleep' was precisely what it did; there was no message, just the bleep to indicate that someone in the force operations room wanted to speak to me. I was told that their stand-by list showed that I was the negotiator on call and my presence was required at an incident that was ongoing in Tredegar.

I left Shel and her family to enjoy their hot punch or whatever, and sped up through the valley towns and villages to be greeted by the sub-division Commander. There was no sign of snow, but I recall that at this highest point of the South Wales valleys it was cold, very cold, and I had on the lightest clothes and a thin coat, dressed for an evening in the pub. I learned that the incident had started about two and a half hours earlier with a domestic argument involving a family who were not really known to local officers. One of the sons, aged 19, had apparently arrived home in a distressed state, in possession of a double-barrelled shotgun, and after an altercation with his family, had barricaded himself in his bedroom threatening to kill himself and anyone who tried to interfere. Local officers had established that there had been a young lady involved, causing the lad to become agitated. From what the family was saying, there didn't seem to be any influence of alcohol and no drug use was suspected. The young man in question had obtained the gun from a friend and I ascertained that it was owned by a lawful certificate holder, was in good working order and several cartridges had been taken with it.

I purloined a heavy Gannex police overcoat from the station and made my way to the scene, which was a semi-detached house, set in a cluster of about 12, near the edge of a fairly run-down estate, one of several owned by the local authority. The local Inspector, who was at that moment the officer in charge of the scene, briefed me that a firearms team had been in a containment position for the past hour, and the young man was displaying sporadic bouts of anger and issuing threats through the bedroom window. The incident had been brought to the attention of the local police station when neighbours had heard what they thought was a gun being fired. I noted as many pertinent facts as possible in as few minutes as I could, including his name and importantly, any nickname he was known by, together with brief details of his girlfriend and family. Luckily, the estate was quite compact, so taking an armed officer with me, I made my way with some difficulty along alleyways, over fences and through gardens until we were as close as possible to the bedroom window so that the young lad could hear me, but out of his line of fire. As we slowly made our way through this maze of wire and brambles, I remember wondering whose coat I had been handed, because the owner wasn't going to be very pleased in the morning.

One of the first rules taught us on our negotiator's training was, whenever possible, try to establish contact with the subject by direct speech, or if not possible, by telephone, and never to use a loud hailer. Well, I'd achieved what I'd been taught, so now it was up to me. The subject and I were on first name terms within minutes and I listened to his problems, which more or less amounted to his life story. He'd lost his job and his girl, and nobody, including his family, understood. I couldn't take any chances throughout this whole episode because he issued threats to use the gun quite often and although the police resources in position were sufficient to ensure that it was only he who would have been harmed, my role was to protect life, no matter what.

After just over three hours the young man, who by now considered me one of his mates, threw the gun down onto the front garden and two of the firearms team met him at the front door and whisked him away to Tredegar police station. I called at the station on my way home to return my life-saving Gannex and felt that I wanted to go and have a quick chat with my 'friend', but that was not the thing to do.

I winged my way back home to a house which, at four o'clock in the morning, was dark and fairly cold, with everyone tucked up in bed. Never mind, it had been a successful night. The only disappointing aspect was that whilst driving the 20 miles back down the valley in the wee small hours of that festive morning, I never had as much as a glimpse of Father Christmas. Our friend with the gun was taken to Crown Court by the Crown Prosecution Service for unlawful possession of and endangering life with a firearm, for which he was placed under the supervision of the Probation Service for two years. The shotgun owner had his certificate revoked and the Judge kindly issued me with a commendation.

1987 dawned on the Thorne family quietly and without any fuss. Well, none that we were aware of anyway. Shel had settled into her role at the Police Training Centre; she was in quite a prominent position, and I mean that physically as well as metaphorically. Her office was designed as an annexe to the one occupied by the Commandant, so everyone who visited him was forced to pass her desk, and the centre, being new and the only purpose-built one in the country, had visitors almost daily in the early months. I believe Shel knew and was on speaking terms with more senior officers than me, certainly those of chief officer rank. She did in fact, have a personal introduction to Douglas Hurd when he visited in his role as Home Secretary. In time, Shel made friends with the Commandant's wife and we both became frequent guests at the passing out parades regularly held there.

My two lads had grown up; they were now young men, having left school. Michael had secured a job at the Passport Office in Newport and Brian, 18 months younger, was intent on joining the police service, but, like his dad, they rejected him when he applied to become a cadet. As in my youth, the number of cadet vacancies in the smaller forces were few and far between, so the recruitment section could afford to be fussy. They told Brian that he was a little too short and they didn't think he would grow enough to transfer to the regular constabulary. Brian had other ideas. He took a job at Bejam, a frozen food store in Cwmbran, where he was given training in several aspects of the retail trade, and every night he would exercise. Quite often he would hang from the top of the doorframe in his bedroom, in the hope of stretching those few millimetres. He applied to the Gwent Constabulary on his 19th birthday and was accepted. I spoke to no one throughout the whole procedure, but a few days after his final interview I felt quite proud when the Chief Superintendent on the panel told me that Brian was a credit to Shel and me. We exchanged some light-hearted banter for several weeks whenever I reminded him that he would need to address me as 'sir'.

Shel became quite proficient in her role within a short time of her appointment and must have been considered an influencing factor on the Training Centre, because after Brian joined the force our then Deputy Chief Constable, Joe Frost, arranged for him to receive his initial training at Chantmarle, the training centre situated in Dorset, to avoid any conflict of interest in his mother's role.

Life for Shel and me must have been running a little too smoothly in the eyes of our guardian angels, because as soon as spring 1987 had burst out all over, I was smartly despatched back to what I was beginning to think of as 'that bloody police college'. I had been nominated to attend the Intermediate Command Course, which meant another three months away from home. The physical structure of the establishment had seen some radical improvements and because I had now reached one of the higher ranks that were enlisted there for training, the accommodation we were allocated was of a much higher standard. Although the lecture facilities were now much better, the calibre of its academics, in my view, had declined. I was told by one of the police members of staff on my earlier course that most of the academic tutors at the college were second-class misfits who had failed to secure an appointment at any of our country's universities, and that comment was made by a very senior officer who had completed almost two years working alongside them. I was not qualified to endorse or argue against his theory, but the opinion I did have, which was formed after being actively involved in policing the community for over 20 years, was that the liberal elitist aim was to change the face of British policing and mould it into a uniformed branch of the Social Services. I had the view that the country's political establishment was producing cloned chief officers on this very campus, by having their original aims and values surreptitiously twisted so that they would conform to the 'master plan'. And here I was, part of the programme. They could lecture me until the cows came home, I would never change my basic views on policing, although I fully admit that they were successful with some;

several were colleagues in my syndicate, who were happy to comply.

I'd completed roughly half the course and on my return home one Friday evening, Shel gave me the news that she had received a date for one of her follow-up appointments so that the consultant could keep a check on 'the problem', and told me she'd be perfectly happy to make her own way there, which was to be on the following Thursday. It wasn't really up for discussion; I had no intention of letting her go without me. My syndicate director at the college was a woman, Chief Superintendent Whittaker of Greater Manchester, and as soon as I informed her on the following Monday morning that my wife had the appointment, she was going to ensure I attended, even if she had to drive me there herself. Whether the consultant ever told Shel anything different when she was out of my immediate presence undergoing the physical examination, I will never know, but he was always fairly upbeat with the comments I heard. There was no reason for concern, but he would see her again, just to keep an eye on things. My course finished midsummer with no end of course dance – that was reserved for Christmas, so I went back to policing Newport and my ethnic friends.

However, I didn't have time to make my presence felt again, because I was transferred more or less overnight to Pontypool. The Chief Constable had decided to carry out a major reorganisation of the force and he was placing superintendents in command of sub-divisions, as opposed to the chief inspectors who had headed them. I was to take control of Pontypool North, which geographically encompassed two-thirds of the force area. Although my patch included the upper half of the eastern valley, I was also responsible for some of the loveliest scenery in Wales (I'm not taking credit for its beauty, of course), from Monmouth down through the Wye valley, the border town of Chepstow with its Norman castle, and a whole swathe of countryside which included the Usk valley. During my time in that post, I could not be accused of showing bias in my art of supervision because I travelled everywhere, quite often, and therefore kicked my monthly mileage allowance to death.

The only problem with Pontypool was the fact that they made me leave it. I was nominated for another course, and to me, they were becoming a pain in the backside. It was only for two weeks, but this time it was held in Wakefield, the HQ of the West Yorkshire Constabulary. It was entitled 'Senior Officer's Course' and turned out to be a bit of a jolly for the 17 superintendents drafted in from all four corners of the United Kingdom. We had no formal lectures as such, but made numerous visits to locations throughout the north of England, to observe different methods of dealing with policing issues, which gave all the participants the chance to exchange views and ideas. That was the official version of events. However, in my mind it was a course organised by the West Yorkshire Constabulary to try to impress on us how good they were. Once we had had our obligatory end of course photograph, I was glad to get home.

I must have been enjoying myself too much in my sub-divisional posting, because after only seven months, my old friend Derek Helps retired and I was moved into the position he left vacant, Deputy Commander of the division I was in. It meant a move of office up a flight of stairs and I was now responsible, operationally, for about three-quarters of the force area. Whilst I had been looking after my sub-division downstairs, I was aware that arrangements were being made by the Divisional Commander, probably at the suggestion of the Chief, to hold a large-scale exercise with the scenario set around an inter-city train accident in the Severn Tunnel. This link between London and West Wales, and ultimately Ireland, is an important cog in the rail network of the United Kingdom, but I would suggest that, apart from the passengers who use it regularly for commuting to and from Bristol, hardly anyone gives it a second thought and most non-rail users will be unaware of its existence. It is in fact a crowning achievement of Victorian civil engineering, over four and a half miles in length with two and a quarter miles of it actually under the River Severn. The little village of Sudbrook, on the Welsh side, houses a pumping station which, on average, pumps 50,000,000 litres of fresh spring water every day from the tunnel's lowest point back into the river flowing above it. One can imagine that if a derailment or even worse, an explosion were to occur as a train travelled through, there would be a major rescue mission to be undertaken.

The planning for this exercise started, at quite a timely moment I thought, with my move to the office which would be prominent in its execution, so my first month or two were fully occupied. The efforts of many individuals and literally scores of organisations helped to make it a success, with much learned by all the emergency services and ancillary supporters.

Part of my role as Deputy Commander was to vet all applications and renewals for firearms certificates and give final recommendations before submitting them to the Deputy Chief Constable for the ultimate decision; also, to give the final police decision on whether there should be a prosecution or otherwise on the more serious or complicated alleged offences before submitting to the Crown Prosecuting Solicitor's office. These matters required a little peace and quiet at the desk so that you could muster the amount of concentration they deserved. To this end, I was in the habit of starting my working day at around 7.30 am so that I could devote my first hour to this important task before the daily hustle and bustle got into full swing.

At about 8.15 on a Tuesday morning I was disturbed by a telephone call from the switchboard informing me that one of the sergeants, Bernie Scrivens, who was the officer in charge of our sectional police station in Blaenavon, was dealing with an incident where a man had entered a house and was threatening the occupants with a shotgun. The call had been put through to me because apparently there was no other supervisory officer in the building. I doubt that my staff in the police station would have known at that time that I was a force negotiator, as they had no reason to, but I knew from the initial message that I would more than likely be required. I issued instructions that Sergeant Scrivens should keep the scene contained and made my way there.

Blaenavon is a desolate little town which sits on the southern slopes of the Blorenge Mountain, some 1200ft above sea level. Its landscape bears the relics of its past history, of being in the forefront of the industrial revolution, with old colliery machinery and waste tips, together with the remains of ironworks buildings dotted everywhere. To capitalise on this, it has now created a museum which gives a very broad insight into the 19th century iron industry, and has reopened its last deep-mine colliery, known as 'Big Pit', to the public, which attracts thousands of visitors, including foreign tourists, throughout the year.

On my arrival, the incident was still ongoing, centred on a mid-terraced cottage of 15 dwellings. The cottages were quite modern, having been constructed by the local authority some 15 years previously, but they had attempted to retain the old-fashioned character of the town's past. However, to contain the cost, they were capped with artificial slate roofs, there were sections of plastic fascia and for the comfort of the occupants, uPVC double-glazing.

I conferred with Sergeant Scrivens, who updated me with his local knowledge, which was somewhat different from my switchboard message, but nevertheless still serious. The tenants of the house were a young family, the male being a 26-year-old man known to the Sergeant, and apart from being a bit of a tearaway in his teens, he had no criminal record. Inside with him were thought to be his wife of similar years and their 14-month-old baby daughter. Sergeant Scrivens had been made aware of the problem by neighbours who had heard shouting, and when he had made a telephone call to the house, a male voice had told him to go away, using Anglo-Saxon terminology. The Sergeant informed me that this man legally owned a shotgun, which he knew was used most weekends for sporting purposes, and when he had knocked on the door on his arrival, he was told that the gun was going to be used on everyone. There was no adequate cover to the front or rear of the cottages, so I, the Sergeant and his constable kept the scene under observation from a safe distance, the main reason being so that I could think for a few minutes.

Our minds went into overdrive. Our first action was to update force HQ and not only request but ascertain the estimated time of arrival of a firearms team. I knew that this was going to present a problem, because as I expected, I was told that firearms officers could not get to us for at least an hour. That was an issue for me. My training told me that I should make contact with my subject as soon as possible and bearing in mind the circumstances, I was not prepared to wait that long. I did mention earlier that in my first such incident at Tredegar, I only had the safety of a foolhardy youth to consider; here I also had a young wife and baby daughter and furthermore, my instinct told me that this man needed help, and sooner rather than later.

Back in 1988, although firearms were carried by the odd individual officer for royal protection duties and specific operations, they were not carried around in the public domain as a matter of course, even out of sight. The issue of firearms in the metropolis was a slightly different matter; there they were far more readily available and in fact, because of the escalation of the IRA and terrorist threats, officers stationed at Heathrow Airport were now being armed with automatic rifles. In the lowly shire counties and especially Gwent, for which I can speak, they were safely housed in the armoury at police HQ and only issued if and when required. Firearms-trained officers, of which there were relatively few, were stationed appropriately around the three divisions, but some may well have been off duty and would have needed to be summoned from home. Our society has evolved and today, firearms are carried securely in the rear of several patrol cars touring the county around the clock, with sufficient officers to hand.

My short conference with Sergeant Scrivens ended and I decided to make contact with this desperate young man. I'd noticed a telephone wire leading to one of the end cottages, so I disturbed the occupant, an elderly lady, and without hesitation she allowed me to use her telephone. The fact that she was being confronted on her doorstep at 8.45 am by an anxious police officer with a crown on each epaulette and scrambled egg on his cap probably had something to do with her agreeable attitude. The telephone was answered by the wife, who sounded as though she was trying to calm her husband as she passed the receiver to him, but on learning that my object was to bring this matter to a peaceful end, he took the opposite attitude and resumed his threats to 'finish everyone off'.

Our conversation continued for approximately 25 minutes, during which I learned that he had recently lost his job in one of the local unit factories, he was in debt up to his neck and basically, his mental frame of mind had convinced him that he was a failure to himself and everyone else, particularly his immediate family. He knew and respected Sergeant Scrivens, who I had told him was outside, and after accepting that causing injury or worse to his wife or baby was not going to help the situation, he agreed to open the front door, place the gun on the doorstep then walk out with his hands out in front of him. I assured him that Sergeant Scrivens would do all he could to help.

Whilst speaking to the young man on the telephone, I was in contact with Sergeant Scrivens via UHF radio and the arrangements went as planned. The Sergeant conveyed him to Blaenavon police station where, I was later informed, they enjoyed a cup of tea. By this time, other uniformed officers had arrived who dealt with the distraught wife and baby while I made my way back to my desk and prosecution reports.

I was just half a mile outside Blaenavon when I passed, travelling in the opposite direction, the Sergeant who was the force full-time officer dealing with firearms training, and knew he would be really uptight on arrival at the scene to learn that it was all over. I am not suggesting for one minute that these officers had no concern for the safety of individuals, but the possession and use of firearms by the police in public was in its infancy. The term 'firearms training' and 'firearms officer' were new buzzwords and, because, during these early years, the few officers selected for training were usually those who had a fetish for guns in any event, they were always anxious to become involved in a real live operation. Well, that's the impression they gave me, and I apologise if in any way I'm speaking out of turn.

In the days following the incident, I picked up a few rumblings on the grapevine that Superintendent Haines, the officer who had an overall watching brief of force firearms training, and if you remember, the one in Ebbw Vale so fixated on found property, was casting aspersions because I hadn't waited for firearms officers to arrive. He didn't, and I knew he wouldn't, say anything to me directly, but I would have been ready with my response. The young father, by the way, who succumbed to my persuasion, was allowed to retain his liberty; the magistrates issued a probation order, but we of course revoked his shotgun certificate.

At about this time, the British Government had invited tenders for the construction of the Second Severn Crossing. The original bridge having been opened in 1966, it was becoming clear that one river crossing would not be sufficient to deal with traffic capacity into the 21st century. The policing of the initial crossing, which was constructed as a four-lane motorway, had been given to the Gloucestershire Constabulary and right from the start, before the construction company had been selected, it was announced that we in Gwent would be responsible for the second, which was going to be a much longer structure. Although the Second Severn Crossing would not be opened by the Prince of Wales until July 1995, in my role as Deputy Commander at Pontypool the Chief Constable called me to his office and we discussed, in broad outline, the policing requirements, particularly in relation to traffic enforcement. Our talk concluded with him asking me to chair a small working party to consider all the issues, and submit a report. To be honest, there wasn't really a great deal to contemplate, but it was obvious that the Chief considered it something of a coup to be given the responsibility and he seemed to want to make a show of it. I chose three other officers to join me and over the following months we met occasionally to keep progress ticking along. There was no real hurry – they hadn't mixed the first load of concrete yet!

CHAPTER 15

I would now like to describe an incident in which initially I had no involvement whatsoever, but whose ramifications would later bring me untold misery and heartache.

It all started with a telephone call from that man who seemed to follow Shel and me wherever we moved to. Yes, it was Mr Green, the man who loved badgering me for help. As I have mentioned, he gave me the impression that he was strangely concerned about any advancement I made in my career.

When I left my divisional HQ I was not in the habit of telling the switchboard operator of my intended destination, because you could guarantee that within minutes everyone concerned would know I was on my way. So it was one afternoon when I left to visit Cwmbran police station. My Sub-Divisional Commander there was on annual leave, so I had decided to visit his office to ensure there was no paperwork lying idle which should have been winging its way to HQ. I was enjoying a quiet cup of coffee in his office when the switchboard operator rang to say she had Mr Green on the line for me, and he wouldn't speak to anyone else; it seemed to be a personal matter and only I would do.

When we were connected, he apologised somewhat, but explained that it was an urgent issue. His son, who I have mentioned a little earlier, was now old enough to drive that MGB sports car on public roads, and earlier that afternoon he had been driving it in Chapel Lane, which I knew was controlled by a set of traffic lights at its junction with the main thoroughfare carrying traffic in and out of the town centre. Whilst at the stop light, he had been approached from behind by a male pedal cyclist who had used abusive language and threatening behaviour, and when his son had remonstrated with the cyclist, he had been punched, causing injury to his upper lip.

I listened patiently to this account, wondering why this young man about town in a sports car had not driven into the parking area outside the front door downstairs and made his complaint of assault as any other citizen of Cwmbran would have done. It was then that Mr Green revealed that this man on the bike had appeared to his son to be an off-duty police officer. This put a slightly different slant on things, and I assured Mr Green that action would be taken.

I relayed this information to the superintendent who was in charge of the Complaints Department at that time, whose identity escapes me, but I remember insisting that he should inform the Deputy Chief Constable. In view of this allegation against a serving officer, I would have thought the matter would have winged its way straight to the Chief himself.

Obviously the matter was fully investigated; the man on the bike was indeed a police officer. He was a young man well known to me as one of my traffic officers from a few years previously. He was a Police Constable Davies, who was still serving on traffic. Not only would I describe him as a knowledgeable, competent officer, who would not in my estimation have lost his cool unnecessarily, but he was a first-rate athlete, having recently won the middleweight class in the National Police Judo Championships. He was no more than five feet eight inches tall, but built like the proverbial brick outhouse.

I naturally took a close interest in the investigation. It transpired that the version of events given by Constable Davies did not exactly coincide with those of the young Mr Green. He related that he was cycling home from work and as he approached the red traffic light, it was the sports car that approached him from the rear in a rather speedy manner. The officer further said that he thought the car driver had not observed the red light until the last minute; the car braked sharply and in doing so it swerved slightly to his nearside as it came to a halt, just nudging the officer's leg and causing him to lose his balance. He was fortunate not to fall to the floor. Naturally, Constable Davies remonstrated with the driver, and according to Davies it was the car driver who had started hurling abuse at the officer. When the officer was interviewed, he fully admitted giving the driver some stern words of advice, but totally denied hitting him in any way. There were apparently no witnesses.

Chapel Lane is narrow, with little traffic, only really giving access to properties and, strangely enough, a chapel. I suppose each of us would surmise differently what really happened in those few moments before the amber light flickered on.

I have no knowledge of any injuries that Mr Green's son may have suffered, but I do know that the Crown Prosecution Service decided to prosecute the officer for an offence under Section 47 of the Offences Against the Person Act 1861, alleging that he committed an assault occasioning actual bodily harm. I was certainly not privy to their reasoning, but in my experience of the law up until that time, I would never have recommended taking up the time of any court in the circumstances. Constable Davies, through his legal representatives, elected trial by Crown Court, as was his right, and ultimately the jury found him not guilty. The case against him was dismissed, and I know that John Green was not at all pleased.

I had now been in my position as Deputy Commander at Pontypool for about 15 months, working under another Alan, who had been promoted into the force some 10 years previously from the South Wales Constabulary. Alan Roberts was about my age. We worked well together and as in other divisions, he left most operational matters to me, but to his credit he did involve me, whenever possible, in the appraisal process of qualified officers and would have me sit in on as many interviews as my work allowed. Chief Superintendent Roberts had spent a little time as a staff officer to Her Majesty's Inspector of Constabularies, and I am not being in any way sarcastic when I say he was always on the lookout for gimmicks – new ideas, new buzzwords.

He really was ahead of his time and was always up for anything which would promote or advertise our division and in turn, its officers. There was nothing selfish in his actions, it was all aimed at improving the image of the force and our service to the community.

Late one afternoon he called me into his office and informed me that the Chief Constable wished to see me at nine o'clock the following morning at Police HQ. Apparently, he wanted to have a verbal update on my deliberations concerning the new Severn bridge. I was somewhat taken aback because our working party had only been convened for about two and a half months, the bridge was years away and he had given no indication that he wanted such a quick response. Not to worry, I would draft a few paragraphs that evening as some briefing notes and I'd be fine.

I was waiting patiently with his secretary at 8.50 that following morning – you never chanced being late for the Chief – and when he arrived, he asked me to follow him into the inner sanctum. Having allowed him to settle at his desk, I broached the subject of my visit only to hear "The bridge? Oh, I don't want to talk about that". He immediately went on to tell me that he was promoting me to the rank of Chief Superintendent and that he was going to take the opportunity of reorganising several sections of the Force into a new division to be named the OSD. I was to be the Commander of this Operational Support Division, which would encompass traffic officers, public order support units, dog handlers, firearms officers and all other groups that carried out a support function to their divisional colleagues. He also told me that I would command Special Branch officers. I had immediate concerns about that, but thought it best to hold my peace and digest this news at my leisure.

As I was leaving, he told me to call into the Deputy Chief's office, where he would allow me to make a private telephone call to inform my wife. This seemed strange to me, but it may have been part of his usual routine, so I complied; I would have telephoned Shel from the first convenient office I found anyway. My friend the Deputy, shook hands with me and nodded towards his telephone, so it must have been pre-arranged. One little expedition I made before returning to my office in Pontypool was to visit the force workshops to share my news with Tom and the other staff, who would now be under my umbrella once again.

As if my new role was not going to keep me busy enough, I had only been in situ for about three weeks when I was told that I had been nominated to sit on a permanently-constituted working party set up under the auspices of the Home Office, whose role was to advise on legislation and monitor operational implementation on the conveyance of hazardous and dangerous loads. What a mouthful, and what a load of wasteful bureaucratic nonsense. I was now seeing at first-hand how our democratic system of government plods on, financially supporting a plethora of quangos, working parties and any other kind of group in vogue at the time, just creating jobs for the boys, who have no responsibility and usually don't have a clue what their objective is apart from not allowing the boat to rock.

I attended the bi-monthly meetings for about a year and was the Police Service representative on the panel. The others, who on average amounted to 20 people in number, consisted of one or two from the scientific field, who seemed fairly well qualified, and civil servants from various departments. We were chaired by a mandarin from the Home Office, who could have doubled for Sir Humphrey in *Yes Prime Minister*. The meetings were held at the regional HQ of the Health and Safety Executive in Bootle on Merseyside, which meant an overnight stay each time for me, so my secretary, who I shared with the Detective Chief Superintendent always booked me into the Adelphi Hotel in Liverpool. Well, if I had to go, I might as well go in style! During my whole association with that particular working party, nothing was ever concluded or achieved, apart from the chairman ensuring that the lavish buffet laid out for each lunch break was not too repetitive.

Another ongoing extra-curricular activity which fell to the superintendent rank was the investigation of the more serious complaints referred to the force, either by another constabulary or the Police Complaints Authority. If our force was asked to provide an investigating officer, then it was down to our Deputy Chief, who would nominate the individual, and with our particular Deputy still holding that office, I had a sneaking suspicion that I was having more than my fair share; or was it that he knew he'd get a thorough report, even if he didn't like the conclusions? Quite a lot of these were concerned with alleged malpractice in various forces, but some did emanate from the public and one such incident was directed my way which necessitated me rushing off to Cardiff Central Police Station late one afternoon with my gofer. It involved a male in his mid-twenties who had been arrested the previous evening for drunken behaviour, which had resulted in several officers allegedly manhandling him in the custody unit. Even after regaining some sobriety the following morning, he furthered his allegations, claiming that he had been assaulted inside the cell and identifying an officer who had thrown him to the floor, causing him to strike his head on the bare concrete. The custody sergeant had decided, after he had complained continually of pain, to have the prisoner seen by the police surgeon, who admitted him to hospital. The tests and examinations had taken a little while and by midday the staff within the Accident and Emergency Department had taken X-rays and diagnosed a fractured skull. As you can imagine, the balloon went up.

The Deputy Chief of South Wales Police contacted the Police Complaints Authority, who asked my Deputy to provide an investigating officer. I was chosen, so I winged my way to Cardiff. It was the category of incident which had to be referred to the Authority, and I would not only have to submit my final report to them but keep a nominated supervisor fully briefed about every stage of my investigation.

My assistant, Inspector Edwards, went to work collecting witness statements from anyone who could shed the slightest glimmer of light on the matter, and two days later we unearthed a connection between the complainant and the notorious little town of Ebbw Vale. Inspector Edwards had served there as a Detective Sergeant for several years after I had left and probably knew the nuts and bolts of the community better than I did. We ascertained that our injured prisoner had lived in the town throughout his earlier life and had moved to Cardiff at the age of 19. My inspector spent a full day in Ebbw Vale ferreting into the complainant's background, and found that he had been involved in what some people termed an accident, but was, in reality, a serious altercation outside a public house late one Saturday night. A visit to the local GP revealed that his registered patient had received injuries on the night in question and after referral to hospital it was found that he had suffered a fractured skull. The GP provided a statement, obviously not being too worried about patient confidentiality, and when the X-rays taken in Cardiff were examined by a registrar, it was clear that the image shown could well have been of a long-standing injury. When the complainant was confronted with these facts, he accepted that he had not been thrown to the floor of the cell and at the time of his arrest, he had become quite agitated, and had been the author of his own misfortune. The Authority was satisfied that the true facts had been revealed, and three rather relieved officers in Cardiff slept a little easier that night.

In between my trips to Liverpool and complaint investigations, I was busy trying to organise the new division created by the Chief. On top of that, Shel suffered a small relapse. We had visited Velindre Hospital in Cardiff, which specialises in cancer care, for one of her routine checks. This revealed that a course of radiotherapy was needed, which necessitated six weekly sessions of about an hour each. We both knew, Shel particularly, that her body's systems would be hit, and hard. I will never, ever understand how she managed to stay so bright and optimistic. In fact throughout the whole series of treatments, apart from the three hours she lost each week to attend, she never had a moment off work.

During our first visit we bumped into Roy Ellis, the officer who had retired and left my current post vacant, whose wife was there for exactly the same treatment as Shel. The staff, who were exemplary in every aspect, kindly arranged all their future appointments together, so that I could drive them both down each week. The company of another woman with the same medical complaint helped them both cope over that six-week period.

It was six months after my promotion; Shel was back to her normal bubbly self and we had settled back into a period of stability when once again I was despatched to the police college. It was for a two-week course on the Management of Disaster and Civil Emergencies. The Home Office had invested in a new training wing equipped with all the latest technology and this was a hands-on fortnight with each student being given the role of 'Gold Commander' (in total and overall control) in various scenarios. One of mine, I recall, was to deal with a cargo boat loaded with a highly flammable and toxic material, which was docked in a small port on the South Coast of England and which somehow, had blown up taking half of the town with it. All good fun!

These two-week courses were a doddle after those lasting months, but I was aware that no matter for how short a time, I was again away from home and family. Everything on the domestic front was again being left to Shel, and although the boys were now actually young men, I was once again absent from their journey through life. On my return to the force, I was a little surprised when, after one of our chief superintendent's conferences, the Chief Constable asked me join him in his office and said how pleased he was to have received a call from the Commandant of the Police College, who he said was singing my praises about my performance on the course. He commented on the credit it brought to the force and said that in his whole term as Chief Constable it was the first ever occasion that he had received such a communication.

There is one more brief encounter with the Chief Constable I would like you to know about, because, although not significant on its own, it acquired a bitter resonance for me as time went on.

Shortly before my promotion to Chief Superintendent, which had been in late autumn, the division was gearing up for the festive season. Each sub-division held its own dinner-dance and its officers expected the Divisional Commander or me to attend. The Chief Constable would always receive an invitation and he, or more likely, his wife, would choose which ones they fancied. The function organised by Chepstow was always popular; the town and surrounding countryside were a tourist trap, the chosen hotel was always of a very good standard and the meal provided was good quality. Probably because of these combined factors, the Chief and his wife attended and from a divisional point of view, I drew the long straw and took Shel. The night was, as expected, very enjoyable and Shel and I were seated at a separate table of six, together with the Chief and his wife and the Sub-Divisional Inspector and his good lady. It wasn't a case of snobbery, it had always been the practice, which I remember from the days when I had organised functions, to seat any high-ranking officers on their own at a little distance so that everyone else could 'do their own thing', within reason.

As we sat making idle conversation waiting for the first course, the Chief Constable invited us all to have a glass of wine. In the course of asking each of us which wine we wanted, he suddenly stopped and looked straight at me, as though some magical notion had consumed his mind. "Mr Thorne" he said, "you have something to celebrate" (I had visited his office three weeks before and my promotion was to take effect on 1st January). He continued "I feel that you should have the privilege of buying us the toast this evening". At the next opportunity, he asked for two bottles of house white and two bottles of house red to be brought to the table, and I settled the account later in the evening.

I had no problem with picking up the tab, in fact, I'd have had no problem whatsoever if he'd ordered eight bottles, if we'd all arrived in a pre-arranged coach with no concerns about getting home. But we hadn't and he knew that. With his experience of traffic policing he would have known that four bottles of wine shared equally between the six of us would have been sufficient to put each of us over the legal limit, when you consider the thirst quenchers we may have consumed as we danced the night away. It was a blatant case of 'you and me' or 'them and us'. The Chief Constable was of course, provided with a personal car, together with a full-time driver, which was part of the force fleet, but reserved for his exclusive use and he not only used it for day-to-day work purposes but to attend official functions. Our Chief had decided to appoint a police constable as his full-time chauffeur, a man who was part of the Traffic Department establishment and had more than 15 years' experience of policing. I had the view that there would have been hundreds of unemployed men within the county who would have been qualified and only too grateful for such a role to support their family.

Constable Knight, his driver, would have been provided with refreshments somewhere in the hotel as he patiently waited for the summons to carry Mr and Mrs Over back to their abode whilst the Chief was blissfully drinking with his officers the alcohol he himself had ordered. However, as far as our night in Chepstow was concerned, Shel had two or three glasses of wine with her meal (she wasn't going to forgo something we'd paid for) and continued the night with orange juice before chauffeuring me home across our fair county.

CHAPTER 16

It was Sunday 6th January 1991; I was off duty and Shel and I had visited both sets of parents in their respective villages. I made arrangements to visit the village pub that evening with my friend John Baillie, of Royal Naval Reserve fame, and unusually, our next-door neighbour had indicated his intention of joining us when we had been chatting that morning. Before leaving the house my younger son, Brian, who was also on rest-day, told me that he was spending the evening with his elder brother, and said that perhaps they would join us later. This was a pleasant surprise; it wasn't often that the two offspring, now both in their early 20s, offered to spend some leisure time with their dad without some specific reason. The Dorallt was no more than half a mile from home, but I took the car because too often in the past, my bleeper had alerted me to some sort of emergency, and I had been marooned without transport.

We arrived at the pub around 7.30 pm and enjoyed a quiet social gathering, putting the world to rights and generally chatting with the odd regular who joined us for a while. At about 10.15 pm I was ready to head homewards, giving John a lift, while both of my boys accepted the offer of a lift from our neighbour so that they didn't have to rush their drinks. I had not driven 15 yards from the car park when I saw in my rear-view mirror, a traffic patrol car pull out of a bus stop which I had just passed on my nearside. The bus stop had been adapted from an old section of roadway some years previously and was obscured by a small hedgerow. Anything smaller than a large van would have been almost totally obscured from passing traffic.

My immediate thought was that the crew had been parked for a quiet smoke and were now on their way, so I continued down the slight incline at about 15 mph and briefly flashed my left indicator so that they could pass. They would have known it was my vehicle. There was no response; the traffic car stayed behind me. It tailed me for about 500 yards, then the blue light started to flash. It is surprising how quickly the human brain can assimilate thoughts, and within seconds I had considered numerous reasons why they were apparently attempting to get my attention. I gave it two or three seconds to see if the observer had hit the wrong switch by mistake, as every traffic officer has done this at some point, including me. There was no mistake; the blue beam continued to illuminate what seemed to be the whole village in the cold, damp, winter air, so I pulled in and stopped.

We had now entered John's estate, so as I opened my door to alight, I told him to make his way home on foot, as it was only about 150 yards away. I took a few steps towards the police vehicle. There was no immediate response, and then slowly but surely the rear offside door opened and out stepped a man in his mid-fifties, of small stature, around five feet seven inches in height and in full police uniform. It was Mr David Purkiss, the Assistant Chief Constable.

My mind went into overdrive, but there was no need for me to think too hard – it was abundantly clear that I had been set up. I approached him and he immediately said "I have reason to believe that you have been drinking and I wish you to provide a specimen of breath". He had obviously rehearsed this several times, because he would have known that he was dealing with someone who had far more knowledge and experience than he did about the breathalyser law. Actually, I found out later that he would have had three or four days to practise. He should, however, have realised that you can't practise for real-life situations because from the distance that was still between us, over six feet, it would have been impossible to detect whether I had been drinking. He should have researched a little deeper beforehand; the fact that he'd seen me leave a public house was insufficient reason in law to demand a breath test.

I said to myself "keep your cool, Al", and then he asked me how long ago I'd had my last drink. I'm afraid that in answer to that question, I lost it. The inbred traits of discipline, rank and superiority vanished from my mind and I pointed out to him, in the vernacular, "If you'd been parked any bloody nearer the front door of the pub you could have looked through the window and watched me drinking." With that, I got into the rear seat of the car, behind the driver. I saw Temporary Inspector Jones, who I had interviewed only two weeks before for his annual assessment, sitting in the front passenger seat. The driver was a constable, also under my jurisdiction. The Assistant Chief sat beside me in the rear and explained that, in view of my answer, he would wait 20 minutes before administering the test. This was normal procedure written into police guidelines, as suggested by the machine manufacturers; there should be at least this time delay between someone's last drink and the sample being provided.

I am sure that there are many who know what it's like to sit anxiously for a long period waiting for time to tick by, but that 20 minutes in the rear of that vehicle was the longest of my life. All I could do was think, and I thought quite quickly. First I considered my intake of alcohol that evening. I was pretty well read on the effects of alcohol consumption on the body, the number of units one should or should not consume and the way the body dissipates it, and I was careful not to drink above the limit when there was a chance of me having to drive. As I sat there at 10.45 pm, I ran the facts through my mind. I'd had my first drink over three hours earlier and had steadily consumed two and a half pints of bitter in half pint measures (half pint of bitter being my usual tipple whenever I visited a pub). Everyone's blood alcohol concentration (BAC) reaches a certain level at different rates depending on one's build, metabolism and a few other minor factors, but alcohol has one of the most predictable chemical reactions in the human body and virtually everyone breaks it down at precisely the same rate, equating to one unit every hour, so I was fairly satisfied as I sat there that my BAC would have levelled at two units, or two halves of beer; I was happy that I was under the legal limit.

The second issue I seriously pondered was, who was it? This operation must have been authorised or initiated by the Chief Constable, but he must have been prompted by something or someone. Although senior police officers throughout the country, because of their position, attract dislike and animosity from both inside and outside the force, I was satisfied that this had not originated internally. Whether it was intuition or some sixth sense, one name sprang to mind almost immediately. I was certain it was my supposedly friendly acquaintance, Mr Green. Over several years, I had formulated the opinion that he was a manipulative, jealous man. His attitude would have been exacerbated by the feeling that Gwent Police, through the justice system and with the involvement of 12 just persons, had branded his son a liar. I knew Green used the Dorallt Inn, which really was a community pub, and had seen me there. I went there probably two Sunday evenings a month, so Green and his wife would have had no problem adding two and two together. However, in life, we all know that sometimes, that particular sum comes to five. My suspicions were confirmed the following day when an inspector engaged in office duties at HQ, told me that he had personally seen Green visit the Chief Constable in his office on the previous Thursday afternoon.

I also ascertained the following day that the police patrol car, under the control of the Assistant Chief Constable, had secreted itself at the hidden bus stop at approximately 7.40 pm to await my departure from the Dorallt two and a half hours later. It was a 10-minute drive from Police HQ to where they were parked and the following day, our one-time neighbour 'Big John', who was on duty in Operations Room on the Sunday night, told me that the radio log indicated that the Assistant Chief Constable had 'booked on' at 7.32 pm precisely. Furthermore, a casual acquaintance told me that he had noticed the parked police car in position as he left the pub at 8.15 pm.

I had answered the two questions I had asked myself initially, and now my mind began to wander. I looked at the Assistant Chief from the corner of my eye and viewed what I could by the light being shed from a street-lamp and the piercing glow of the green 'on' beam from the VHF radio set. I saw a man who didn't really want to be there; we'd got on reasonably well since he'd transferred to the force. He was doing what he had been instructed to do and was scared stiff that he'd make a mistake. I saw a Temporary Inspector who had been selected to undertake this task because he would do exactly as he was told; he desperately longed for promotion. The third person, the man I was sitting behind, was the poor constable, who I bet was cringing, as embarrassed as hell.

The seconds were ticking by and the thought suddenly flashed into my mind that whatever was going to happen in the next few minutes, I was not going home; I had to be taken to a police station. I was sitting in the back of this patrol car because a man employed in a senior position in the Magistrate's Clerk's office had told my Chief Constable that one of his most senior officers was visiting a public house and driving a motor vehicle, and, for whatever reason, the Chief had instructed his Assistant to endeavour to administer a breath test. There was no way he would accept that I had provided a negative result and let everyone go home to bed happy. That wimp of a man Green wouldn't accept it, and the Chief would know that. I knew the Chief well enough to know that he would be afraid of facing all kinds of suggestions and innuendos. No, I would have to be arrested and taken to a police station, where justice could be seen to be done with official written documentation to corroborate it.

The temporary Inspector turned in his seat and stretched out his right hand. As the electronic breathalyser came towards me, he advised me that he required a sample of my breath and continued with the verbatim guidance that it should be in one continuous breath, I should hold the mouthpiece firmly in my mouth etc, etc, etc, as per the training manual. He knew I was fully aware of the procedure, as I had gone through it dozens of times in the classroom, lecturing probationers and dealing with drunken motorists who really needed police intervention. I begrudgingly gave up a lungful of life-saving air through the tiny disposable shred of plastic and in the silence that followed, the temporary Inspector slowly moved his stare away from the machine and glanced at the Assistant Chief sitting next to me. Whether or not there was a specific need for that visual contact, whether it was a secret acknowledgement of proposed action, only those two will ever know, but the Temporary Inspector then returned his gaze to me and clearly stated that the machine had not registered correctly; I had not properly provided a breath sample and he was therefore arresting me for failing to comply.

As the constable started the vehicle and slowly

manoeuvred out of the cul de sac, I thought to myself 'I've not only been set up, they are out to stitch me up as well'. I'd just lived through the longest 20 minutes of my life in total silence, with my mind analysing my immediate past, and I was to have another 10 minutes of total silence being driven to the police station, analysing my future. I'd made my mind up before we'd reached the main road that whatever happened now, I could no longer work with these people. Shel would surely understand that.

Cwmbran police station was not a bit like Maindee. It was relatively new, light and airy. No clanging of heavy doors or musty smells. Actually, to the uninitiated, on entering the reception room where the breathalyser procedure was carried out, it was like a visit to a doctor's surgery. One of the regular reserve officers was Constable Wright, who I knew very well, and it was he who was charged with dealing with this unexpected and exalted prisoner. Like my chauffeur, only somewhat more so, he was highly embarrassed. Anyone who has the pleasure of sitting in front of a registrar to notify a birth or register a death would experience a similar situation if they had the misfortune to be arrested for a drink-driving irregularity. The officer conducting the procedure would be sitting or standing opposite you, asking a myriad of questions with numerous forms spread across the table, some in duplicate, some in triplicate and others, not quite so important, in single sheets. That was how it was organised in 1991, but perhaps the computer is now king.

It has been an offence to be drunk in charge of a horse, cattle or carriage since 1872, but with the onset of the motor vehicle, legislators made it an offence to drive or be in charge of such a dangerous article in 1930 and since that time, with occasional amendments to cater for the advancement of society, the law itself had been pretty straightforward. An officer on patrol would need to prove you were the person responsible for the initial act and then a medical practitioner would have to give his considered opinion that you were drunk, but this need for human intelligence was superseded by scientific instruments as the decades progressed. A legislative minefield has been created, enabling solicitors and barristers to get very rich on the protracted, time-consuming court cases which have resulted.

So there we were. I was left in the capable hands of Constable Wright with a sergeant looking on, because probably, if the truth be known, he wouldn't have known how to operate the intoximeter, which according to law had to be used. My earlier companions, the temporary inspector and the constable, were probably availing themselves of a cuppa, and the Assistant Chief, so I was told the following morning, had gone to a quiet office to update the Chief.

Constable Wright now had to make a specific statement, addressed to me, as clearly outlined in legislation, requiring me 'to provide two specimens of breath for analysis by means of a device of a type approved by the Secretary of State'. The approved device was, and still is, an intoximeter, which is much larger and provides a far more accurate indication of a person's BAC than the machine carried by patrolling officers. However, Constable Wright did not make this statement. He quite officially asked me to provide a blood sample for a laboratory test. I immediately realised what he had said and knew that he was wrong. I replied

"No", then kept my own counsel. I knew that if I mentioned that it was unlawful, it would have prompted the sergeant and goodness knows who else to check and recheck their actions, and maybe they would have taken stock and restarted the whole procedure. In any event, nobody reacted to my answer with concern, not even the Assistant Chief who was now just outside the door, keeping himself aware of everything that was going on.

The legislation governing the drink-drive law and some aspects of the request for samples has been amended slightly over the past two decades, but the incident in which I had a prominent part was enacted on 6th January 1991. The legislation in force on that particular evening was the un-amended Road Traffic Act 1988. Section 7 (1) (b) of that Act does allow the police to request a specimen of blood, but Section 7 (3) (a) makes it perfectly clear that *'a specimen of blood cannot be made at a police station unless the constable making the requirement has reasonable cause to believe that for medical reasons a specimen of breath cannot be provided or should not be required'*. The Act also gives the officer permission to request a blood sample if the intoximeter equipment is unserviceable. I, thankfully, was a perfectly fit and active police officer with no known health issues, so they could apply no part of that exemption to me and the intoximeter machine was in perfect working order. If you're interested in the legal nuts and bolts, a copy of the relevant legislation is attached at Appendix 1.

One or two working colleagues who kept in touch with me in the following weeks did ask why, if I was pretty certain that I was under the limit, I didn't just provide a sample and let them analyse it. Well, as I've explained to you patient readers, I'd been quietly contemplating several issues during the half hour before I arrived at the police station. I was certain I'd been set up; I had a very strong suspicion there was some serious malpractice being contemplated and my feelings during that short period of my life were certainly anti-police. I saw that request for blood from the constable as a legal and legitimate lifeline, and I grabbed it.

Because of my refusal, the proceedings were terminated and I was charged with 'failing to supply a specimen when required without reasonable excuse', contrary to Section 7 (6) Road Traffic Act 1988. My excuse, I would maintain, was more than reasonable; the request was unlawful. Before I left the police station, the Assistant Chief Constable suspended me from duty at the direction of his superior, who was at home, probably worrying and pondering his next move.

It was gone midnight when I arrived home. Shel was still up and aware that something had occurred because my lads had told her I'd left for home before them. We sat holding hands across the kitchen table as I described the evening's events. I knew she would support me through thick or thin, but I could see deep concern and worry in her face, which was not natural for her. As we sat there, I thought of the first consultation we'd attended after Shel's operation; the doctor had been up front and told us that cancer was a terrible disease but it could be beaten. The answer was partly to adopt a positive frame of mind, live life to the full and try to avoid stress and anxiety. We went to bed and I finally got to sleep after hours of thought, most of it about how much Shel had endured since I'd joined the Police Service.

We were able to discuss the whole issue in a more settled frame of mind over the next few days, having put the turmoil of the previous Sunday evening behind us and as I knew she would, Shel made it clear that we were going to face the future as one. Michael, now almost 22, although fully appreciating the situation, had begun to mould his own future as any young man of that age would. He knew that his mother and I could handle whatever was thrown at us, so he would just offer help and support if asked for it. Brian was my biggest concern. Although now a man himself at 21, he was a serving officer in the Force and I was fearful of any backlash that could be flung his way; I knew some would have been. I clearly remember one of the discussions we had when I, most unlike my usual self, let my emotions get the better of me. He calmed me down and made it clear that I had nothing to worry about regarding his career. I should concentrate on myself and his mum; he could look after himself.

Shel and I spoke almost daily about our future when she arrived home from work, until the second Friday evening in my role as house-husband. She came into the kitchen and looking straight at me said, "Do you know what we could do? Buy a pub". I didn't answer straight away, but thought to myself 'a pub?' We stood there, our eye contact never wavering, and the invisible thought waves reverberating around the kitchen screamed "YES!" I knew the licensing laws backwards and had the temperament to stand no nonsense from disgruntled customers. Shel, by now, had several years' experience of working in the catering field and neither of us was afraid of hard work. That decision endorsed itself as the days went on because my life had become a living hell. The morning following my arrest, our house was besieged by television crews and press reporters. We were bombarded with telephone calls from people shouting abuse, and after a call from an obnoxious, drunken person at 3.30 am woke us both up, I told the family that I would only replace the receiver for half an hour each day so that they could make contact if necessary. You would have thought I'd been charged as a serial paedophile.

This bombardment, most of which came from unstable members of the community, was negated somewhat by the numerous calls of support I received from colleagues and members of the Police Authority, including the Chairman. I'm sure Mr Over would have liked to know that. This period of harassment not only convinced Shel and me that the move we'd planned was right, but that it had to be away from Cwmbran, out of the county.

Before leaving the police station on the night of my arrest, I was charged to appear at Cwmbran Magistrate's Court in three weeks' time, which would have been normal practice because there were no further enquiries to be made which would have prevented the prosecution from proceeding. The prima facie case against me was, in law, complete. However, when I consulted my solicitor, which is always a wise course of action in serious matters, and mine was certainly serious, he knew almost as much about the circumstances as me from the gossip and innuendos that had been spreading throughout the judicial system across the County for several days. He agreed with my synopsis of the defence and advised me that there was considerable alarm and discord between the Crown Prosecution Service and the police chief officers about certain procedural issues surrounding my case. My police experience told me that my case would have already been discussed in depth by all and sundry. The solicitor I chose, who, I would add, was not one of the Legal Aid hacks I used to argue with in the County's Magistrate's Courts, had been recommended by Des Jones, the magistrate's clerk who used to goad me in the witness box in front of my young wife. My solicitor could tell me, at our first meeting, that the Crown Prosecution Service was to engage a High Court barrister to present their case and although he was relatively satisfied with my account of proceedings, he thought that in the circumstances, we should seek a second opinion from counsel also.

This we did, from one of the leading lights on the Wales and Chester circuit, who practised out of chambers in Cardiff. The feedback I received through my solicitor was encouraging; the barrister agreed with our deliberations and, if I wished, he would be more than happy to present my case in court.

That was how my case proceeded. When I appeared to answer my bail after the three-week period, I was entirely satisfied that the prosecution was concerned, because they informed me in advance that they would not be in a position to proceed and would be seeking an adjournment. This would not have happened with any other member of the public; there was no valid reason to warrant the delay. However, my intuition told me that the adjournment would be granted, and it was.

To save on legal fees I represented myself at the preliminary hearing and told the magistrate, when asked, that I had no comment. My bail was extended, this time for only two weeks. To be honest, they could have kept seeking adjournments till kingdom come. Shel and I had mapped out our future, and it did not include Gwent Police. We had lots to do. Whilst I was dealing with my 'Great Matter', like the infamous King Henry VIII, I was still receiving the full pay of a Chief Superintendent, which would help support us in the interim.

Before my case was finally heard with the fairness that should be ensured by the British judicial system, the matter was adjourned twice more, still with no valid reason as far as I could see, and I finally answered the charge made against me on Monday 11th March 1992, more than two months after the alleged offence. You will note my cynical quip about the fairness of British justice, but I will draw your attention to the fact that the man who had some responsibility for ensuring the correct implementation of justice at Cwmbran Magistrate's Court was Mr John Green, the man who I am totally convinced set this whole sad affair rolling, hoping to satisfy some warped animosity he may have had against me and Gwent Police. There had been a reorganisation of Petty Sessional areas throughout Gwent about 18 months previously and Green had secured a post covering the east of the county, based in Cwmbran.

From the amount of television and newspaper coverage I had generated in preceding weeks, I knew there would be a gaggle of reporters at the court entrance to cover my arrival, so I telephoned the Sub-Divisional Commander, Superintendent Tony Watkins, the day before to ask if he would have the prisoner's back entrance door to the court opened so that Shel and I could quietly slip in unannounced. I'd know Tony Watkins for many years and in fact, had kept a watchful eye on his lad when he had served as a cadet in

Pontypool. He responded by saying that it was the least he could do; he gave me his good wishes and said he hoped to see me in the near future.

As we surreptitiously walked from one of the town's multi-storey car parks shortly before 10 am on that Monday, we could see quite a commotion at the court's entrance which I was glad I'd arranged to avoid. Shel and I arrived at the court's basement door, adjacent to the police station, only to find it locked and unattended. After a ten-minute wait, we were forced to walk to the front of the building and scramble our way through the rabble with notepads and microphones being thrust at us from all directions. None of their rude and unethical behaviour bothered me, as I had been a divisional public order commander for several years in my younger service and I gave as good as I got, but it was Shel I felt for. I will never forget the actions of that man Watkins on that morning. He probably sought guidance after receiving my request, not having the courage to act on his own volition, and of course was told not to go along with my request. That was one of several moments, the memory of which will stay with me for the rest of my life, which when combined, were responsible for me losing all faith in the Police Service and in some part, human nature itself. I understand he passed away recently and while I would be eager to pass on my condolences to his family, I myself lost no sleep.

The morning of my hearing in Cwmbran Magistrate's Court was something of an occasion for everyone apart from Shel and me. She stood by my side the whole day and even when it was prudent for me to sit next to my counsel she was only two seats away. They had reserved the vacant

Juvenile Court room so that the usual workload would not be disrupted, and in an attempt to let the world at large see that justice was being done, the 'establishment' had arranged for three magistrates and their clerk to be brought from the Cardiff City Bench to hear and adjudicate on my case. When I use the term 'establishment' it would have included the Crown Prosecution Service, but primarily arrangements would have been made by the Magistrate's Clerk's office, where John Green worked, and tacit approval of Gwent Police, viz. Mr John Over. Furthermore, to transfer magistrates to other Petty Sessional areas, especially outside their home county, is a most unusual practice and I can be certain in my own mind that these good people must have been more than a little surprised by their allocated task. In the days beforehand, they would have discussed the matter amongst themselves and asked as many questions as humanly possible to find out all about their unique selection. Being quite influential individuals themselves and asking the right questions, they would have found out all the details of my case before leaving the Capital city. That was supposed to be justice!

The hearing, with all the preliminaries, took no more than an hour and a half and my barrister was quite concise in his assertions:

I had drunk a small amount of alcohol but was not over the limit and there was no evidence to the contrary.

In the patrol car, I had provided a sample of breath but it was alleged I'd failed.

At the police station, the request for me to provide a specimen of blood was totally unlawful.

My barrister posed only two questions to the prosecution

witnesses. He asked the Assistant Chief Constable if, at any stage, I had shown any signs of being under the influence of alcohol, to which he replied that I had not, apart from a slight indication on my breath. He asked Constable Wright why I'd been requested to provide a sample of blood in contravention of the legislation and he replied "To be fair to Mr Thorne". My counsel pointed out to the Magistrates and the Clerk that it was not the officer's role to determine fairness, but to comply with the law.

I have thought long and hard over the years why on earth Constable Wright asked me to provide blood when the Act clearly states that, apart from medical reasons or defective equipment, I should have been asked for two samples of breath. I knew the constable very well. I had been his Divisional Superintendent for over 18 months and he was an experienced officer who had been carrying out the role for years. He knew the procedure backwards. I usually come to the conclusion that he took that course of action knowing it was wrong, and not knowing how much alcohol I had consumed at that time, he thought he might be giving me a lifeline. I will continue to ponder the question, and will ask him if I ever have the pleasure of meeting him again one day.

My barrister produced two witnesses in my defence, the proprietor and the barmaid from the Dorallt Inn, the two people who served me drinks that night, and both substantiated my evidence.

The magistrates retired for quite a while, at least 30 minutes, certainly enough time for a nice cup of tea, before finding me, yes, guilty. They fined me £300 with the mandatory disqualification. My barrister took Shel and me into a side room, where he expressed his disgust at the verdict and strongly advised me to appeal, saying he was confident that the judge would rule the procedure unlawful. I told him that I would let him know in due course, then attempted to leave the building. Somehow, two or three camera crews had been able to gain access to the court's interior corridor and my most vivid recollection is having the then BBC Wales reporter, to whom I'd given numerous interviews over the years at many incidents, asking for my comments whilst thrusting her microphone as close to my mouth as possible. Through the melee, I guided Shel into a corner, stood in front of her and although completely in control, 'lost my rag'. I told them all that they were a disgrace to their profession and to society in general and that I was going to say nothing. It seemed to have the desired effect, because Shel and I walked out unmolested across the three-lane carriageway of the town's one-way system and disappeared into the car park. Throughout the whole period of that unruly gathering we saw not one police officer.

We started to get our thoughts together as we meandered between the parked vehicles and my racing mind slowed down a little, as I was sure that the mob wouldn't find us now. In fact we couldn't find the car ourselves; with the bustle of the morning's events, neither of us could remember where I'd parked it. We eventually located it and sat there for several minutes in the quiet of that concrete jungle, contemplating the thousands of thoughts flashing through our minds. In that short period of solitude, I just wished our two boys had been with us.

The one thought that was foremost in my mind over the

next few days was the question of an appeal. My solicitor had also had a word with me before we faced that onslaught on leaving the building. He reiterated what the barrister had said and was quite forceful in his advice, instructing me to advise him well within the 21-day period allowed.

Our joint decision was not to appeal. Whatever the outcome of the disciplinary procedure, I was leaving the Police Service. There was no way I could work within its ranks again. I knew my defence costs to date were going to be in the region of £3,000 and the Crown Court route would be triple that. Furthermore, Shel and I had suffered tremendous pressure during the two months leading up to this day and a pending Crown Court appeal could take even longer. The only real benefit if my appeal was allowed would be the lifting of my driving disqualification, and that had to be weighed against the anguish and anxiety that the coming months would bring. I was not prepared for Shel to endure it.

I have pondered over the years why John Over instigated such devious tactics against me on that Sunday evening, after I had given the police service over 25 years' service and him, personally, since his arrival in Gwent, over 20 years of dedicated loyalty, helped in no small way by my wife and family.

I suppose human nature contains many unsavoury traits, and we all know that acts of betrayal date back more than 2000 years, to that man Judas. I have mentioned much earlier in this story that I deduced, shortly after he came to Gwent, that John Over seemed to have one main concern, and that was the reputation and well-being of himself, to the disregard of everything and everyone else. The information given to him by that man Green could have been dealt with in a far more appropriate manner. However, I know that John Over was far from the upstanding, integral pillar of society that he would have everyone believe.

Even when Shel and I had reached the safe haven of our home, we were pestered for the following two days by television crews who were encamped in our close; some reporters hoped beyond hope to get a response when they rang the doorbell, but the majority were content with taking a few shots of our house and waiting in anticipation of catching some movement on film. We just sat tight until something else occurred which they thought would grab the headlines in the evening news.

I knew that my involvement with the Police Service had not come to an abrupt end with that hour or so in court. They had yet to drag me through the disciplinary procedure, and after their deliberately protracted activities before the court hearing, I was determined to play it at my pace now. I knew the Chief Constable would be intent on having me removed from the Force; if I were to continue he'd feel as if he had a stick of dynamite in his ranks. Several senior officer friends who I was still in almost daily contact with held the view that the circumstances did not warrant my dismissal, but the decision had been made – Shel and I were to start a new life.

The Chief Constable would definitely want the disciplinary procedure to be completed as soon as possible, to get the Force back on an even keel. In effect, all he had to do was have me appear at police HQ before a presiding officer, have a presenting officer produce a copy of the Court

Register and he would have achieved his aim. I would be dealt with under the Discipline Code, for 'Having been found guilty of a Criminal Offence'.

The first thing I did was to visit my doctor, Dr Sharma. I had not been sleeping well for some weeks, and he diagnosed anxiety. He gave me some medication to help the small hours drift by and a sick note to produce to the manhunters at HQ. I turned my attention to becoming self-employed.

CHAPTER 17

To become self-employed in the licensed trade, you really have to purchase your own free house so that you are not hampered by any terms and conditions set by any other party. The first step in our venture was to meet up with a man called Alwyn Morgan. Alwyn had been Shel's boss in charge of the company's property estate when she had worked at Rhymney Brewery, and the advice he gave us was invaluable. We spent a good two hours with him at one of the free houses he serviced in the Goytre area. He told us that before we considered any other aspect of buying a likely hostelry, we should tour the immediate area and count chimney pots – chimney pots mean houses, houses mean people and people mean regular customers.

We started to scour the adverts, principally in the brochure issued weekly by Sidney Phillips, the commercial estate agents, who were recognised nationally as experts on the purchase and disposal of all types of licensed premises. I believe it was the first time I'd used our small study for its intended purpose; I would spend most of each day poring over facts and figures about likely premises and making lists so that Shel and I could concur or discard them each evening. Shel was still busily employed at the Police Training Centre receiving all the support and understanding we could wish for.

After lengthy discussions, we both hit on the type of premises and business we'd like, which was probably the epitome of everyone's ideal local hostelry; olde worlde, charming, inviting and providing pleasant service with a good selection of liquid refreshment. Shel was adamant she wanted to provide food, which had been her forte for several years. We were aware that the country's financial climate was not conducive to the self-employed at that time. Interest rates were climbing above 10% and there was an unusually large number of country pubs closing for all kinds of reasons, but we took the view that it could therefore be the time to seek out a prime deal.

We must have discussed hundreds of adverts in the following weeks and made the decision to visit a few that we thought were possibilities. The first was near Betws-y-Coed in North Wales, but first impressions dashed any initial enthusiasm we had. Shel described it as tall, thin and shabby and it was much further from the famous tourist-attracting waterfalls than the advert would have had us believe. We visited a possibility in Castlemartin, Pembrokeshire and one that really caught our attention in Salcombe, Devon. It was the Ferry Inn, a large imposing building right on the water's edge nestled over the estuary.

We made all of these visits unannounced, posing as customers to avoid any special preparations or treatment. The Ferry Inn was certainly in a position to attract customers, in a much sought-after seaside setting, but I had concerns that during the peak summer months a substantial number of staff would be required to cope, and I imagined scores of youngsters trying to consume as much liquor as possible before staggering back to their caravans or other abodes. Too much hassle!

We took a ride into mid-Wales one weekend with a few premises in mind, most of which were merely en route, but the object of our day out was to visit the Lamb Inn in the village of Kerry, about four miles to the east of Newtown. Although the building itself was lacklustre and we both had concerns about the lack of chimney pots in the area, the proprietors had created what appeared a very pleasing bed and breakfast outfit. It was a five-bedroomed property with four of them decorated in a colour-themed fashion for paying guests. Shel was quite taken with the set-up and it was the only time we identified ourselves on an initial visit, primarily to inspect the accommodation. However, we decided it was not what we'd originally planned and reluctantly kicked it into touch.

Shel had arranged to take a couple of odd days' leave for a few weeks, either a Friday or a Monday, so that we could go gallivanting around Britain on long weekends, searching hopefully to cement our future, and that month or so really reignited our relationship. We were in each other's company for longer than we had been for years and thoroughly enjoying it. It made me realise just how much of our lives had been surrendered to Gwent Police.

Our next expedition, which ultimately proved to be our last, was to a country pub in Bromyard, Herefordshire. The town is on the A44, 14 miles north-east of Hereford, but I had to refer to my book of maps before setting off because I'd never heard of it. The tourist board described it as Herefordshire's most unspoilt market town, a jewel in the Downs, the name given to the acres of common land surrounding it, and it had a population of about 4,500. We knew from the advert that it was not trading and was being sold by Barclays Bank, who had repossessed the property. We found it nestled on the edge of a meadow which gently sloped down to the banks of the River Frome. It was shaded by the rambling slopes of the Downs and just a hop, skip and a jump from the town itself, which was in clear view, with St Peter's Church, of Norman origin, set nicely in the centre of the picture.

Now the pub. It was called the Holly Tree, an old stone building with a large rendered extension at the rear. It looked run-down, dismal, dejected and forlorn, and that was just the outside. We had arranged to meet the bank's representative to afford us access, and the inside was even worse. It was dirty – no, filthy – dark, drab and dank. I remember seeing, perched on the bar, a half-empty jar of pickled eggs which were trying to spring to life with the aid of some aged green mould. Shel and I slowly walked around without saying a word. We didn't have to try to soak up the atmosphere; it hit us. And yet, there was something about it; I just didn't know what.

As we stood in the car park watching the man who had secured the premises drive into the distance, Shel admitted that she had the same feeling. The whole plot, building, car park and small garden were an utter mess but somehow, we could both see a hint of potential. The bar and lounge areas had character although a little forlorn, and the large extension at the rear, which had a new commercial catering kitchen attached, could provide ample space for dining or other entertainment. The three-bedroomed living accommodation, with redecoration, could prove suitable.

As we stood there, we were joined by a passing member of the West Mercia Constabulary, a Constable Wood, who, like any good copper, wanted to know who we were and what we were doing on his patch. I was eager to engage him in conversation, but like a good ex-copper, I wanted to know all about this abandoned public house without giving too much away about myself and Shel. It appeared that the previous owner, who apparently had no idea of running a business, especially one selling alcohol, had added the extension about six months earlier and instead of increasing profits it had become a millstone round his neck, hence the bank's repossession.

As we drove home, I became convinced that we could make it work. I could inject the muscle-power with the help of a few tools, filler and paint and I was more than satisfied that Shel would inject the heart and soul it so desperately needed. However, we needed to return home to Cwmbran; Gwent Police and I had to meet one more time.

I was feeling a lot better thanks to Shel diverting my attention and Dr Sharma keeping a watchful eye on me, so I let it be known that I was ready to catch whatever John Over wanted to throw at me. The date was set for my disciplinary hearing at HQ and I found out that the Chief

Constable of North Wales, Mr David Owen, had been appointed presiding officer. In normal circumstances, it would be the officer's own Chief Constable who sat in judgement, which is why all Deputy Chief Constables take overall charge of internal investigations, but in my case, I had been working far too closely with John Over for several months, so it was obvious he had to try and demonstrate impartiality and it had to be a chief officer from another force.

However, if things should be impartial, then let them be seen to be so. This is where I will mention that third application for promotion I made to another force. Less than 12 months before my hearing I had been interviewed in depth by Mr David Owen, the Chief Constable of North Wales, in his office in Colwyn Bay, as he was considering appointing me as a Chief Superintendent in his force. I had been placed on the shortlist, along with another Gwent officer (who, incidentally, was subsequently appointed) and on my return John Over called me to his office to advise me that I was David Owen's second choice. My initial selection for interview meant that Mr Owen would have had every detail of my service record and without doubt, would have discussed me in depth with John Over before my trip to his office.

The second point to be aired; it was a publicly-known fact that the Chief Constables of North Wales and Gwent led Welsh forces, were roughly the same age, and it was natural, if not desirable, that both working in the Principality, should be harmonious working colleagues. What was not so widely known was that they were also very friendly on a personal basis, a fact that John Over made clear to his top executive team, of which I was one. I was told in confidence, two days before my hearing by a close colleague of similar rank to myself, that David Owen was travelling to Cwmbran the following day and was to be entertained by Mr and Mrs Over whilst staying at their home. There were 44 other chief constables outside Wales, all of whom would have been far more impartial. I was, and always will be, convinced that John Over chose the Chief Constable of North Wales because he knew it would help to achieve the outcome he desired.

I stood before David Owen represented by a solicitor financed by the Superintendent's Association to speak on my behalf, and it took no more than 20 minutes of official claptrap before the man who John Over had asked to come and do his work said "You are required to resign". I arrived home 30 minutes later to be greeted by Shel, who had arranged a day's leave, and the rest of our lives began.

We spent the following two weekends in and around Bromyard. We left on the Friday evening as soon as Shel could wangle herself away from work, and spent two nights in the Travel Inn right next to Hereford racecourse, which allowed us two full days to scour the area and its amenities and assess the points which would affect our proposed business. We visited almost every shop in Bromyard, hoping to gain as much information as possible from conversations that Shel would try to encourage, and visited every public house within a three-mile radius. To be honest, I was a bit concerned about the number of drinking establishments in the town itself. However, on reflection, I became satisfied that they were just 'watering holes', most of them attracting the less desirable individuals, which would not help them to attract a wider customer base.

The Holly Tree was about 500 yards from the edge of the

town, which I thought would enable us to make it into something a little different. It became clear that this particular area of Herefordshire was attractive to tourists, especially 'Brummies' coming from the metropolis of the Midlands to seek solace in the tranquil countryside. In fact we found a large caravan park only two miles up the road, which attracted hundreds of temporary residents from Easter right through to the autumn when the evening light diminished. To put a little icing on the cake, as it were, the pub's rear boundary fence abutted several acres of open land, which housed two pitches used by the town's amateur football club. Surely there would be a few spectators who would bring us custom on a Saturday afternoon? On our way home after the second weekend, we made the decision. This was 'the one'.

At this point I will mention one small thing about my wife. Most people who knew Shel well, her family and close friends, were aware that she hated driving. It took me months and months to persuade her to have lessons and she only succumbed after the two boys were born, and only then because I arranged for a good friend, Bob Hitchins, a police driving instructor, to impart his knowledge. She was quite happy tootling back and forth to work in her immaculate Fiesta, but no further.

As I've explained, Shel and I were discussing our future within days of my arrest, because of the circumstances. We did exchange a few words before embarking on our nationwide tour and Shel reluctantly agreed, with the proviso that I refrain from any type of comment on her driving. I duly complied and throughout our journeys she impressed me with her tenacity.

There followed a few anxious weeks of negotiating with the Birmingham branch of Barclays Bank, who were selling the property, and they eventually accepted (with the usual urgency of an organisation who didn't really care whether they sold the place or not) our offer of £100,000, some £20,000 less than the advertised price. We had secured a purchaser keen to buy our house, but there was another anxious period when we had to negotiate a business loan from our bank because our mortgage company would not allow an advance on commercial premises. We both let out a sigh of relief when our bank manager (yes, we actually had one to talk to then) happily agreed, but not before spending an afternoon travelling to Bromyard to satisfy himself of the feasibility of the project.

We started to formulate a list of jobs which we thought were essential before we started trading. Although 75% came under the general heading of cleaning and decoration, there was one major issue which I knew had to be tackled; the unpalatable subject of sewage. Although the pub was only 500 yards from the town, which obviously had the benefit of mains services, our newly-acquired home was technically in the country and serviced by a Calor gas tank and a cesspit. The gas was no big problem, but although a cesspit had been adequate in years gone by, even when it had been turned into a roadside inn during the 19th century, I was concerned it would not be sufficient to cope with the use which Shel and I envisaged. I got several quotes for a 'bio' sewage system, large enough to deal with all the waste and foul water that would be generated both domestically and commercially. This involved the installation of an underground tank on the periphery of the car park, which the experts said would treat the water to a standard good enough to drink. I never actually tested that claim, but it was certainly good enough for Welsh Water to certify it acceptable to be discharged into the nearby river (I was also surprised, like you, that Welsh Water covered so much of England).

Another major expenditure was crockery, cutlery and catering equipment. The building was left with very few fixtures and fittings, so we really had to start from scratch. With Shel still working I spent time attending auctions and, quite often, when discussing the day's activities over our evening meal, I was quizzed and often castigated about why on earth I'd bought this or that.

We didn't see a great deal of our sons at this time. They were both still single with no serious attachments, much to the dismay of their mother. Brian was serving on the beat in Newport and had just moved into his own house, not too far from us in Cwmbran, and Michael was sharing a flat in Newport, still employed in an administrative capacity at Her Majesty's Passport Office. Actually, my claim to fame some months earlier, when I had to renew my passport for a holiday in the South of France, was that the signature on it as the issuing officer was that of Michael. I still have it today as a keepsake.

One evening when Michael visited us, he broached the subject of our impending move and asked if he could come along to help run the business. He was then aged 22 and explained how bored he was with his pen-pushing role. His mother was quietly delighted, but I had reservations that he was reading too much into this new role he saw and whilst I was as careful and diplomatic as possible, I tried to put him off and did my best to point out the pitfalls and disadvantages. This would not be employment in one of the latest nightspots with all the excitement that offered a young man just out of his teens, but a boring job with long, tedious hours, with sometimes nothing to entertain you but the ticking of the clock. He was having none of it, so with more than a little persuasion from his mum, I embraced the idea and included him in all future discussions.

CHAPTER 18

We were now owners of a pub which was still closed, although the repayments on the business loan would have to be met every month. My last payday from the Police Service was 30 April 1991 and we now had to rely on our contingency fund, a small amount of savings and Shel's meagre salary from the Home office. I did in fact, receive several tax rebates over the next few months, which helped. I had no idea why and never questioned it.

It was now the first week of May, so things had to move up a gear. We decided that I would encamp in our new property in Bromyard and Shel would stay in the house in Cwmbran so that she could continue working to help the financial situation. She joined me each weekend to get stuck in with the cleaning, and it seemed to me that we were spending most of her wages on sugar soap! I set up camp in one corner of the restaurant with my bed assembled from a lot of bench seating I'd bid for at an auction. I surprised myself with the amount of work I got through working at it full time and with Shel's input every weekend we soon had it looking something like a place that the public would want to enter.

There was obviously some work that had to be undertaken by craftsmen, such as electrics and gas, which had to be certified under the myriad of legislation that we had to comply with. Wherever possible I employed local tradesmen, which paid off when a number of them and their families became regulars in the fullness of time. There was one issue that came to light in the form of a leak in the lead flashing on the roof over the toilets, which seemed to unearth more problems the more we delved into it. For this particular task, we engaged a friend of Shel's nephew, who also contributed a considerable amount of graft. Apart from these two, all the workmen we took on were from Bromyard itself.

My monastic existence lasted for approximately six weeks, after which you could see quite a transformation in the building, indeed the site as a whole, and I became concerned that we now had to concentrate on preparing the business launch. That proved to be more time-consuming and stressful than the physical side of things. There were menus and prices to compile, suppliers to organise, a suitable brewery to approach and negotiate with and an opening night to consider, which would need to be impressive. In the light of all these thoughts and perceived problems, we decided that Shel would leave the Police Training Centre and embark on a new full-time career alongside me. Michael took a similar step, and his first job in the family business was to freshen up the paint on the outside of the whole building, which was no small task. It suited me down to the ground because I've always had an aversion to heights – well, certainly since our honeymoon flight across the Channel.

I was surprised and obviously delighted when I received an energetic response from the breweries I approached; all were keen to do business and anything I asked one company to provide, another offered more. I would have loved to have struck a deal with Rhymney Breweries, Shel's former employer, but we were just too far out of their territory. Although cost was an important factor when purchasing our beer, consideration had to be given to the palates of the people who were going to drink it in this area of Herefordshire. I also had to bear in mind that I had learned that a fair percentage of future customers would hail from the West Midlands. At the last hurdle it was between Ansells and Bass, both brewed in the Birmingham area, and my final choice was Ansells, partly due to the discount offered, but also because they undertook to completely refurbish my cellar and provide new signage for the building free of charge.

The house sale went through relatively smoothly, thank goodness. We had enough to concern ourselves with our new acquisition, but there was one issue I needed to resolve before leaving Cwmbran. On our way home from town on the evening before we had arranged to move, I had Shel pull up outside John Green's house. His car was on the drive and I knew he would be aware it was me before I'd reached his front door – his wife would have had her radar trained on me through the front curtains. He came to the door with his wife a few feet behind him, so they must have been expecting me. Without any preamble, I told him that I was totally satisfied it was he who had visited the Chief Constable with his malicious message and that he was nothing but a 'jealous wimp'. I turned my head towards his wife and said that I actually felt some sympathy for her for being married to him. Green coloured up but neither of them said a word. Without any more ado I walked back to Shel and we drove along the close to our house. Some might say my behaviour was a little churlish, but I needed him to know, and I felt just a tad better.

We all beavered away over the ensuing weeks and I suppose we could have continued for the next six months, because in our new and unique situation, with naïve business minds, every task we completed seemed capable of improvement. However, during our daily discussions we came to the conclusion that enough was enough. Our financial reserves were running low and it was important that this hostelry started to provide an income. We analysed the tasks that needed finishing and set an achievable timescale before setting our opening date for the first Friday in July. If unexpected glitches or other problems arose, then we would just have to deal with them in time.

I'd had one more essential task, perhaps the most important aspect of our purchase, and that was to apply for a Protection Order from the local magistrates which was, in reality, the licence to allow us to sell intoxicating liquor with the requirement to have my name emblazoned above the front door. The local police in any area have a duty to ensure that all licensed premises under their jurisdiction are run in a law-abiding manner and that the licensee is a 'fit and proper' person. Well, they certainly did in 1991 before they started to abdicate their responsibilities due to an apparent lack of manpower. The magistrates therefore required the local police commander to air his views on the suitability of any new applicant appearing before their bench. I'd had a very bitter experience of one injustice and I wasn't going to let that happen again. I made arrangements to meet with the Chief Inspector at Leominster to put him in the picture and ask if I had any cause to be concerned about pressure being put on him from his supervisors. He assured me that there would be no objections raised at court; he was pleased to see the Holly Tree being passed into good hands and hoped to sample our wares when he was in the area.

We didn't advertise our opening night widely, but kept our invitations to word of mouth. We made a general list, which included family and friends, and I was particularly pleased to see some of Shel's former colleagues take the trouble to travel the considerable distance from Cwmbran. We asked our neighbours in a small group of houses nearby and the occupants of several farms within about a mile radius. It turned out most of these had large families, but it was important to include them because I had assessed over the preceding months that they could well become the bread and butter of our business. I was right; within weeks of opening, we started to receive visits every Friday and Saturday night from a sizable group of Young Farmer's Club members who decided that ours was the venue where they would get fuelled up before the weekend's activities.

Everyone we'd employed to work on the project was invited as a gesture of thanks, and a few employees of the local newspaper, who were keen to prepare a full-page advertising feature the following week. My brewery representative came, along with two of his managers, kindly donating two kegs of best bitter, and to round the gathering off, the Mayor of Bromyard agreed to carry out the opening ceremony. Actually Mr David Cave, The Mayor, could have been there in his capacity as a close neighbour – we were now living in exalted company. Shel, with the help of her family, prepared a superb buffet which, when laid out in the restaurant, looked as professional as anything I'd seen. The centrepiece was a large dressed salmon. The provision of a buffet was the main reason we restricted those present to personally invited guests; an open invitation would have attracted punters from far and wide, enticed by the free food and with no intention whatsoever of bringing us custom in future months.

We had opened our establishment to the big wide world and our first evening was a resounding success, but the coming weeks would really tell. The first month or so went reasonably well, with weekly takings in accord with our pre-determined business plan; we just had to ensure that our gross and net profits were in line. Our Sunday lunches thankfully proved popular and, as with other eateries, they tended to concentrate quite a large number of customers into a relatively short period of time, making sufficient staff to provide acceptable customer service a priority. Michael seemed to cope with the liquid bar sales adequately, with me, as they say 'floating', trying to keep all the strings pulled together, but it became obvious that Shel needed help serving in the restaurant. We took on three part-time waitresses on a casual basis, all recommended by word of mouth, who were rostered to work set days, but they were all quite happy to respond to a telephone call if an emergency arose. We took on two more as the months went on and fortunately, they proved to be a grand bunch of girls. We never had a moment's trouble with any of them and they would respond to any request in the interests of the business. I am quite convinced that it was in no small measure due to the way Shel treated them.

One was Lisa, 16 years old and the daughter of a local farmer, who was also a regular customer, and she tended to be excitable and a little bit ditsy. I say that with no slur on her character, because she was a lovely young girl. However, when Shel broached the subject of employment with her (after being approached by her father), Lisa was at pains to say that it was only to be a casual arrangement because she really wanted 'to be a model'. I can hear her saying it now, in that heart-warming voice that so suited her character, which has given me pleasant memories over the years whenever I think of it.

The other area of the business where it became clear that we required assistance was the cleaning. In my previous role, it had become abundantly clear to me how uncooperative and disruptive a fair proportion of the general public can be and in the pub, it became just as clear how dirty they are too. How such a supposedly advanced and educated form of creature as a human being can make such a mess eating a meal, taking a drink or paying a visit to the toilet was, until I'd seen it for myself, beyond comprehension. I believe that it was me who nagged Shel to enlist some help, and several applicants replied to an advertisement Shel had placed in one of the town's newsagents. We chose three to interview, arranged for one afternoon after closing time, and offered the post to Gillian Greaves who, incidentally, was the wife of a self-employed upholsterer in the town who we had engaged to fit the bench seating I had used as my bed for all those weeks. That connection had no influence whatsoever on our decision to take Gill on. Shel thought she was a capable and pleasant young woman and I was impressed by her honest answer when I asked her why she wanted the job. She told me "I need the money".

It was not intentionally arranged, but we opened our doors to the public right in the middle of the town's busy period. Shel would report that she saw large numbers of tourists in the town during her morning escape, when she would take the opportunity of shopping for the day's fresh produce, and it seemed that we attracted our fair share of their custom before they left the area. I was wary during the early weeks about the more undesirable characters that might grace our doorstep, because this type of individual will always test out any new licensee arriving in the area. We had a few, but they were given short shrift, especially if the information about them I gleaned from our regulars gave me cause for concern.

One idea we implemented came to fruition through our joint love of music. We were both brought up in the 50s, and the 60s saw us right in the midst of the British pop era, so we had a professional music system installed and Shel would spend hours of what I called her 'upstairs time' condensing all our suitable records onto cassette tapes, which we would then play almost every evening in both bars. There were some afternoons when our private lounge resembled the Decca recording studio! The pub's music became quite a talking point with customers, and many were attracted to spend their evenings listening to, and very often singing along with, the songs of their youth, which also had the side benefit of keeping the yobs away. And yes, I did cough up for a performing rights licence!

It wasn't long before the static caravaners came to suss us out and we attracted a group of families who made us their destination most evenings. Because the majority of caravans were used as weekend and holiday homes by their owners, we would see the same folk throughout the whole season.

One of the more welcome surprises we received towards the end of August was an approach from a Mr Edgar Whitely, who one Friday evening asked if he could have a word with me in private. Edgar owned a bed and breakfast business in town, but he spoke to me in his capacity as Chairman of the Bromyard Town Football Club. He explained that they were in the local Hereford league and played their home games on the ground behind the pub almost every other Saturday afternoon and the occasional Wednesday. They had invested in recent years by building a small pavilion, but it only provided players with changing facilities. He asked me, with some trepidation, whether I would allow both teams to visit the Holly Tree for post-match drinks. Before I could utter a word, he assured me that the club would take every measure to prevent any unsociable behaviour. I explained to him that I had other customers to think of, with which he fully concurred, but I had no wish to be a doom-monger to the lads, so I was prepared to give it a trial for two games and then appraise the situation. He shook my hand and returned to the bar to finish his drink. I, meanwhile, nonchalantly walked through the door to our private area, closed it slowly behind me, and gleefully pulling two imaginary lavatory chains with my clenched fists exclaimed "YES!"

The following Saturday afternoon I warned the locals using the bar and suggested to one or two of the older gents, who I thought might take umbrage, that they might be a little more comfortable in the lounge. And then we were hit – 22 players and several officials descended on us within the space of about 20 minutes, with a nucleus staying for about an hour and stragglers until about 6 pm. Actually, as the months went by, there were occasions when I had to suggest to three or four of the younger element that it was time for them to leave so that we could clear up and prepare the bar area for our evening customers. Experience gave me a cut-off time of 6.30 pm, and no one ever complained.

For that first game Shel decided, probably out of the goodness of her heart (although I considered it a loss leader to secure their future custom), to provide our visitors with bowls of freshly-cooked chips and chunks of crusty bread, and if my memory serves me correctly, as time went on, for special occasions such as cup matches and so forth, she also provided bowls of sausages. Bromyard Town must have had considerable success and climbed two or three divisions in as many years, because Shel always seemed to provide bowls of sausages. The lads loved the gesture, while the officials were most appreciative, and they always presented Shel with a big bouquet of flowers at Christmas.

After we had been trading for about four months, I was conscious that Michael wasn't really at ease living in this backwater of Herefordshire. On occasion, perhaps too often,

I would vent my feelings and tell him I expected more drive and vigour from him. I wanted him to take more of a leading role in taking the business forward, but he really was not happy. The only time he'd show any sparkle was when he was serving the football teams on Saturday afternoons. Shel had to try to mediate over our increasingly frequent arguments. I recall that it was only a few days after opening when a customer, who in time became a very good friend, asked me why on earth I'd moved to that part of Herefordshire. I was honest in my reply that I thought the area was very pretty. His response was, "Pretty it may be, but I've lived here man and boy. They say Britain is 10 years behind America – well, take it from me, Bromyard is 10 years behind Britain!"

In the fullness of time I came to completely agree with him, but I was then 47 and in many respects, I liked it; Michael was 22, and he didn't. I had tried to point out these pitfalls to him when he'd first suggested his move and I suppose that was what really annoyed me. However, Shel supported him as only a mother could and we parted company. Fortunately, he got his old job back at the Passport Office.

Michael's exodus back to the bright lights of Newport left me with a problem. Although both public and lounge bars were served from a central servery, I could never have handled both on my own during busy periods and it was essential that I provided adequate service for the football entourage. To make things worse from a staffing point of view, Nola Moses, the bubbly and energetic lady secretary of the football club, had tipped me the wink that I was going to be asked if the second team, which was about to be formed, could also use the premises. That not only meant that we could look forward to a game every week, but the club had two pitches and that could mean, with two home games, well over 50 people every Saturday afternoon. Shel would have to double her order of sausages!

It was essential I took on someone to serve behind the bar and I knew I had to be careful with my selection. Without being over dramatic, I was a retired police officer and knew that it was probably the easiest place to lose profit. With a less than totally honest employee, the business could suffer dramatically from misappropriated cash or free drinks – to put it another way, thieving.

Before I took steps to achieve my goal, Shel suggested that I should ask Gill. She had approached her some weeks earlier about the possibility of waitressing and had received a resounding "no thanks", but Shel had a feeling that she'd be happy to give bar work a go. Shel asked her, she would, and she did. She took to it like a duck to water and I had no qualms about her loyalty. She was able to keep the few noisy footballers in order because she knew them all and they were well aware that she probably knew their wives or parents. The last thing they wanted was complaints drifting back about their behaviour.

Gill became so competent behind the bar that during the quiet hours mid-week I was able to sneak away for the odd game of golf with neighbouring licensees who I'd become acquainted with. I got to know quite a few fairly quickly after being whisked away by the captain of our cribbage team to make up the numbers at some of our away matches. I was also often absent on Friday mornings, far more than I had envisaged, attending court in Leominster applying for extensions to cater for the increasing number of functions we were being asked to arrange. We had also been asked by one or two local factories to provide the occasional outside bar for their social activities. This left Shel to run the ship with Gill's assistance, and as far as I am aware, there was never any problem. Because of this close working relationship, they really bonded, and as time went on they became very good friends. We did receive visits from family, as I will unveil shortly, when Shel could catch up on domestic issues, but there's nothing like someone outside family, who you can trust implicitly and talk to about those innermost thoughts that you need to air. I now know that as time progressed, the two of them would occasionally discuss my shortcomings and for Shel to do that, Gill must have been someone she felt she could confide in.

One lazy sunny afternoon, during the first full summer we'd spent at the Holly Tree, there came a loud rap on the door. I was annoyed at the disturbance, as I had only just locked up after the lunchtime session and Shel and I were planning to spend a little time together in the privacy of our lounge, which didn't happen very often. However, as I pulled the door ajar my face must have lit up with delight. Standing there was ex-Superintendent Derek Helps, my loyal and trusted friend, who had been my companion in that tenacious and psychological battle against that tyrant of a Deputy Chief Constable. He had heard that we had moved away, and on the spur of the moment he and his wife had decided to seek us out. Shel knew and liked Derek and along with other memories, she recalled that police social dinner/dance when they had attempted to perform a foxtrot with Derek having two left feet. We reminisced for more than an hour over afternoon tea and as we waved them off I wished, as I had before, that more people in this crazy world could be like him. Sadly, Derek passed away in 1996, but not before he'd accomplished his ambition of taking an extended holiday in Australia, which he used to drool about over coffee in the office.

CHAPTER 19

Almost the first thing we did after moving into the Holly Tree was to register with Dr Boddington and his team at Bromyard surgery. It was of the utmost importance that someone should monitor Shel on a regular basis considering the medication she'd been prescribed. The doctor advised her at one of her visits, probably after studying her records, that in view of the change of practice, he thought a hospital check would be prudent, for his benefit, if not for Shel's. Cheltenham General Hospital was the regional cancer centre covering Herefordshire and the Cotswolds, but the general practitioner who was dealing with Shel at that time thought it prudent that she should continue to visit her original specialists in Cardiff, as they would have much more intimate knowledge of her condition. Arrangements were made, and on the day Shel and I journeyed back to our homeland, regretfully closing the restaurant for lunch, Gill quite happily took charge of our hostelry and dealt with all the liquid refreshments.

Shel was her usual calm, collected self during the whole afternoon, while I sat, as always, full of trepidation. She was seen by a new young registrar who, it seemed, had been recently assigned to the medical team, but he appeared as competent and thorough as they always were. The examination and checks carried out on Shel during these hospital visits could take anything up to three hours, and I was always asked to keep myself busy. There was time to take a stroll in the pleasant grounds surrounding the hospital, followed by at least two cups of coffee. The consultation always ended with a short discussion, to which I was always invited, and on this occasion, the young doctor seemed to be unusually upbeat. He appreciated that Shel had been what he termed 'living under a cloud' for some considerable time and previous tests had indicated that the cancer was in remission. It was his considered opinion that everyone's efforts over the years had proved successful and the disease had been eradicated.

We turned and looked at each other, our eyes flooding with a mixture of excitement and relief. I shook the doctor's hand with some relish and as we walked along the corridor towards the front entrance, we put our arms around each other and I swear we both did a little skip. The drive home seemed to take just minutes, we were so engrossed in conversation. However, back at the ranch, as they say, there was work to be done.

In 1991, we began trading at the Holly Tree as the first week of July began to sink over the horizon, only about seven weeks before an event Shel and I would come to quietly dread every year of our tenure – Bromyard Folk Festival. We moved to Herefordshire having undertaken what I thought was substantial research and planning concerning our venture, but we somehow managed to display a fair degree of incompetence about this festival, which had been held every year since 1967, attracting over 3,000 dedicated music lovers each day over its three-day span. It was held in the ten-acre field lying alongside the River Frome, only about 300 yards from our pub, with a large percentage of those attending camping in surrounding fields, with recompense to local farmers of course. Apart from the more devoted ones submerging themselves in non-stop folk melodies with the occasional tinge of jazz, just about everyone took part in one long drinking session. When local police officers demanded the closure of entrance doors of the town's public houses as soon after closing time as they could accomplish, festival goers would take as long as possible to slowly drift homewards and the thousands who were destined to spend the night stargazing would ensure that they'd bought sufficient quantities of intoxicants to see them through until dawn.

Intoxicating liquor was not the only thing consumed to blur the senses during the three-day festival, and I'm sure West Mercia Constabulary had drafted in drug squad officers from all over their territory. I was fully aware that small amounts of cannabis were being smoked in my public bar each evening, but when you're confronted with the number of customers we were dealing with, the issue of public order and personal safety was foremost in my mind and I had no intention of provoking an argument which could get out of hand. What was and was not an entitlement to an individual citizen was no longer my concern or any responsibility of mine.

That first year we were totally unprepared for the onslaught. Not only were we left short of staff for the odd hour or two, but I'd totally underestimated the amount of beer I needed in my weekly order. In fact, I had to dash to my cash-and-carry on two out of the three days to supplement the cellar. It wasn't that Shel and I were completely ignorant of the festival's existence, because Gill, along with all our locals, gave us warning a few weeks beforehand. It was the sheer volume of custom that took us by surprise. On the Saturday night, the revellers were 'packed to the gunnels' as the saying goes, and customers we chatted to during the weekend came from all over the United Kingdom. On one occasion, we found that an energetic young man who was enticing people into the bar with his fiddle playing had arranged a two-month trip from Australia to coincide with the festivities.

We were, however, fully armed for the following year. There is no better way of learning than by experience, and I was able to stock up with sufficient quantities at my trade prices. We also closed the restaurant for the weekend from midday on the Friday because nobody, but nobody, within five miles of Bromyard would consider trying to take a sedate meal whilst this celebration of music was in progress. However, Shel did utilise the space up until noon each day by offering the traditional cooked breakfast for those who'd managed to get a little shut-eye and were fuelling up for another full day. I think our highest morning total reached about 95, and our bank manager was most appreciative on the Monday morning!

As any licensee worth his salt will tell you, Christmas is the time to take the farmers' advice and 'make hay while the sun shines', and I had plenty of farmers to talk to. We embarked on a small advertising campaign which proved fruitful in securing several pre-season social functions. I'd envisaged the possibilities and within weeks of moving in I had arranged for a neighbour, who was a self-employed carpet fitter, to lay a small wooden dance floor in the restaurant so we could have a disco and our customers could really let their hair down. As the months went by we also arranged buffet dances, but these had to be carefully planned because financial loss and profit were keenly balanced.

There were no such fiscal considerations when it came to Christmas Day itself. We placed a small advertisement in the town's free advertising publication and we were fully booked, with all deposits received before the end of November. Shel prepared the usual Christmas fare with, I recall, two choices of meat and of course, the compulsory vegetarian dish. This diverse dietary requirement must of course be totally accepted by anyone contemplating the catering trade, but I did feel for Shel quite often because a local girl who was a regular visitor to functions was often accompanied by a male friend who was a dedicated vegan. Shel had many frantic moments when his pending visits were announced and would try and extract some earth-shattering menu suggestions from Gill, and sometimes me. It would however, usually end up being a nut roast, which in fairness, he always said was delightful. Together with the premium charge for Christmas Day table d'hôte, an extraordinary amount of wine and bar sales, it proved a very successful 24 hours, again to the delight of the bank manager.

I've mentioned that the caravan park, which was only some three miles along the Stourport Road, provided us with most welcome custom. Well, it was owned by a middle-aged couple of Dutch extraction, Mr and Mrs Kopechne, who, I would guess, had bought the site as an investment and had no real intention of providing any kind of labour towards its upkeep. To run the on-site social club, hey had employed a couple who, though not actually born within the melodic tolls of Bow, were from the Greater London area. The social club only opened in the evenings, so Terry and Brenda, along with some of their punters, would visit us most lunchtimes for refreshments and also give us the pleasure of their company on the evenings when they could arrange cover for their own establishment. They really were a match made in heaven; they enjoyed good company, which they obviously found under our roof, and although they sometimes had 'one over the eight', like everyone, they were never, ever a moment's trouble. They seemed to get along really well with Shel and often brought tapes of music for her to copy. Like some other customers, they were always happy to strike up a conversation with the man whose name was above the front door, but it was as if I had a gossamer-winged sign above my head reading 'ex-police officer', because they always seemed to have an air of apprehension when Shel was occupied elsewhere.

There seemed nothing unusual the evening when Tel, as he was known, came in with Brenda and brought along their employers for a sociable couple of hours. The game of quoits was quite popular in the bar, but in addition to testing his skill, I found Mr Kopechne to be most interested in my establishment; what kind of trading terms we had with the brewery, how many employees we had and how long we'd been in the trade. These queries weren't posed as direct questions, but came out in the course of conversation, so I thought no more of it, imagining he was just trying to extract some useless information from a competitor.

Some weeks later, our right-hand lady, Gill, stepped into the breach once more and after closing the restaurant at 9 pm, Shel and I visited the caravan park social club at the invitation of Brenda and Tel. Our findings surprised me somewhat. The large room was clean and tidy, but had no atmosphere whatsoever. There were formica-topped tables and upright chairs placed at slightly offset angles in an attempt to give the area some ambience and atmosphere, but to me, it made matters worse. It highlighted to me what an uninviting room it was and reminded me of a supermarket cafeteria. No wonder their leisure seekers came down the road to the Holly Tree.

Brenda and Tel entertained us and I had a tour of the engine room – the cellar. At that point, I admitted to myself that I was jealous. It was more than an adequate size, and it's room you need to lay down sufficient kegs of real ale for several days without them being disturbed, in addition to all the other draught products and gas bottles. This cellar however, provided no real ale, just two products, keg beer and lager. My cellar, although fitted out with the latest equipment by the brewery, was small. I could stand in the centre, stretch out my arms and almost touch both walls. I only had room to lay down three kegs of real ale, so it was a time-consuming task to keep all the balls in the air, so to speak.

We had been at the Holly Tree for just over two years and seemed to be well accepted. Whenever either of us ventured into town it appeared that everyone we passed acknowledged us; we had made a few good friends and had dozens of acquaintances. It was at least three months after our visit to the caravan park when Brenda and Tel sauntered through the front door as usual, but this time they were accompanied once again by Mr Kopechne.

After the usual courtesies, Tel's boss quietly asked if we could have a word in private. I chose a table in the restaurant and he explained that Brenda and Tel had decided to retire in the very near future; he was sure they would tell me about it quite shortly. He then hit me with the question "Would you be prepared to manage the social club for me?" That was quite an ask, and I had no intention of giving him a reply there and then. I – no, we – had to think about it very carefully. Over the following few days Shel repeatedly insisted that the decision was mine; she was right behind me if I thought we could make it work, although she did say that there would have to be more help at the pub if I was to spend what would be a considerable amount of time three miles down the road.

The first thing that shot into my mind when he proposed the arrangement was the advantageous financial implications, but it didn't take long for me to realise there were other, perhaps more important issues at stake. We hadn't been at the Holly Tree that long and when trying to establish a business venture, it was merely a blip. We'd undertaken a lot of hard work, both before and after we'd opened, and the next few years would be crucial in enabling us to consolidate and make a comfortable living for the future, even perhaps to our retirement. I'd taken the chance to have a quiet word with Tel about the subject, and although he said it wasn't the main reason for retiring, he and Brenda found their Dutch employers difficult to work with on occasions. I concluded, with Shel's full agreement, that if our plans stayed on course and I were to be approached again in a couple of years' time, we would seriously consider it. I spoke with Mr Kopechne and told him that at the moment, it was thanks but no thanks. Brenda and Tel did retire within months and the caravan park's general handyman and his wife took over.

CHAPTER 20

Unless you're a born entrepreneur and your genes dictate that you are destined for the world of the self-employed, or it is unquestionably expected that you will continue to steer the family firm that has been shaped and nurtured by previous generations, it takes a little something to embark on your own business from scratch. Just what that something is, I'm not quite sure: desperation, foolishness, some personal driving ambition which is being denied you by the world of general employment, or just a basic self-surviving desire to beat the taxman. The problem with the latter is that Mr Average never will. In my case, I believe it was 10% desperation and 90% a desire to experience a feeling that everything, and I mean everything, I (we) achieve was down to me (us). I include those short words in brackets because mine was a joint venture with perhaps more than 50% attributable to Shel. In my view, I had been denied the career to which I'd devoted everything by the twisted jealousy of one man and the self-centred attitude of another, who had both used their publicly appointed positions for personal reasons. I was not going to let that happen again. In retrospect, I can now endorse the sentiments of others who have stated over the years that you have such a great feeling as your own boss that although the buck stops with you, the last and final word can always be yours.

Although I've perhaps painted a rosy picture of our first two and a bit years at the Holly Tree, the waters were not always calm and untroubled. We had the constant, almost daily problems encountered by any business providing a service to the public; equipment malfunction (always at the most inappropriate time), suppliers being late or completely missing a desperately-needed delivery and the incessant pestering by trade organisations and sales representatives offering the world but not paying a penny for your wasted valuable time. In addition, never a month went by without some department of the local authority visiting to check that specifications were being met, as laid down in the public safety certificates that had been issued. Of course, last but not least, the lovable general public who entered our establishment to partake of our wares.

I thought I had seen all there was to see of folk after 27 years in the police service, but the Holly Tree proved me wrong. As they've been saying in Yorkshire since time immemorial "there's nowt so queer as folk". To observe individuals in their unguarded moments, often in varying degrees of sobriety, gives you an overview of life sufficient to compile a series of sit-coms. You only have to consider that some of the best comedy programmes and soap operas shown on our television sets over the last 30 years have been based around the local pub or other community watering hole. As far as our customers were concerned, obviously we had to provide them with service and refreshments that were hopefully unrivalled in the area, but when any unwarranted comments or behaviour came to light, I did not defer to the generally accepted premise that 'the customer is always right'. I was legally obliged to keep an 'orderly house' and our livelihood depended on it.

One comical little episode, although it didn't seem so at the time, involved a near neighbour who, I would assume, had experienced a few problems with previous owners about the pub's septic tank situated next to his garden fence. He obviously became aware that the premises were about to reopen for business, and the amount of refurbishment we were undertaking probably indicated to him that we hoped to achieve a level of custom unseen for quite a while. So he complained to the town's Mayor, who I've mentioned lived locally, about an alleged strong odour emanating from the sewage tank which was apparently affecting his family's well-being. The Mayor referred him to the District Council, which in turn referred him to the County Council. I was later told that the Department of the Environment became involved, but that could have been exaggeration. However, the appropriate department of the local authority initiated tests which included taking soil samples from his garden, suspecting possible contamination. I believe everyone who had an input into this complaint and investigation was instructed not to approach me for fear that I would cure any fault that might exist and thwart prosecution.

This matter progressed for over six weeks without any hard evidence being found to substantiate the complaint. It culminated one afternoon when two officials came to the Holly Tree to confront me and became highly embarrassed when I revealed that my bio-tank had been installed for more than two months and every drop of waste water was being taken on its long journey to the sea. The whole expensive episode could have been sorted in five minutes if he'd just walked 100 yards up the road to discuss it with me. I decided to let bygones be bygones and we invited him to our opening night buffet, where I saw him sitting in the lounge in high spirits.

Like any other married couple, Shel and I had our ups and downs, and our joint venture at the pub did not help us in that respect. Very often, with deadlines and pressure of work, nerves tended to stand on edge and in the early days it was difficult to keep any cross words between us purely to ourselves. Michael, working with us in such close proximity, very often felt the edge of disagreements between me and his mother, with some comments from me directed at him, which he didn't always deserve. His less than ebullient enthusiasm towards the business really upset me sometimes, because I'd nurtured a somewhat vague aspiration in the back of my mind that in a few years' time he could continue to run the business on his own when it was time for his mum and me to gracefully retire. As I've already mentioned, this was not to be.

This irritable period of our marriage soon passed as we both gained in knowledge and experience. However there was one issue that I viewed as serious, while Shel couldn't seem to give it the importance it deserved; the issue of costing our activities and products with the ultimate bottom line of net profit firmly imprinted in her mind. Shel had made copious notes on all our pre-opening visits to other establishments and had a folder full of competitors' menus, and she seemed to adhere too rigidly to that information without considering our outgoings before setting out our own prices. I tried to explain until I was blue in the face that before we could decide on a menu price for say, sirloin steak and chips, we had to take the basic cost of the meat and potatoes, then factor in a myriad of other things such as gas, electricity, rates, wages etc. Very often, in frustration when the pub was closed, I would draw a half pint, sit in solitude somewhere in the bar and count slowly to 1,000! It was one thing about her that infuriated me, but at the same time, I wouldn't have swapped her for the world. Ever since I'd joined the police service three years after we met, she had been 'the wind beneath my wings' and I wasn't going to hold any of her faults against her. Good Lord, I had enough of my own.

Actually, we both had a far bigger issue than that in respect of the business. Shel couldn't see it, or perhaps didn't want to, and it was such a delicate issue that in fear of really upsetting her, I never pursued it in any depth.

The issue was family. Both sets of parents were in their mid-70s and had a relationship which was most unusual by modern day standards, because ever since they had first been introduced shortly after Shel and I met in that windswept pub almost 30 years earlier, the four of them had really hit it off. Over the years that followed, they grew closer as companions and shared holidays, usually by coach on excursions all over the United Kingdom, and we even took the four of them on two continental adventures. It seemed a little weird at the time that they did click, because my parents were almost teetotal, with my father, although having seen the rough edge of life in the army, only partaking of a small sherry at Christmas and perhaps 'just a half' when he attended his military reunion each year. To my mother, with her strict Baptist upbringing, alcohol was definitely a no-no. Even at the few weddings we attended together, she would raise the toast glass to her mouth with her lips firmly closed, then discreetly pass the glass with its contents to Shel or me.

Shel's parents, Trevor and Bette, on the other hand, were another kettle of fish. Trevor had been a miner all his life and was something of a boozer well into his 60s. I use the term with no disrespect because Shel knew he was, Bette and the rest of the family knew he was and Trevor himself would jovially advertise the fact. His main social activity could well have been influenced by the demanding physical effort and danger associated with his occupation. In his younger days, he would make his way to the local hostelry straight from the pit-head baths, and I heard from family members how his mother would sometimes have to visit his drinking den herself to escort him home for his dinner while it was still edible. However, he grew into someone who took his family responsibilities seriously and was deeply loved by his wife and children. Shel's mum, in contrast, was the epitome of sobriety. She did enjoy the odd glass at social occasions and broadened her experience of life somewhat when she secured domestic employment at the Russell Hotel in London for several years before her marriage. She must have seen something of the party scene in those few years, because once I had settled my feet under the kitchen table at Shel's home, I soon found that she had a few treasured bottles of quite sophisticated liquor in her well-guarded front room sideboard. These prize exhibits were really just for looking at, so I must have been considered a suitable match for Shel because I was one of the few individuals who, on special occasions, was offered a small glass of green Chartreuse or blue Curaçao. I believe that it was just the once I accepted, not wishing to offend!

It followed that when Shel and I announced our intention to purchase a public house, her father made no secret of the fact that he thought it was a wonderful idea and her mum, although a little bemused by our decision, supported her husband without question, as she always did. My mother and father were totally non-committal. As I've mentioned, neither had displayed any interest in my law-enforcement activities and they were probably totally deflated when my services were dispensed with. They never had a single word of dialogue with me over either. However, during the three months when we were renovating the pub, the four of them, always together, made the journey twice to appraise our progress, which we appreciated, Shel in particular, because she was quite close to her parents, especially her dad.

The journey was not the easiest for people of their age; some 60 miles, with an unavoidable route through the centre of Hereford city, which, incidentally, still has no bypass to this day. My father always drove because although Shel, some years earlier, had persuaded me to teach Trevor to drive to a standard high enough to pass his test, he was never really keen on driving and by this time had given up altogether. In reality, Trevor could drive to a far safer standard than my father, who'd had his licence issued by the military during the war years. He had never passed a civilian test and I can say, quite categorically, with my professional background, that his driving was dangerous, but he was blissfully ignorant of the fact. He was always in the wrong position on the road, in the wrong gear and travelling at the wrong speed. I learned never to get in the car with him as I knew we'd be arguing within 100 yards.

During the first visit they made, their feedback was negligible; Trevor voiced enthusiasm at first, which waned somewhat when he realised that the beer was not yet actually on tap, and it was obvious to me that they were all a little disappointed and I believe, a little concerned about the amount of work there was to do. They did, however, give us bags of encouragement, which was important. The four of them seemed to thoroughly enjoy themselves on the opening night, with Trevor not being content until he was able to commandeer the Mayor's ear for a few minutes to advise him in a very proud manner that he was the father of the proprietor's wife. My parents were far more reserved, but I could clearly tell, as the evening progressed, they were both proud of us.

I am sure that if anyone had viewed the building with Shel and me on that very first occasion, they would have had no hesitation in stating that the place had been transformed, and I'm convinced that our parents thought likewise. Once we were up and trading, the four of them were not long in formulating a routine. They would come and stay for a long weekend at least once a month and the two mums seemed to be enthralled and captivated by the ambience of what appeared to them to be a domestically-orientated commercial scene. After a pleasantly relaxed breakfast with their male counterparts, they would enquire of Shel as to how they could help, and she would assign them some chore, usually in the kitchen, which would in all honesty be of little help to our daily objectives, but in reality was designed to keep them occupied and out of Gill's way, as she would be well into her morning ritual of cleaning away everyone's mess from the previous evening. Timing was crucial for Gill, as she would have to finish the cleaning, then travel home to the other side of town, change, and be back for bar duties by noon.

The two dads had far more time on their hands. They would religiously take a constitutional stroll after breakfast, taking in the small garden and the entire perimeter of the car park adjudicating on what they thought needed some attention before wandering up an adjacent country lane that led to several farms. Their main concern at this time would be to accurately gauge the distance they walked to ensure that they would be back at the pub to coincide with the opening time of 11 am. I had made it quite clear that although I did on occasion supply the odd glass a few minutes after closing time in the evenings, I had no intention of serving early in the mornings, unless of course, the odd charabanc full of punters pulled up seeking refreshments. The two of them would sit quietly supping their half pints for a short while until their arthritic joints forced them to go on a slow tour of the downstairs public areas. They both smoked and I could fully accept Gill's agitation on many mornings when she found herself constantly cleaning ashtrays, often the same ones more than once. I was forced one morning to suggest, in a jovial manner but with serious intent, that they could carry their own around. This helped for a very short while, but what's that saying about old dogs and tricks?

Shel was the youngest of three children. Her brother Clive, as I've mentioned, was in the Air Force and we were unable to attend his wedding after he returned from abroad to a base in Norfolk, because the timing was just seven days before ours and work commitments, together with wedding arrangements made it impossible. We did however, drive to Norfolk to meet his new wife, Dianne, shortly after our honeymoon, which turned out to be a disaster. Shel had arranged for us to stay with them in their bungalow, which was on a small residential estate in Louth, quite close to the air base where Clive was stationed. We were to stay for two nights. On the first morning, while our hosts were at work, Shel decided to clear out the remains of the previous evening's open fire in the lounge, cleaning the surround before laying fresh kindling for the next use. Her attempt to be helpful was totally and quite rudely rejected that evening when her sister-in-law came home. Without a word of explanation, she removed all the contents of the hearth and scrubbed the whole area, including the fire basket, with soap and water. Shel, understandably, was upset, but she laughed the matter off when we retired for the night, and accepted that the new addition to her family was one of those people who are completely devoid of any diplomatic attributes.

However, the following day was to herald something even more astonishing. On a leisurely sightseeing drive through the local countryside, my car developed an expensive-sounding knock. I was positive that it emanated from the drive-shaft, but I would need a ramp to investigate fully. The local garage confirmed my thoughts; the centre coupling had fractured, it was nearing total failure and incapable of supporting our drive home to Wales. Now, Louth isn't exactly in the heart of a large conurbation, so the necessary replacement part could not be obtained until the day after our proposed departure. That was no real problem; Shel and I had nothing preventing us from staying an extra night, the part could be fitted in half an hour and we'd be on our way. Well, that's what I thought and that's what Shel thought, but unknown to us at the time, that's not what our hostess thought. When we explained the situation to Dianne that evening, she went ballistic; there was no way we could stay another night in her home! We had the option of taking the train home and returning later in the week to collect the car or, we could book into an hotel.

I couldn't believe what I was hearing and Shel's brother was simply standing idly by, not wanting to get involved. Well, he did get involved, Shel made certain of that. I was all for walking out there and then, but Shel convinced me that she needed a family conference with her brother. That prompted a private domestic argument between the two Norfolk residents and about an hour and three cups of coffee later, Dianne must have relented. We stayed the night, my car got fixed and we wound our way home.

I've kept the story of that visit to myself at Shel's request, but it didn't stop me deciding that her new sister-in-law was someone I would never share a friendship with, and her brother – well, he was just a plonker and still is.

Shel's sister, Frances, was the eldest. Frankie, as she'd been known all her life, had married before I came on the scene. Shel's brother-in-law, another Clive, was also in the military and as my relationship with Shel was beginning to blossom he was posted to Aden with the Pioneer Corps, leaving his wife and baby daughter in army accommodation in a picturesque village just outside Stratford-upon-Avon, with a promise from his regiment that they'd join him within a year. Quite naturally, Shel was eager to visit her sister whenever we could; this occurred every couple of months or so, when work permitted.

I'd only met Frankie two or three times when it became obvious to me that she had, shall we say, a soft spot for me. Her suggestive comments and innuendos when Shel was out of earshot, coupled with her obvious attempts to be near me or touch me at any opportunity, grew more frequent as time went by. After two or three visits I mentioned this behaviour to Shel, only to be told, in a light-hearted way, that I'd better behave myself! It seemed she thought that it was my imagination and that her sister wouldn't behave in such a way. But it wasn't her on the receiving end. My stance was that I'd mentioned it to Shel and she was indifferent about the issue, so I just played along. I was a young man of 21 with my testosterone at its peak, and I could take all the chatting up that came my way.

By the time we were trading at the Holly Tree, 26 years later, Frankie and Clive were living on the outskirts of Banbury, their daughter Julie was married and son Glenn, born a couple of years or so after Julie, was living at home with them. We had kept in close touch over the intervening years, making Christmas and other celebratory visits to each other. Frankie, even with her husband now back in the bosom of his family, was still excitable in my company.

Like our parents, Frankie and her family attended our opening and their visits continued on subsequent weekends without Julie and her husband Mark, but often accompanied by Glenn. At this stage our living accommodation could just about cope with this influx of three or four visitors; we had reconfigured the living quarters during our renovations and we now had four bedrooms. When I think back, we maintained equilibrium because the parents would visit on alternate weekends to Frankie and the family, but there were occasions such as Christmas, the folk festival and our charity auction nights, when they all descended together and to be honest, I just cannot fathom now just where we all slept. It was another organisational achievement by Shel, as usual.

Shel and I had now been running this establishment in this unique trade of 'licensing' for long enough to realise that it was hard graft. The hours were long and the tedious quiet periods could be just as tiring as a busy Saturday afternoon, and there was always something to accomplish, even out of 'permitted hours' in the periods when some people imagine licensees put their feet up. With this constant stream of family visitors I often wondered what on earth prompted them to repeatedly spend their weekends in this effervescent and noisy atmosphere.

Whatever enjoyment they all extracted from their trips to Bromyard, none of them seemed to realise the difficulties they were creating for Shel and me. They were of no practical use to us, in fact, as I've already explained, they caused more work just by being there. I suppose to them it was a weekend away at a seaside hotel, but without the sea and the sand! The regular weekend customers were so used to seeing them that they would quite naturally assume that the pub was being run by the whole family, and an awful lot of customers in pubs all over the country are there to get away from just that – the family. I felt on occasion that Shel and I were in danger of losing our unique identity, which is such an important part of every 'local'.

I was just a little easier in my mind when Frankie and her family arrived, because Shel's sister was only about four years older than her and could assist in the general running of the kitchen to a level which was of benefit, especially if there was any kind of function to cater for. It also gave Shel the opportunity to discuss family issues, as only sisters can, and as I became aware later, to unburden personal problems which were playing an important part in Shel's mind. Clive, her husband however, was a different matter. He was one of those chaps who you just cannot help but like, a professional soldier all his working life, and he had but one speed, just a tad above dead slow. Within minutes of arriving he would ensconce himself behind the bar, occupying a tall stool and believing that he was being of the utmost assistance in the customer service department.

Throughout their middle years Frankie and Clive had been ardent caravanners, and if any of the folk from our local site were in early evening, Clive would become engrossed in conversation about their common interest. Fine, but it would be to the detriment of anyone else patiently waiting to be served. Whenever I went near the servery I would have to prompt him into action, but in the nicest possible way, not to disturb family harmony. Come

Saturday afternoon, with the football onslaught pending, I would have no option, family or not, but to dispatch him to some other area of the building to prevent utter chaos.

Gill on the other hand, being a paid employee, very competent and with the right amount of diplomacy, would tactfully move Clive out of her domain whenever she was on duty.

There was, however, one task undertaken by my now departed friend for which I was most grateful. Clive would, without fail, restock the bar shelves every morning he was with us, which was no mean task because my bottle store was some distance from the building at the other side of the car park. It was a task which took roughly 45 minutes to complete and throughout its duration I was able to remain prostrate in my bed – heaven!

In presenting my case against the onslaught of family visitors, which I continued to raise with Shel on frequent occasions, I have to mention the issue of feeding all these people, which had financial implications. The number of family members visiting each weekend was between four and seven and I will completely discount those times when up to 11 would arrive for special events. I was prepared to accept those occasions as reciprocal family gatherings which do and should occur periodically.

Shel and I were working our socks off trying to make this venture a financial success and the cost of providing board for everyone for two and a half days a week was significant. From a business aspect, it was akin to running a bed and breakfast enterprise with a dozen or so nightly boarders making off each week without paying. I'd defy anyone to make a commercial success that way. What the family didn't grasp, or didn't want to grasp, was the fact that the Holly Tree and its activities were mine and Shel's only source of income and therefore our lifeline. With the accommodation factor and the 'subsidised' drinks (and I mean that in the nicest possible way), together with the detrimental effect that some family members were having on our customers, Shel and I were being presented with problems.

There may be a few, or hopefully more than a few, who would say that there is no sentiment in business and that I should have put a stop to it. Maybe, but I had to tread a very fine line. The woman I loved had been through, and was still experiencing, a very difficult period, both physically and emotionally, and although she would never tell me, I knew that she appreciated the support from the two mums and her sister. It was something I just had to live with. Shel knew my views only too well, but refrained from taking part in any argument between us, for both our sakes. There were, however, two visitors she would have liked to see far more often, but never publicly voiced her view; her two boys, but they were living their lives quite a few miles away.

Gill had become a stalwart of the business by this time; she dealt with the cleaning in its entirety and bar work two or three afternoons during the week and most evenings at the weekend. She had the confidence to take sole control of the establishment and was happy to do so quite often so that Shel and I could make the odd shopping trip or attend to the myriad of business matters that seemed to crop up. Gill and her husband regularly used the Holly Tree socially, bringing their young son with them to challenge his dad to a game of quoits in the front bar. It gave Gill the chance to switch off and chat with those folk she'd got to know, and was now able to converse with in a much more relaxed manner.

It came as a total surprise to me when one afternoon when Shel and I were travelling back from an expedition to Worcester, she told me that Gill and her husband were experiencing some marriage problems. Apparently the atmosphere between them was becoming far more strained, far more often, and Gill was concerned that the situation was reaching a crisis point. Shel was telling me so that I wouldn't unwittingly put my foot in it with some flippant remark, and I took heed of her warning. As I've mentioned, Shel and Gill had become very close, and I wasn't sure whether Shel was holding back any further information that Gill had told her in confidence, so I encouraged Shel to support Gill and ascertain, if possible, whether her work at the pub was a contributing factor. Being good employers, as I hoped we were, we not only ensured safe working conditions but accepted social and moral responsibility towards our staff, which today is enshrined in law as 'a duty of care'. Within a day or two, Shel took the opportunity for a further quiet chat with Gill, who confirmed that her work had no bearing on her domestic life.

CHAPTER 21

By July 1994 we had been installed at the Holly Tree for almost three years and had really settled in. At least, as well as we thought we could with all the little trials and tribulations I've outlined. I felt that as a couple we had become part of the town and indeed the surrounding community, and most folk knew us. I say 'us' because in the early days I was known to a few people, especially those that Shel met regularly each day on her walk through town as 'Shel's husband', just as I had been 'Nurse Thorne's son'. Shel's personality seemed to walk six feet in front of her. Our faithful old retriever, Ben, was still with us and quite often, on a summer's afternoon between licensing hours, we'd take him for a shuffle (he was now 15) up Burying Lane and onto the lower slopes of the Downs, where Shel, on almost every occasion, would remark how much she loved the area. "I couldn't live in those dark, depressing valleys again" she'd often say.

It was at that time that I noticed that Shel was carrying a slight limp in her left leg. It was nothing pronounced, but I could see it if I stood and watched her walking through the restaurant. She admitted to having hit her thigh on the corner of one of the tables as she was changing a cloth. It wasn't too much of a problem for her and she shrugged it off by telling me it would be fine in a day or two. I deserve to be castigated for admitting that it wasn't until 10 days later that I asked if her leg had recovered. It wasn't through a lack of concern, but so many things cropped up so often in the working day that it was easy for something to slip one's mind, and I'd had total faith in what Shel had told me.

Well, Shel's leg wasn't any better. There was no bruising, but slight pain was still causing her discomfort. She attended the surgery the following morning, but the doctor was unable to diagnose the problem without an x-ray. This was carried out at Hereford General Hospital two days later, the surgery staff having organised a speedy response because of Shel's history.

I left the consultant's room after that meeting in total turmoil. Deep inside I was fuming at Shel for giving me a load of bunkum about a mishap with a table. The examination had revealed that her left femur was diseased and a small section of the bone was weakened. The consultant, Mr Rosser, in his totally professional manner, had explained that the bone only required a short pin to be inserted and Shel's leg would be as good as new, but I was furious. However, I knew I had to keep my unhelpful thoughts to myself at that particular moment. I had learnt over the years that my role was to encourage and support whenever the need arose, and the need had just arisen.

During the short journey home Shel was soon back to her normal self, and I found myself fully endorsing her devil-may-care attitude. Mr Rosser was going to do his best to slip Shel's small operation into his orthopaedic list, and if everything went well with the post-op physio, she'd be home in three days.

The hospital rang the following morning to direct that Shel should attend two days later. Mr Rosser's bedside manner, which was a credit to him and his profession, was aimed at lifting the patient's spirits, but I knew this was serious, and I knew that Shel knew too.

Shel did brilliantly and had first-class care; she was back at the Holly Tree in three days and hobbling around without her stick in four. I'd closed the restaurant and was coping with serving bar meals whilst Gill dealt with the drinks distribution, both lunchtime and evenings. Frankie and Clive arrived earlier and left later on their weekend visits so that Frankie was able to give assistance in the kitchen. Shel's temporary handicap did not prevent the parents visiting though.

That year's folk festival seemed busier than ever, and it must have been a little special for Shel, as a result of both Michael and Brian visiting. I cannot remember how long they spent with us, but they were definitely there on the Saturday night, at the height of the Festival's activities, as that was the evening I commandeered both of them to help me eject a most despicable member of society from my establishment. It was about 8 pm and both bars were packed when some caravanners in the front bar drew my attention to a young man in his early 20s, who was making suggestive remarks to some ladies present, with the intermittent use of obscene language. He failed to respond to two verbal warnings from me and on the third occasion, I made it clear that he would have to leave, but he refused, point blank. I made the decision to physically eject him, because there was no hope of a police attendance with all the Festival's goings-on in the area. We had two doorways to negotiate and I believe that Brian was assigned the task of ensuring a clear exit. After one more refusal to leave, Michael and I took one arm each and lifted him off the floor. He was manoeuvred through the passageway and out through the front door in seconds, landing sedately on his rear in the roadway, having cleared the four-foot pavement. The three of us walked back into the bar to cheers and thunderous applause from our customers.

Shel seemed to take on a new lease of life after that brief stay in hospital and we were making tentative plans about our ventures over the forthcoming Christmas period. However, only about four weeks after the festival she had a relapse and felt sufficiently unwell to stay in bed for a few extra hours on two or three mornings one week, which prompted me to ask for a doctor to call. He adjusted her medication, took blood samples and agreed to visit again. From that moment, Shel was confined to bed. We told all those who enquired after her that she was a little anaemic and, as the doctor put it, 'she needs a little rest'.

The doctor had promised to call again at 2 pm on Tuesday 28 October. After leaving Shel's bedside he asked if we could sit somewhere, and said that he'd really enjoy a cup of our coffee. He had satisfied himself that I realised just how ill Shel was at that moment and strongly suggested that he should arrange for her to go into hospital, where she could receive effective pain relief.

He then told me as sympathetically as he could that he thought my wife had no more than about three weeks to live. The tests carried out whilst Shel was having surgery on her leg had revealed that the cancer had spread to her liver and kidneys.

I have no recollection of anything else that day apart from driving sedately behind the ambulance, which seemed to take forever to reach Hereford, and kissing Shel goodnight as she dozed, lying in the assessment unit waiting for her ward allocation.

I set off for the hospital first thing the following morning, as soon as Gill arrived to take possession of the keys, and eventually, after scouring the vast complex of corridors in the old pre-war building, I found Shel in her own little side-room, snugly tucked up and apparently enjoying a morning piece of toast.

My God, what on earth was I going to say? Throughout her life, Shel had always said exactly what she thought. Not quite as blunt as the proverbial Yorkshireman, but she would never hold anything back. However, the one thing she didn't talk about was her 'problem'. She gave me the unquestionable impression that she didn't want to – it was part of her way of coping with it. I had no idea if our doctor, the consultant, or indeed anyone had told her the prognosis, so I decided not to mention anything unless she brought the issue up.

I sat with Shel for a few hours during that first visit to try to build up her spirits, but most of the time was spent trying to answer the questions and queries she raised about the pub. However, I did convince her that on her discharge she needed to recuperate properly, and I meant properly. We had achieved our goal at the Holly Tree and the building, together with the business, was worth considerably more than we'd paid for it; we should sell up and give ourselves an extended holiday. I was expecting her hackles to rise and for her to shout me down, but there was no response other than one of her smiles.

Travelling back to Bromyard, I just hoped that Gill was coping. How did we ever manage in those days before mobiles?

Once we had discussed the issue of the hours she could dedicate to her role, Gill assured me that she would continue to provide her present cover and would help in any other respect if at all possible. I also phoned Frankie to confirm that she would be making her regular visit; they actually came the following day. I had worked out that if I picked up my pace before Gill arrived at 9 am each day, I could be at the hospital for two hours in the mornings, getting back in time for the lunchtime session, and as soon as I closed the doors at 4 pm, I could go back to the hospital to spend another three hours, or more if Gill was prepared to open the pub at six. Irrespective of whether the family were there, I needed Gill to be present for my peace of mind.

Before setting off for my second visit to Hereford, I contacted an estate agent in Birmingham, who I had randomly picked out of Dalton's Weekly and who specialised in the sale of business premises, especially in the licensed trade. They would soon be in touch to arrange a visit.

On that second morning's visit, my travelling time was

cut by at least 15 minutes because I knew exactly how to negotiate those corridors, but I was soon brought down to earth when I saw Shel lying in her bed, which had been wheeled out of the side-room and was now positioned to one side of what was a pretty busy corridor. The room Shel had vacated was occupied by an elderly lady lying motionless, surrounded by at least five people. The explanation I received from the Staff Nurse made me livid. The elderly lady's condition had deteriorated significantly during the night and she had only hours to live, so they had commandeered Shel's room so that the family could be allowed to spend her last moments together. However I knew it was not the time or the place to express my feelings. I was within both sight and hearing of the grieving family and the last thing they wanted was me performing.

Shel, although conscious, didn't really know what was happening, due to the morphine she was receiving. Wasn't anyone reading her notes to keep abreast of the situation? Did the ward staff not know the seriousness of her condition? Surely, in a hospital of that size with all the staff and resources, an idiom of compassion and common sense wouldn't have gone amiss. The corridor where they'd parked Shel's bed was about as peaceful and dignified as a railway station.

I left her lying there in the corridor and just went. Where to I had no idea, but I knew who I wanted. I needed to speak to Shel's consultant, Mr Rosser, and I knew that he had a secretary accommodated somewhere in this hospital complex. I enquired of anyone who looked as though they could assist me as I hurried along, and finally reached my destination. Mr Rosser was expected back shortly, after his rounds, so I sought out my first cup of coffee of the day. I had made my mind up that Shel wasn't going to stay in this hospital for a minute longer than necessary and Mr Rosser, when we spoke, had no hesitation in agreeing to move her to the Nuffield Private Hospital, which I knew was on the crest of Aylestone Hill, only a stone's throw away. He arranged for a private ambulance and by mid-afternoon Shel was settled in her large en-suite room, where we were both carefully looked after by the staff. Shel's expression said everything to me; she was far more comfortable.

I spent many hours over the next week or so in that room chatting away to Shel, both of us being fed and watered when meals were served, and when she closed her eyes for that little nap I would stand at the large window thinking about everything and nothing, with the nicest view from the building of their landscaped gardens.

My routine of hospital visits and running the Holly Tree seemed to work well without any serious problems. I obviously couldn't have achieved it without, in part, the help of Shel's sister, but mainly the efforts and dedication of Gill. I had very little time to speak to or even see her on some days, but she was always there so that I could be away first thing in the morning and would always brief me when I arrived back each evening before she left for home. The estate agent had now been to obtain details and take photographs and a call from them a few days later sounded promising; a family from Wolverhampton were showing keen interest.

Shel had been growing visibly weaker by the day and spending less time awake, but the staff assured me that she was comfortable due to the morphine syringe driver they had inserted. Mr Rosser called every evening on his way home, and although I knew he could not achieve anything, his brief presence helped us both mentally.

I made my usual morning trip into Hereford on Thursday 24 November, which seemed like any other morning at that time of year. It was dry, but the sky was full of thick, dark, angry-looking clouds. I received the usual cheery welcome from the staff at their station, which was just outside Shel's room. Shel acknowledged me with the biggest smile she could muster, but it was left to me to do the talking because she had so little energy. She took a few sips of water as I sat there, but her eyes were telling me that she was tired. I told her, as I always did, to have a little rest and said I would pop over to the window to see how many more leaves had fallen.

As I stood scanning the lawn, something made me turn and glance at the bed. I didn't need a nurse or Mr Rosser to tell me that Shel had passed away. I just froze for what seemed an eternity before moving to the bed to kiss her forehead. As I opened the door, one of the nurses looked at me and seemed to sense what had happened. They sat me in an easy chair next to their station and within what seemed to be seconds, one of them came over, pressed something into my hand and said "you'll be wanting this". I looked down at Shel's wedding ring. I just broke down and quietly sobbed.

I must have been there for some time, because Mr Rosser was the next person to speak to me. I'd composed myself, and he patiently explained all the formalities that were necessary. I can't remember driving home, but as I entered the pub through the side entrance, a local, who could see me from his seat at the bar called out "How's Shel?" I couldn't speak; I climbed the stairs to our living quarters.

The funeral service took place in St Peter's Church, within sight of the building we'd made part of the community once more, and it seemed to me in my comatose state that the whole town had turned out, matched by the number of people who had travelled up from Gwent to Hereford's crematorium. I do recall that there were a number of my former serving colleagues, along with many of Shel's friends and acquaintances, who cared enough to make the long journey. I was particularly touched on my return to the Holly Tree, where I had arranged refreshments, to find there six of my young mechanics who I had supervised 28 years earlier. They were not so young any more of course, like me.

To lose a daughter so suddenly in the prime of her life must have been devastating for Shel's parents, and Michael and Brian had lost their mother. I have constantly had reason to think deeply about the impact her parting had on their lives. Both of my sons were forced to return to work directly after the funeral, so we had no opportunity to share each other's company and allow grief to come out in any kind of natural way. They say that sons are far closer to their mums. Well, I can tell you: dads need them too, sometimes.

Looking back, the weeks leading up to the Christmas after Shel's passing passed in a blur. I was in a kind of vacuum, carrying out just the daily tasks that were needed to keep the business ticking over. Frankie and family, together with both sets of parents, came to stay over the

Christmas break, but it was the support of my regulars that really got me through, together with the loyalty and dedication of Gill.

The property market had gone to sleep over Christmas, but I was still intent on selling if the right deal was presented. There was no extended holiday to plan for now, but I'd made up my mind well before Christmas that I had no desire to continue running the Holly Tree without my wife. Any enthusiasm I could muster to show prospective purchasers was going to be a total sham. I kept my decision to sell to myself for business reasons, but the one person I did tell was Gill. I wanted to display the same concern to her that she'd shown to Shel and me over the years, and I knew I could trust her to keep her lips sealed. I did tell her that if it was at all possible, I would make it a condition of sale that her job remained safe, but I knew that was legally impossible.

I really needed to have the restaurant functioning again, because whilst its income was not crucial, it was significant most weeks, and I had to keep my accounts looking healthy for my hoped-for sale. Then, as if by magic, I received a telephone call out of the blue from Vi Norman, the wife of Shel's last boss at the Police Training Centre. Her husband had retired and they had returned to their home in North Wales. After expressing their condolences and discussing my difficulties at the pub, she offered their help for a short while if it would be of any assistance. Vi, in her earlier life, had been a school cook, so I bit her hand off.

They came down and stayed with me for two weeks and their help was invaluable. Keith had experience of serving in the staff bar at the Training Centre, and with all this assistance and Gill at the helm, I joked that I felt like the CEO of ICI! During Vi and Keith's stay, my prospective purchasers came to view the premises, which I thought went quite well, but there was bad news from Gill, who told me, before I gleaned it from any other source, that her marriage had taken a turn for the worse; she had moved out and was lodging with her sister in another part of town.

Vi and Keith bid farewell, but not before Vi had helped me discover all those articles which are stacked away but which make up the fabric of a home. We rifled through cupboards and all the other nooks and crannies where Shel would have kept and known the location of every single item, but I was a man; I had no idea what was where, apart from the basic necessities of life. I do recall that Vi was delighted when I offered her any of Shel's cookery books that took her fancy, of which there were quite a few.

The New Year of 1995 had truly left us and we were marching towards the end of January when the Hewitt family, from the heart of the Midlands, asked if they could all come for a second viewing of the Holly Tree. This resulted in me having a most detailed discussion about my trading figures with the son-in-law of the family. I supported my comments by allowing him to scrutinise my accounts. George Hewitt, the head of the family, and his wife were the actual prospective purchasers and they were bringing with them two daughters, one of whom was heavily pregnant, and the son-in-law, who, as I have pointed out, seemed to be the one who was going to steer the business. The Holly Tree as it stood would not support the lifestyle of six people, of that I was convinced, but *c'est la vie*; I had my own problems.

Before leaving, and without any discussion with his legal representative, George shook my hand on the sale and some relief swept through me. The really enjoyable bit would come when the legal papers had been exchanged. Neither George nor any other member of the family had any experience of the licensing trade, so I suggested two things. The first was that they retain the services of Gill for continuity and essential ongoing local knowledge, which would keep Gill gainfully employed; the second was an offer from me to stay in the locality for two weeks so that they could summon me if any problems arose. I would also, if at all possible, visit the pub for an hour or so each evening to introduce the regulars that I thought they should nurture to help achieve a smooth transition. George eagerly accepted both suggestions and when the time came I booked into the Travel Inn in Hereford. The prospective purchasers and I had agreed a sale figure of £130,000 and there was I, already starting to spend part of this most acceptable sum.

Once the solicitors really became involved, matters seemed to slow down. My cynical view of life told me that this was always necessary to justify the time they listed on their final invoice. However, I was told by my solicitor that completion should be towards the end of February. I therefore had a busy few weeks in front of me. Within days, things seemed to be piling up and overpowering me; there were scores of little jobs that I'd put aside after Shel had gone, and I just had to get the premises and all the fixtures in top order in time for the handover. I had nowhere to move to, so it was going to be necessary to put most of my domestic items and furniture into storage, and even in the best of circumstances, all these things take time to arrange.

All this pressure must have taken its toll on me, which apparently became noticeable, because one weekend during their visit, Clive asked me whether it would be any help if Frankie came to stay for a few weeks. Frankie was at that time working in what they termed the 'rag trade', sitting monotonously stitching small garments together to be supplied to large retailers. She often said that the pay was pathetic and she gained no enjoyment from the role whatsoever. Clive continued to explain that they had talked it through, Frankie had persuaded her very understanding employer to allow her a few weeks unpaid leave and that he himself had no objection. It was a very gracious offer. I had been giving Clive a few pounds every weekend to cover his travel expenses, and I accepted the offer on the understanding that Frankie would not be out of pocket through her absence from work. We went forward on that basis and I made sure that she received £20 to £30 more than her usual wages.

Those few weeks went a lot more smoothly than I had expected. Although Clive was still employed as a County Court bailiff, he took a couple of days off each week to make a very long weekend when he came to join his wife at the pub. Frankie was only unaccompanied by family for three days a week at the most, but after the first week she started the nonsense of our earlier years. I say 'nonsense' because it was nothing untoward; a lot of water had passed under the bridge, we were much older and far more sensible. We had a few serious words and spent the remainder of our working relationship in complete harmony. Actually, with Frankie covering the kitchen and Gill doing almost everything else, I was able to devote most of my time to preparing for my pending move.

Once the sale had been finalised on paper, I systematically announced my intended departure to the regulars, who all gave me their support, with many offers of assistance if physical effort was involved, hoping, obviously, for that odd pint in payment! To be honest, everyone was as good as gold; I knew they all still had Shel in their minds.

I say everyone, but there was one person I really fell out with. We met him a few weeks before we started trading; he lived on the Downs just up from the pub and he was the proprietor of a small bakers in town, named Loafers. Shel went there six mornings a week and every ounce of bread we used in the business was purchased from him. Like most of our suppliers, his account was settled monthly. It was only five days after Shel had passed away, about 11 am and I was upstairs, when Gill came to inform me that he had arrived and was asking for his account to be settled, stating the amount due right down to the last penny. It was another week before the payment was due and I wasn't exactly feeling on top of the world at that moment in time. I blew my top in front of Gill, which was wrong, and whilst I collected together the amount in cash, which was rarely more than £100 a month, Gill had advised him of my demeanour. He tried to flannel his way around the situation by alleging that he'd heard that I was leaving within days. I stormed downstairs and with great restraint not to physically remove him from the premises, I thrust the money into his hand and just like Barbara Windsor in *East Enders*, told him to "Get out of my pub!" I bought not one more crumb from him for the remainder of my tenure and recommended a competitor to the new family when they moved in.

The date for my departure was set, and I faced it with some apprehension. It had been a little over three months since I'd lost Shel and although a lifetime of memories had flashed through my mind each day, I did still have the comfort of living in our home, her home. I'd given my word to the new licensee that I would be staying in Hereford for the next two weeks, but what was I going to do then? I had nowhere to go and wherever I did eventually find, there was no Shel to go with me. I was frightened.

The Friday morning I left saw me rise well before 6 am with a very strange feeling. George Hewitt had travelled down from Wolverhampton early with his family to follow, but my solicitor had clearly instructed me not to relinquish possession until I had received a telephone call from her personally. It came at 10.10 am; the money had been transferred. With as theatrical a flair as I could muster, I sauntered over to George and sedately presented him with what was probably the largest bunch of keys he'd seen in his life. I calmly said, "You are now the owner of the Holly Tree". I briefly said farewell to Gill, knowing that I would probably see her several times over the next two weeks, and drove west along the A465 to Hereford. The last time I'd made that journey, it was to say a final farewell to my wife.

That fortnight spent at the hotel in Hereford was a difficult time; on reflection, perhaps I should have made a clean break on that Friday morning, but the sale of a business, and in particular licensed premises, is a complex issue. You not only sell the business with fixtures and fittings, you contractually sell the goodwill, and I was anxious that nothing went wrong. The Travel Inn, now a Premier Inn, was and probably still is, the busiest hotel in the city with enough activity to secure someone's attention for hours, but I couldn't sit in the public bar from breakfast through to evening meal, so I sat in my room with the television churning out mostly rubbish. I would sit, reflect and become totally depressed. I would only lighten up towards the evening when it was time to drive to Bromyard, where I could chat to a few friendly faces. I thought, it's only the last few days of February, the pub may be empty! Not to worry, hopefully, Gill will be there.

And she was. Most nights, after addressing various queries from the new owners, I found that Gill was a godsend. She would fill me in with all the local gossip and I found that I could talk to her, without any inhibitions, about how I felt without Shel, and I really needed someone to listen. Towards the end of the first week, Gill told me that she wasn't really happy working with the Hewitts and, as I had thought initially, she had a feeling that they couldn't afford to continue employing her. She also had a problem on the domestic front, which caused me the most concern really. Her sister and brother-in-law were at loggerheads about Gill's temporary lodgings and she had been banished to sleep on the floor of their empty garage. Nice sister!

Those few hours each evening chatting to Gill and the locals kept me going on a temporary basis. In fact it was more temporary than planned, because after 10 days I told the new licensee that I saw no further need for my presence, so we bade farewell. I told Gill that we'd keep in touch.

I was having great difficulty formulating a plan of action for the future; my mind was in turmoil. My younger son, Brian, was living in his own house back in Cwmbran, and I knew that he was not destined for a single existence because he had come to the pub several months previously, accompanied by what seemed to be a much-admired girlfriend to be introduced to his mum and dad. However, that relationship had fallen by the wayside and he was currently unattached. He had no hesitation in allowing me to install myself in his humble abode on, what I assured him, would be a very short-term basis.

With Brian working continental shifts and leading the very busy social life of a 25-year-old, I was left more or less to my own devices, and as decorating was at the top of Brian's list of dislikes, I occupied my time in that respect. I telephoned Gill after several days to find out how she was coping and to let her know of my new domain, but if the truth be known, and there is no need at this stage for it not to be, I felt a compulsion to do so. I felt so at ease talking to her about Shel and somehow, I needed to. I didn't, or couldn't, explain my feelings about Gill to Brian, or anyone else for that matter, because they would read far too much into my words, and I didn't want to hurt anyone's feelings.

As the weeks progressed, I made a couple of trips to Bromyard, inviting Gill out for a meal, and in fairness to Brian, he agreed to allow her to visit his home on several occasions with a cordial welcome. However, I knew he wasn't completely happy. After all, he had lost his mother only some four and a half months before. It was not a situation that could prevail. I was prompted into action when during a telephone call to Gill, she revealed that, probably because she had left the marital home with her husband retaining custody of their young son, her mother had taken umbrage, so her sister had given her notice to quit the salubrious surroundings of the garage.

I gave the matter a lot of thought; after all, I had plenty of time. There was one course of action which I didn't particularly want to pursue, but in the circumstances, there was little choice. My mother and father had adopted my loyal and trusty Ben, as he'd got to know them well over the years, and I decided to ask them if they would consider allowing Gill to lodge with them too. The answer was a resounding yes, as I'd assumed. Both of them had got on well with Gill during their visits to the Holly Tree and I knew that Gill had a soft spot for my father.

The arrangement worked out a lot better than I expected. Gill and I both had uncertain futures hanging by a thread, and my parents realised that. We all therefore, trod very carefully and avoided thin ice. As time went by, perhaps because of our situations, perhaps out of concern for each other or perhaps because of that something in life that you can't put your finger on, I developed a very soft spot for Gill. My love for Shel would always be in the forefront of my mind, but Gill knew that, and it seemed to me that she didn't particularly want it to diminish. I knew we had to at some stage move from my parent's home. Would my feelings for Gill flourish, or fade? Would her feelings reciprocate mine? I wasn't looking for everlasting love – I'd already got that – but could we share a future?

It became clear that Gill was also developing feelings for me, and after discussing the situation, we agreed to pursue our relationship and see what evolved. I decided that our decision should be promulgated to those that mattered straight from the horse's mouth. I arranged to take my two lads out for a meal, just the three of us. I told them of my intention that Gill and I were to become 'an item'; I asked for their blessing and told them with every ounce of honesty that I would never stop loving their mother. They looked at each other and we sat in silence for what seemed ages, but was probably only a few seconds. Their reactions and mannerisms told me that Brian was more concerned than Michael, as I knew he would be. However, they neither laughed nor cried, and that was good enough for me.

My mother and father obviously already knew, so Shel's parents were the other two I needed to speak with. I mustered every bit of diplomacy, concern and tact I had, because I knew that they would not readily accept it. Trevor said absolutely nothing, which indicated to me his total and utter disgust, and Bette utilised the diplomacy she had nurtured throughout her earlier working life by saying that it was a matter for me, and wishing me all the best. Not that I had any concern about the views of Frankie and Clive, but they had been so close to Shel since her childhood that I arranged to spend a weekend with them in Banbury, on my own. Frankie was not happy, as you'd expect, but Clive was pleased for me that I had formulated a future and swiftly shook my hand before suggesting that we adjourn to his local. What about Shel's brother? As I said, he's a plonker.

My sons and I each dealt with Shel's death in our own individual ways, because of the different relationship each of us had nurtured over the years, and I would not dare to try to explain their feelings. What I can and will say is that each of us, in our own special way, dearly loved her. I had loved her, I was convinced, from that first evening I saw her in that windswept pub, and I had grown more in awe of her every day from there on. In the weeks that followed the funeral I knew, whatever my future held, that I could love no one else in the way I had loved Shel. The morning after that fateful day at the hospital I was in the most desperate state and I dread to think where the path would have led if my bond with Shel had not driven me on to keep the business on an even keel, as I knew she would have wanted, and that led to the support I received from Gill. In the space of a relatively short time, my career had been ruined, which had forced us to sell our home to seek an alternative income and now I had lost what I considered to be the most important thing in my life. As I write, our political masters are debating in the Mother of Parliaments the somewhat ignored problems of mental illness, and reflecting on the months that followed Shel's passing, I can sympathise with those arguing the case.

I will only mention what I observed of my two sons, knowing that they had and still have deep-rooted feelings that will remain with them for ever. However, it appeared that Brian handled the situation a little better than his brother. He immersed himself in his work and kept his feelings pretty much to himself. But it did hit them both hard. They were young men in the prime of their lives, looking forward to their mum playing a very important role in their futures. But she was snatched away, aged only 50, and they were left with just memories to share with their families in later years. Michael, our first born, displayed his grief far more than his brother. He turned in on himself, became insular and, like me, developed short periods of deep depression. After I had relinquished the Holly Tree, Gill was invaluable in helping me to offer him support.

EPILOGUE

I decided that I wanted to settle back in the Cwmbran area; most of my life with Shel had been spent there, and that's where my memories were. That my two sons lived near was also a factor. Gill seemed to like the town and was happy with my decision. The village of Henllys and the surrounding area had been earmarked for expansion when the New Town was first committed to the drawing board and I signed for a house 'off-plan' on a new estate that was being developed. The chosen dwelling, into which Gill had an input, was less than half a mile from the house Shel and I had sold four years previously.

Gill and her husband had both consulted solicitors and had started on the long, harrowing journey to divorce, which was not made any easier by the acrimonious attitude of her husband. He certainly used their son as a pawn in what became a very upsetting episode in Gill's life. For several years she was presented with unwarranted obstacles whenever she attempted to see her young lad. I gave her the support I could and was able to help her wade through all the legal correspondence. The situation wasn't helped by her sister, who kept bombarding her with totally unjustified letters, making all kinds of accusations of a domestic nature. The best advice I could offer was to completely avoid the temptation to reply. That won through eventually, but not before it had caused Gill a great deal of anguish, which she bravely shouldered.

As time went on Gill and I slowly started to bond, and she explained to me that she had married far too early, at just 19 years of age with the full support of her parents, before her heart and soul were really ready for such commitment. It followed that her marriage did not have the necessary qualities to withstand modern-day pressures.

Gill and I occupied our new home in June 1995 and she soon made her mark on it, which was not that different from the way Shel would have gone about it, so I was at ease. I had mentioned to Gill before actually moving back to Cwmbran that I intended to return to work and that I thought she should seek employment too. I didn't want anyone suggesting that she was looking for a 'free ride'. In fairness, it had been her intention anyway.

Within about three months I'd secured a position in a new water treatment works which was under construction in Newport, owned by a multi-national company named Browning Ferris Industries. The term 'water treatment' was laughable really and was, in my view, just a sop to con nearby residents, who would undoubtedly have objected if they had known the true use to which the new building was to be put. The Local Planning Authority obviously knew, as did the Environment Agency, who had a legal duty not only to set its conditions of operation, but were to physically monitor it daily activities. The facility certainly treated liquid, but it wasn't water. Its role was to take delivery of hundreds of tons of waste chemicals daily, such as hydrochloric and sulphuric acid, and neutralise them to such an extent that they could be pumped into the estuary.

It was a busy and dangerous place, and I was in on the ground floor. I had the ability to prove myself and within three years I had become the company's transport manager, with a fleet of 17 20-ton tanker lorries collecting spent acid from all parts of the United Kingdom. I had very little assistance, and most of my group of drivers had difficulty in thinking for themselves. The only objective the company had was to make as large a profit as possible, and in the dangerous business we operated, that was a recipe for disaster. My role became too busy, and that comes from a man who had relished work and responsibility all his working life. It became ridiculous; I was being awakened by my mobile phone at all hours of the night, and the only way for Gill and me to have a peaceful break was to leave the Country. I was denied any assistance, so I kicked that role into touch and left them to sort it out.

The one real benefit I gained whilst working with this company was to have financial support to study for my DGSA examination. The Government quite quickly and unexpectedly introduced legislation which made it compulsory for all undertakings that transported hazardous materials to have a fully qualified 'Dangerous Goods Safety Advisor', either employed directly by them or officially seconded to advise their company. The subject matter was extensive and the exam very stiff, so they paid for me to take some instruction in work time to supplement my home study and I was chuffed, yes, very chuffed, to gain my certificate at my first attempt.

The last and final cog in my working life was as the rating officer at the Caldicot and Wentlooge Drainage Board, whose only role, although a significant one, was to prevent South East Wales from being swallowed up by the Bristol Channel. This task was like chalk and cheese when compared with my acidic adventure. I had very little to do and all day to do it in. I could easily have become bored enough to seek pastures new, but the Board Engineer who held the position where the buck stopped was so weak, wet and pathetic it was unbelievable. The Board had a workforce of 15 when I joined and because of his total lack of management skills, the tail was wagging the dog. I surreptitiously took over more work, which satisfied me to the extent that I was happy to continue in the post. I finally retired in 2008 when my calculations indicated that my accrued pensions would provide me with the living to which I had become accustomed. Shortly after I left, the Engineer's shortcomings were identified by a concerned local councillor, which led to the Welsh Assembly disbanding the Board and placing all its functions under the umbrella of the Environment Agency.

Gill took no time at all in finding employment once she was a resident of Cwmbran. It was unskilled, working in the rag trade making gentlemen's' neckties, but I often bolstered up its importance by announcing to family and acquaintances that they were really upmarket – for Marks and Spencer! Gill had no real qualifications, but she'd proved to me that she had a shedload of common sense and the wisdom of life, and it wasn't long before she enrolled on a year-long evening course in business administration which gained her a diploma in keyboard skills. She set out to improve her employment status and secured several positions over the following 15 years, each one bettering her conditions and salary. She has now settled into an administrative post with the Stagecoach bus company, whose regional offices are only five minutes from our home. One of the perks is unlimited free bus travel throughout the United Kingdom, which is not to be sneezed at by a pensioner like me!

My two sons seem happily married. Brian is living a stone's throw away with very little time left to serve in the local force and Michael found his way to Hebburn, which is in the heart of Geordie land. Brian and Pam are the proud parents of two daughters, Beci and Hannah, while Helen, Michael's wife, presented me with a grandson, Alfie, nine years ago. Helen had a difficult pregnancy and they were both fully aware that Alfie would be born with Down's Syndrome and a congenital heart defect. I was able to hold him in my arms just before he died at only eight months old. I know with absolute certainty that the three of them would have been the pinnacle of Shel's life.

Gill's son Edward is married, living in Bromyard, and has given her a granddaughter. Fortunately, in latter years, certainly since his marriage, he has found the need to reconnect with his mum, and we pray it will continue.

The four parents who gave me palpitations whilst I was attempting to grow my business are no longer with us. They left their families peacefully, my mother sadly passing on only six months ago. It was Gill, with my love and grateful thanks, who cared for her in the nearby bungalow I moved her to 13 years ago, until she was hospitalised for her final weeks.

Gill's dad died in 2002 when he sadly succumbed to heart problems and her mother passed away last year without ever allowing Gill to repair the family wounds caused partly by her leaving, but mostly by her sister's malice. Clive, my friendly brother-in-law who enjoyed getting in the way at the Holly Tree, died in 2004, also with heart failure for which he was being treated, leaving Frankie living near their daughter, who without question will care for her when necessary.

Gill and me? Well, we are still in the home we set up on my return to Cwmbran and I must, as I have done throughout this tale, be honest and say that our first couple of years together weren't always a bed of roses. We couldn't expect them to be really, with some members of each family not prepared to give us a chance, plus the trauma that each of us brought from our past. We have, however, forged a bond which I am convinced will last and have found a love which will endure. We have a relationship where three is not a crowd, Gill, me and Shel, and for that, Gill has my eternal thanks.

Shel never did have to go back to those dark, dismal valleys. I scattered her ashes at the highest point of Bromyard Downs, and Gill and I visit the spot at least every two months. I still have that favourite chair, and quite often sit with my eyes lifted, looking at nothing in particular and feeling those small, delicate tears meandering down my cheeks. My mind takes note and I whisper to myself, "What a bloody life".

(2) If an accident occurs owing to the presence of a motor vehicle on a road or other public place, a constable may, subject to section 9 of this Act, require any person who he has reasonable cause to believe was driving or attempting to drive or in charge of the vehicle at the time of the accident to provide a specimen of breath for a breath test.

(3) A person may be required under subsection (1) or subsection (2) above to provide a specimen either at or near the place where the requirement is made or, if the requirement is made under subsection (2) above and the constable making the requirement thinks fit, at a police station specified by the constable.

(4) A person who, without reasonable excuse, fails to provide a specimen of breath when required to do so in pursuance of this section is guilty of an offence.

(5) A constable may arrest a person without warrant if—

    (a) as a result of a breath test he has reasonable cause to suspect that the proportion of alcohol in that person's breath or blood exceeds the prescribed limit, or

    (b) that person has failed to provide a specimen of breath for a breath test when required to do so in pursuance of this section and the constable has reasonable cause to suspect that he has alcohol in his body,

but a person shall not be arrested by virtue of this subsection when he is at a hospital as a patient.

(6) A constable may, for the purpose of requiring a person to provide a specimen of breath under subsection (2) above in a case where he has reasonable cause to suspect that the accident involved injury to another person or of arresting him in such a case under subsection (5) above, enter (if need be by force) any place where that person is or where the constable, with reasonable cause, suspects him to be.

(7) Subsection (6) above does not extend to Scotland, and nothing in that subsection shall affect any rule of law in Scotland concerning the right of a constable to enter any premises for any purpose.

(8) In this section "traffic offence" means an offence under—

    (a) any provision of Part II of the Public Passenger Vehicles Act 1981, 1981 c. 14.

    (b) any provision of the Road Traffic Regulation Act 1984, 1984 c. 27.

    (c) any provision of the Road Traffic Offenders Act 1988 except Part III, or 1988 c. 53.

    (d) any provision of this Act except Part V.

7.—(1) In the course of an investigation into whether a person has committed an offence under section 4 or 5 of this Act a constable may, subject to the following provisions of this section and section 9 of this Act, require him— Provision of specimens for analysis.

    (a) to provide two specimens of breath for analysis by means of a device of a type approved by the Secretary of State, or

    (b) to provide a specimen of blood or urine for a laboratory test.

(2) A requirement under this section to provide specimens of breath can only be made at a police station.

(3) A requirement under this section to provide a specimen of blood or urine can only be made at a police station or at a hospital; and it cannot be made at a police station unless—

(a) the constable making the requirement has reasonable cause to believe that for medical reasons a specimen of breath cannot be provided or should not be required, or

(b) at the time the requirement is made a device or a reliable device of the type mentioned in subsection (1)(a) above is not available at the police station or it is then for any other reason not practicable to use such a device there, or

(c) the suspected offence is one under section 4 of this Act and the constable making the requirement has been advised by a medical practitioner that the condition of the person required to provide the specimen might be due to some drug;

but may then be made notwithstanding that the person required to provide the specimen has already provided or been required to provide two specimens of breath.

(4) If the provision of a specimen other than a specimen of breath may be required in pursuance of this section the question whether it is to be a specimen of blood or a specimen of urine shall be decided by the constable making the requirement, but if a medical practitioner is of the opinion that for medical reasons a specimen of blood cannot or should not be taken the specimen shall be a specimen of urine.

(5) A specimen of urine shall be provided within one hour of the requirement for its provision being made and after the provision of a previous specimen of urine.

(6) A person who, without reasonable excuse, fails to provide a specimen when required to do so in pursuance of this section is guilty of an offence.

(7) A constable must, on requiring any person to provide a specimen in pursuance of this section, warn him that a failure to provide it may render him liable to prosecution.

Choice of specimens of breath.

8.—(1) Subject to subsection (2) below, of any two specimens of breath provided by any person in pursuance of section 7 of this Act that with the lower proportion of alcohol in the breath shall be used and the other shall be disregarded.

(2) If the specimen with the lower proportion of alcohol contains no more than 50 microgrammes of alcohol in 100 millilitres of breath, the person who provided it may claim that it should be replaced by such specimen as may be required under section 7(4) of this Act and, if he then provides such a specimen, neither specimen of breath shall be used.

(3) The Secretary of State may by regulations substitute another proportion of alcohol in the breath for that specified in subsection (2) above.

Protection for hospital patients.

9.—(1) While a person is at a hospital as a patient he shall not be required to provide a specimen of breath for a breath test or to provide a specimen for a laboratory test unless the medical practitioner in immediate charge of his case has been notified of the proposal to make the requirement; and—